T0174376

# Medical Innovation

An essential text for innovators, this accessible book explains how medical and healthcare professionals who are new to innovation in healthcare can best progress their innovation projects. The book provides a clear framework for the innovation pathway, describing step-by-step how projects are taken from concept to marketing. It also includes a current assessment of emerging technologies that will influence healthcare in the future.

**Key Features**

- Wide-ranging and comprehensive coverage of the field, from digital health and AI technologies, stem-cell applications and robotic surgery, to specialty-specific innovations including those in cardiology, public health and ophthalmology
- Illustrated with real-life examples of success and failure and what can be learned from these projects
- Reflects a greater emphasis on clinical innovation within health systems and its inclusion in undergraduate and postgraduate medical curricula and medicine-related courses
- Supports national and international initiatives to encourage innovation in healthcare and maximise the novel ideas generated by university staff and students as well as practicing clinicians

Ideal for students at both undergraduate and postgraduate levels as well as medical practitioners and allied medical health professionals, it will also be of interest to clinical innovators and healthcare businesses seeking to increase the uptake of their products both in the UK and internationally.

**Rahul Kanegaonkar** is the Professor of Medical Innovation at Canterbury Christ Church University, UK, and a practicing Consultant ENT Surgeon at the Medway Maritime Hospital, Gillingham and the Royal London Hospital, Whitechapel, London.

**James Tysome** is a Consultant ENT and Skull Base Surgeon at Cambridge University Hospitals, an Affiliated Associate Professor at the University of Cambridge and has an active role in all aspects of the medical innovation field.

# Medical Innovation
## Concepts, Delivery and
## the Future of Healthcare

Edited by

Rahul Kanegaonkar and James Tysome

CRC Press is an imprint of the
Taylor & Francis Group, an **informa** business

First edition published 2023
by CRC Press
6000 Broken Sound Parkway NW, Suite 300, Boca Raton, FL 33487-2742

and by CRC Press
4 Park Square, Milton Park, Abingdon, Oxon, OX14 4RN

*CRC Press is an imprint of Taylor & Francis Group, LLC*

© 2023 Taylor & Francis Group, LLC

### Library of Congress Cataloging-in-Publication Data

Names: Kanegaonkar, Rahul Govind, editor. | Tysome, James Russell, editor.
Title: Medical innovation : concepts, delivery and the future of healthcare / edited by Rahul Kanegaonkar and James Tysome.
Other titles: Medical innovation (Kanegaonkar)
Description: First edition. | Boca Raton : CRC Press, 2023. | Includes bibliographical references and index.
Identifiers: LCCN 2022030473 (print) | LCCN 2022030474 (ebook) | ISBN 9780367759162 (hardback) | ISBN 9780367703004 (paperback) | ISBN 9781003164609 (ebook)
Subjects: MESH: Biomedical Technology--organization & administration | Biomedical Technology--instrumentation | Inventions--trends | United Kingdom
Classification: LCC R857.B54 (print) | LCC R857.B54 (ebook) | NLM W 82 | DDC 610.28/4--dc23/eng/20221205
LC record available at https://lccn.loc.gov/2022030473
LC ebook record available at https://lccn.loc.gov/2022030474

ISBN: 9780367759162 (hbk)
ISBN: 9780367703004 (pbk)
ISBN: 9781003164609 (ebk)

DOI: 10.1201/9781003164609

Typeset in Minion
by KnowledgeWorks Global Ltd.

This book is dedicated to Dipalee, Amee and Deven
And to Laura, George, Henry and Max

# Contents

# Foreword

All healthcare systems are limited by resources, an issue that has become more apparent and acute during the Global COVID-19 pandemic. An increasingly elderly population with more complex needs, a projected global shortfall of 18 million health workers by 2030 [1] along with the rising expectations for "on demand" healthcare, in the context of fiscally constrained investments in this sector, have made the need for medical innovation all the more important.

In the United Kingdom, Medical Innovation has come to the fore with many National Health Service "Research and Development" departments rebranded as "Research and Innovation" Departments. Frameworks for innovation and translational research have improved, with a number of platforms established both Nationally and abroad, powered by a post-pandemic focus on science and innovation. The subject of Medical Innovation has also been introduced into medical and medically related undergraduate and postgraduate courses, with academic units encouraging students and staff to develop their ideas.

This publication has been designed to provide a guide for innovators. Contributors include leading experts within the field, the NHS's Academic Health Science Networks (AHSNs), the National Institute for Health Research (NIHR), Life Science Industry, Clinicians and Academics. An understanding of the innovation pathway, the resources available and examples of how to avoid expensive potential pitfalls  provide a guide to delivering successful outcomes. Successful projects will ultimately provide scalable and cost-effective solutions, but more importantly, they will improve the quality and equity of care delivered for patients within the United Kingdom and abroad.

**Dr Junaid Bajwa**
Chief Medical Scientist, Microsoft Research

## REFERENCE

1. World Health Organization (2016). Working for health and growth: investing in the health workforce—report of the High-Level Commission on Health Employment and Economic Growth. 2016. [Online] [Last Accessed 25 Dec 2020] Available from: http://apps.who.int/iris/bitstream/ 10665/250047/1/9789241511308-eng.pdf

# Contributors

**Richard Anderson**
Sciad Communications, London, UK

**Sunil Arora**
NIL, London, UK

**Raj Attavar**
Hertfordshire NHS Partnership
Trust, Aylesbury, UK

**Julian Barwell**
University of Leicester, Leicester, UK

**Robert Bell**
University College London,
London, UK

**Mahmood F. Bhutta**
Brighton & Sussex Medical School,
and
BMA Medical Fair and Ethical Trade
Group, Brighton, UK

**John Bladen**
Kings College Hospital, London, UK

**Tom Calderbank**
Nottingham University Hospitals,
Nottingham, UK

**Chirantan Chaterjee**
University of Sussex Business
School, Brighton, UK
and
Center for Management of Health
Services, Indian Institute of
Management, Ahmedabad, India

**J. Yimmy Chow**
UK Health Security Agency,
London, UK

**Chris Coulson**
endoscope-I
and
Queen Elizabeth Hospital,
Birmingham, UK

**Aditya Desai**
The University of Oxford,
Oxford, UK

**Alwyn D'Souza**
London Facial Surgery, London, UK

**Jacques du Preez**
Psephos Biomedica, Brighton, UK

**Dipalee Durve**
Evelina London Children's Hospital,
London, UK

**Jonathan Fok**
UK Health Security Agency,
London, UK

**Geraint Green**
Software Engineer and Solutions
Architect, Reading, UK

**Emma Hodge**
Small Pharma, London, UK

**Raj Jena**
Department of Oncology, University of Cambridge, Cambridge, UK

**Richard Jenkins**
University Hospital Southampton, Southampton, UK

**George Karous**
The University of Durham, Durham, UK

**Sashi S. Kommu**
East Kent Hospitals University NHS Foundation Trust, Canterbury, UK

**Ian McLoughlin**
ICT Cluster, Singapore Institute of Technology, Singapore

**Wesley McLoughlin**
The University of Edinburgh Medical School, Edinburgh, UK

**Vinod Muniswamy**
Genentech, San Francisco, USA

**Athina Mylona**
Kent and Medway Medical School, Canterbury, UK

**Ian M. Newington**
LGC Ltd., Grant Management Group, London, UK

**Jane Ollis**
MindSpire, Tunbridge Wells, UK

**Nigel Sansom**
PinPoint Data Science Limited, Leeds, UK

**Ziyaad Sultan**
King's College Hospital, London, UK

**Richard Webb**
Canterbury Christ Church University, Kent, UK

# Glossary

**Academic Health Science Network (AHSN):** Established in 2013, 15 AHSN's were founded in England to connect the National Health Service, academic organisations and industry to drive the spread and scale of medical innovation.

**Adaptability:** The ability to adapt to changing conditions.

**Adaptation:** The process of adapting to a new environment, medical use or situation.

**Adoption:** The process of users becoming aware of and using a product or process.

**Advance market commitments:** A contractual obligation used to guarantee a viable market for a developed product once generated.

**Angel investors:** An individual or individuals (groups or networks) who provide capital for a business start-up in exchange for ownership equity or convertible debt.

**Architectural innovation:** The creation of an improvement based on the method by which components, which are not all necessarily novel, are put together to produce an improvement.

**Artificial intelligence:** The development of computer systems that have the ability to perform tasks usually requiring human intelligence.

**Assimilation:** The process by which a group or groups embrace the process or product.

**Big data:** Large datasets that can be exploited to analyse and reveal patterns, trends and associations.

**Bottom of the pyramid:** The poorest two-thirds of the human economic pyramid.

**Business case:** The justification for undertaking a process or product and the expected commercial benefits.

**Business model innovation:** The development of new unique concepts that support an organisation's mission and financial viability.

**Business model:** An organisation's plan for making a profit by identifying the products or services the business intends to sell to an identified market as well as any expenses.

**Care Quality Commission:** An Independent United Kingdom regulator for health and social care.

**Centralisation of healthcare:** The reorganisation of healthcare into fewer, specialised units.

**Cochrane database or collaboration:** A healthcare database that contains high-quality independent evidence to guide healthcare decision-making.

**Collaborations for Leadership in Applied Health research and Care (CLAHRCs):** Collaborative regional partnerships among universities and NHS organisations, focused on improving patient outcomes through the application of applied health research.

**Commercialisation:** The process of bringing new services or products to market.

**Commissioning for Quality and Innovation (CQUIN):** A framework that supports improvements in the quality of services and the creation of new, improved patterns of care.

**Compatibility:** A state in which two things are able to exist together without conflict.

**Complexity:** Tasks or systems considered complicated or intractable, i.e. "not simple"

**Complexity of healthcare systems:** The diversity of tasks, processes, healthcare providers and clinicians and other staff involved in the delivery of patient care.

**Continuous innovation:** The process of incorporating modest, incremental and, on occasion, radical improvements to a process, system, technology or item.

**Costs and benefits:** The process of analysis comparing the projected or estimated costs and benefits associated with a project in order to determine its business viability.

**Counterintuitive behaviour:** An action intended to generate a result, that may generate the opposite desired outcome.

**Crowdfunding:** The process of raising capital from a large number of people to fund a project or cause.

**Monetising data:** The process of using data to generate revenue.

**Discontinuous innovation:** An entirely novel product that leads to significant change in consumption habits.

**Disruptive innovation:** An innovation or technology that makes expensive or sophisticated products or services accessible and more affordable to a broader market.

**Dominant design:** An uniform standard often built upon existing and accepted design.

**Early adopters:** Individuals who use novel products before the majority of potential users.

**Evidenced-based medicine:** The use of best evidence in making decisions about the care of individual patients.

**Fast-fail:** The philosophy that values rapid extensive testing and feedback to determine if an idea has value.

**Frugal innovation:** The process of reducing complexity, cost and production of an item i.e. low-cost new products and solutions.

**Health Technology assessment (HTA) Programme:** Funded by the NIHR, a programme that funds research about the clinical effectiveness, cost effectiveness and impact of healthcare interventions and tests.

**Hype cycle:** A graphical representation of the development maturity and adoption of a product or service.

**Implementation:** The process of executing a decision or plan.

**Incremental innovation:** A series of small improvements relating to an existing product.

**Innovation:** A novel method, idea, product or service.

**Innovation champion:** Individuals who promote innovations across businesses and organisations.

**Intellectual property:** A category of property that refers to intangible human creations.

**Invention:** Something that has never been made before.

**Knowledge mobilisation:** The connection between academic research organisations and government to improve and inform policy change,

**Lean thinking:** A transformational framework that provides a new way of thinking, creating the most value for the customer.

**Machine learning:** A branch of artificial intelligence, the development of computer systems that are able to adapt by using algorithms and statistical models.

**Mainstreaming:** The process of bringing something novel to being considered normal.

**Modular innovation:** The redesign of a service or core element within a product.

**National Health Service (NHS):** A complex publicly funded service that provides free-at-the-point-of-contact healthcare services.

**National Institute for Health and Care Excellence (NICE):** An independent organisation that provides evidence-based guidance for health and social care practitioners.

**Normalisation:** Acquisition of a product or process such that it becomes the standard

**Novel:** New and not resembling something previously known.

**Open innovation:** A situation whereby an organisation does not rely solely on internal knowledge and resources.

**Over-treatment:** The unnecessary or excessive treatment of a medical condition.

**Printing, 3D:** An additive process whereby layers of material are deposited to construct a three-dimensional object from a digital file.

**Patent:** The granting of a property right to an inventor, conferring exclusive rights to the patented process, design or invention.

**Patient and public participation:** Research undertaken with and by members of the public.

**Pilot project:** A small-scale study used to prove the viability of a project or idea.

**Prototype:** A sample model of a product or device.

**Public-private partnership:** The collaboration between a government agency and private sector companies to finance and build public services.

**Pyramid of care:** A graphical representation of tiers of influence that result from public health interventions.

**Radical innovation:** An innovation that supplants or destroys an existing business model.

**NHS Research and Innovation Department (R&I):** Departments responsible for conducting clinical research and fostering innovation; based within hospital trusts and replacing research and development departments.

**Randomised controlled trial (RCT):** A study assigning individuals, by chance, to two or more interventions and comparing specific outcomes.

**NHS Research and Development Department (R&D):** Units within the NHS structure responsible for facilitating clinical research.

**Relative advantage:** The extent to which a novel product is superior to an existing one.

**Reverse innovation:** The process by which costly products are reworked as inexpensive versions for developing nations but are subsequently repackaged and delivered as low-cost versions to Western Countries.

**Risk:** Exposure to danger or harm.

**Safe-fail:** A product developed to counteract the effect of possible failure.

**Self-testing:** A test that can be administered to oneself.

**Sensemaking:** The action or process of giving meaning to something new.

**Service innovation:** Innovation in services and service products.

**Small Business Research Initiative (SBRI):** A UK initiative allowing the public sector to tap into new ideas and technologies, hence facilitating their adoption.

**Spreading:** To expand and further reach.

**Stage gate model:** A management technique whereby a new initiative project is divided into several stages and separated by decision points, "gates".

**Systemic dynamic model:** A continuous modelling simulation that uses postulated relations across processes and activities.

**Task shifting:** The redistribution of tasks among healthcare workers, where specific tasks are moved from highly qualified workers to those with shorter training and qualifications.

**Technology:** The application of scientific knowledge for practical purposes.

**Telecare:** The use of technologies to enable remote monitoring and supervision of patients.

**Telehealth/Telemedicine:** The use of telecommunications technologies to provide healthcare remotely.

**Treatment substitution:** The replacement of a substance either a similar or "substitute" drug.

**User-led:** An organisation that is run and controlled by those using its services.

**User-led innovation:** The concept that the lead users of a product innovate faster than the producer.

**Venture capital (VC):** An investor who provides capital in exchange for equity stake in a project in which there may be considerable risk.

**Whole systems approach:** The application of systems thinking, methods and practice to better recognise health challenges and identify collective solutions.

# SECTION 1

# The Innovation Process

# 1

# Introduction

RAHUL KANEGAONKAR AND JAMES TYSOME

The purpose of this book is to provide a framework for innovators embarking on the innovation journey. This process is often protracted and frustrating and, on occasion, may demand significant financial investment. For a variety of reasons, the majority of innovations fail, but the experience gained by an innovator is still of practical value. Hence, this text also aims to identify potential pitfalls and how these may be avoided to deliver a successful outcome.

## WHAT IS MEDICAL INNOVATION?

A new process, product, service, method or technology may be considered to be "innovative", and when applied to healthcare a "medical innovation".

It is essentially something new.

## MEDICAL INNOVATION – A CLASSIFICATION

A classification system for medical innovation is presented in Table 1.1.

Examples of truly novel medical innovations, Class I, are often derived from basic science studies.

Alexander Fleming of St Mary's, London, is best known for discovering the first broadly effective antibiotic, penicillin. In 1928 whilst investigating staphylococcal growth on culture plates, he noticed that one plate had been contaminated

DOI: 10.1201/9781003164609-2

Table 1.1 Classes of medical innovation

| Class | Description | Example(s) |
|---|---|---|
| I | An innovation that is completely new to market that provides a solution to a specific problem | 1. Antibiotic penicillin<br>2. Recording of the electrocardiogram |
| IIa | Adaptation of existing product in a parallel field | 1. Bone-anchored hearing aids and dental implants |
| IIb | Introduction of current product in parallel field | 1. Microdebrider first used in orthopaedic surgery introduced to address nasal polyps<br>2. Balloon dilatation in carotid artery stenosis and Eustachian tube dilatation |
| III | An Innovation that replaces standard best practice or product | 1. Introduction of the intraocular lens following cataract enucleation<br>2. Magnetic resonance imaging as a replacement or complement to computed tomography scanning<br>3. Cochlear implantation for profound hearing loss<br>4. Robotic surgery for specific surgical pathologies |
| IV | An innovation that translates from one species to another | 1. Laryngeal mask used initially in humans and now used by veterinarians to administer general anaesthesia<br>2. External fixation of long limb fractures |

and that colonies of staphylococci immediately adjacent to a fungus had been completely destroyed, whilst those distant were normal. The fungus was later identified as a mould from the genus *Penicllium, P. rubens*. Extraction and administration in humans have proven to be a remarkable turning point in the management of bacterial infection, described as the "single greatest victory ever achieved over disease", and he was subsequently the recipient of the Nobel Prize in Physiology or Medicine in 1945.

Augustus Waller, a physiologist, also based at St Mary's Hospital in London, performed the first human electrocardiograph in 1887. Electrodes attached to the front and back of a human subject were attached to a capillary electrometer, and the bobbing mercury was recorded on a photographic plate mounted on a wooden train. The clinical application of the electrocardiogram was developed further by Willem Einthoven, for which he was awarded the Nobel Prize in 1924.

An example of a Class II innovation includes the transferrable application of dental implantation. Developed by Per-Ingvar Brånemark, titanium implants were known for integrating into bone and could be used to permanently attach prosthetic teeth into jaw. A similar principle was later applied to hearing loss in those with a normal inner ear but disease of the outer or middle ear that prevented sound energy reaching the cochlea. These bone conduction hearing implants allow sound to pass through the bone directly to the inner ear and have transformed the lives of countless patients (note Figure 1.1).

(a)

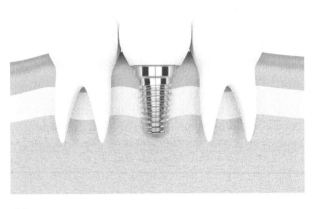

(b)

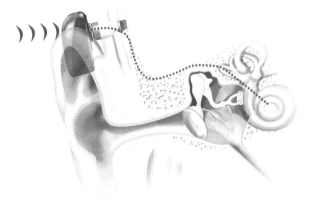

Figure 1.1 **(a)** Dental implantation has led to the BAHA by Cochlear. **(b)** A method of bone conduction aiding in those with hearing loss. (Image courtesy of Cochlear Bone Anchored Solutions AB, © 2022.)

A Class III medical innovation replaces what may be considered to be the current standard or best practice. An example is that of the corrective intraocular lens used in cataract surgery, first performed by Sir Harold Ridley at St Thomas' Hospital in 1949. After seeing RAF pilots with pieces of shattered plastic canopies in their eyes, Ridley noticed that acrylic was inert. The concept of introducing a corrective implant after cataract lens removal did not gain widespread acceptance until the 1970s, but over 30 million cases are now performed annually worldwide.

Both computed tomography and magnetic resonance imaging may also be considered to be Class III medical innovations by replacing X-ray in many situations. Godfrey Hounsfield, an English electrical engineer, shared the Nobel Prize for Physiology or Medicine with Allan MacLeod Cormack in 1979. Hounsfield introduced and developed the concept that one could identify the contents of a box by taking X-ray readings of an object at several angles. Applied to medicine, computed tomography has revolutionised the diagnosis and management of a wide variety of diseases. Similarly, the application of magnetic resonance imaging in medicine by Peter Mansfield has provided unparalleled imaging of soft tissue structures.

An innovation that is transferrable from one species to another, a Class IV innovation, often applies to the pharmaceutical industry, with laboratory studies on animal models preceding human trials. An unusual example of the transfer from humans to animals is the development of the iGel (note Case Study C). Used to maintain the airway in both emergency and elective anaesthesia in humans, the iGel has been repurposed for veterinarians to deliver anaesthetic agents in animals.

## THE NEED FOR INNOVATION

There are a number of reasons why medical innovation should be encouraged and fostered. The cost burden of healthcare alone is a key driver for publically funded healthcare platforms.

### The cost of healthcare

Current and anticipated costs of healthcare remain a keen driver for medical innovation.

In 2018, government and non-government spending on healthcare in the United Kingdom totalled almost £215 billion. This equated to just over £3200 spent per person. In real terms healthcare expenditure increased by 2.0% in 2018, while non-government healthcare finance grew by 7.6%.

Measured as a share of gross domestic product (GDP), healthcare expenditure represented 10% of GDP, an increase from 9.8% in 2017. Whilst lower than many other developed countries (note Figure 1.2), this remains a significant financial burden.

Approximately 64% of government spending on healthcare is attributed to services providing curative or rehabilitation therapy. Health-related long-term

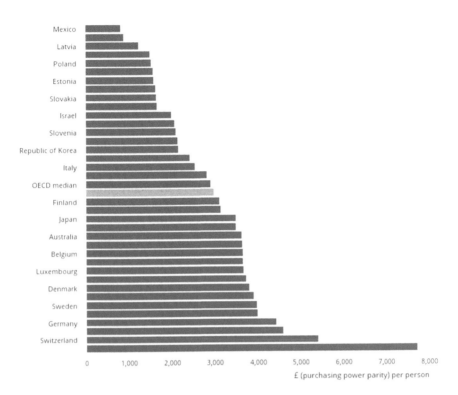

Figure 1.2 The relative national cost of healthcare. (From Office for National Statistics - UK Health Accounts, Organisation for Economic Co-operation and Development - OECD.stat; https://www.ons.gov.uk/peoplepopulationandcommunity/healthandsocialcare/healthcaresystem/articles/howdoesukhealthcarespendingcomparewithothercountries/2019-08-29.)

care and the provision of goods account for 15% and 9% of government healthcare expenditure. Preventative care accounted for 5% of government expenditure, whilst healthcare governance accounted for 1% of spending.

The main provider of government finance healthcare was acute hospitals' trusts, accounting for almost 50% of healthcare expenditure. General practitioner surgeries, dentist and homecare providers accounted for almost 25% of government expenditure. The remainder was due to medical goods 9% and residential long-term care brackets 8%.

Within the hospital setting 97% of hospital spending related to curative and rehabilitative care, of which 57% was spent on inpatient care and 11% on hospital day-case treatment. Outpatient care represented 30% of government hospital expenditure. The remaining costs are related to preventative healthcare services, including screening tests, and to long-term care, including palliative care and transport services.

The cost of healthcare will continue to rise, and healthcare providers are keen to encourage innovation, including specific product development and structural organisational pathways.

## Clinical improvement

Clinicians aspire to provide the best care they can to improve the outcomes of their patients. This may involve developing or introducing a novel product or pathway, which may either extend the lifespan or improve the quality of life of an individual. Novel pathways may also be implemented to satisfy changes in the demand of the local population or may be developed to respond to local competitors.

The National Health Service provides free at the point of contact care to all. Health workers offer an impartial opinion on the management of patients as there is no direct financial benefit from recommending one particular pathway over another. This is not necessarily the case in other healthcare systems where doctors and nursing staff may be incentivised to use a particular product or clinician.

## Rationalising the infrastructure available

Medical innovation may involve reworking networks and pathways to provide a more efficient and effective service.

In many businesses, creative development and innovation are key to survival. This also applies to healthcare on a slightly circuitous route as new developments, innovations and treatments often require validation and publication. In both the Public Healthcare service and private healthcare domain, innovative and effective treatments may allow a unit to attract a great caseload of patients and hence improve turnover.

The subject of workforce planning should also be considered. Recent predictions suggested a 30% shortfall of healthcare workers by 2030. This is likely to be an underestimate. The physical and psychological impact of COVID19 pandemic is yet to be fully established, but anecdotal and initial research suggests that staff are likely to reduce their clinical commitments.

Hence, novel pathways that reduce the need for healthcare staff will be required to address an increasingly elderly population with more complex medical needs.

## Brand reinforcement

The development of an innovative pathway may attract patients to a unit and reinforce the reputation of the hospital as innovative, "world leading" and "cutting edge". This may reward the unit by attracting medical talent, an increase in footfall and hence income. For some, this may also attract a specific caseload of patients who may also be recruited to a research study, hence bolstering their academic profile.

## Unique selling point

The development of an innovation or innovative pathway may provide a unique selling point that attracts patients, referring clinicians and insurers. Publication in classical and social media may further improve the profile of a unit.

## Rewards to an individual

Whilst the foremost reason for developing a medical innovation is that of improving patient care, individuals or teams may profit financially, academically and through improving their reputational and professional status. Whilst there is no specific financial reimbursement in the United Kingdom National Health Service (NHS) workplace, medical innovation can improve the chances of success of applications for Clinical Excellence Awards (CEA) for doctors working in the United Kingdom.

## Research opportunities

Research to assess and validate a novel product is often required. Academic units may attract such commissioned work, with costs covered by the innovation team or through research grants (note Chapter 6).

## RISK

Medical staff are by nature risk averse. A clinical error or deviation from an accepted norm may attract criticism or legal recourse but, more importantly, may harm a patient.

Whilst this is appropriate for the clinical care of patients, medical innovation requires a different mindset. An innovator will need to accept that some projects will fail. This may be due to a variety of reasons such as poor timing, too small a market or poor leadership (note Table 2.1). Whilst failure is disappointing, the experience gained in the innovation process will still be of value. It is often the case that one's first innovation is not necessarily one's best. On occasion, the product may evolve to address a problem that was initially unknown or thought irrelevant (i.e. collateral use).

An innovation requires thought, time and expense. During the early stages of an innovator's career, it is important to commit to a single project. One should avoid a scattergun approach as far as possible. An early-stage innovator will often have several ideas that they would like to pursue. With experience, some innovators may be able to drive several projects simultaneously. Through establishing a team, delegation and understanding of time delays in the process of innovation, one may be able to return to a project to drive it. It takes experience to know when to allow a project to fail. It is often worthwhile having a mentor who can not only act as a guide but also steer an innovator away from an invention that is unlikely to benefit them with regard to both experience and a final product.

## REPRIORITISATION OF INNOVATION IN THE NHS

Hospital trusts are acutely aware of the need to innovate and conscious of the potential cost saving of a successful process or financial return of a successful product. Indeed, some may expect a substantial share of any profits generated (e.g. 70–90%), citing that the innovation arose as a result of the clinician's role within the trust.

Many National Health Service trusts have in recent years rebranded their *Research and Development Departments* as *Research and Innovation Departments*. Clinicians or academics are expected to register their innovation projects with their employers and should note that their employers may expect a proportion of profits generated from any innovation or spin-out company. It is, therefore, important to address these issues prior to embarking on a project.

## CASE STUDY A: D+R HEARING

Tuning forks are widely used by clinicians to assess hearing (Figure A.1). Rinne and Weber's tests are commonly performed to assess the presence of conductive or sensorineural hearing loss in both adult and paediatric patients. These are usually performed using a 256 Hz or 512 Hz tuning fork, as low-frequency tuning forks are "felt" rather than heard and high frequency tuning forks decay rapidly [1]. The accuracy of hearing assessment using tuning fork testing has been found to vary significantly [2].

Tuning forks are also used in the diagnosis of a sudden sensorineural hearing loss. This is an ear, nose and throat emergency, and hence rapid identification is essential [3]. Oral steroids are administered as soon after the loss as possible, as a delay will make recovery less likely.

Low-frequency tuning forks are also used by neurologists, general physicians and physiotherapists to assess proprioception. This involves placing the heel of a struck tuning fork on a peripheral limb and asking the patient if they can feel the vibration.

The sensitivity and specificity of tuning fork tests are affected by the method of presentation of the stimulus as well as the amplitude of the tone presented. The latter is highly variable and dependent on how the fork is struck.

### SOLUTION

We proposed the use of a custom smartphone application and ear jack insert that produced a vibrating stimulus (Figure A.2). An iPhone application written specifically for this project was able to present specific tones at user-specified frequencies (128, 256, 512 and 1024 Hz) and amplitudes (10, 20, 30 and 40 dB). This allowed these tuning-fork tests to be performed in a standardised manner and result in an accurate diagnosis.

Figure A.1 A 512 Hz tuning fork.

Figure A.2 The tuning fork mobile phone insert.

## COST

Whilst a pair of medical standard tuning forks may currently cost £27–£39, the insert and application would be marketed at a similar cost but would provide a standard test of amplitude at four frequencies.

This project was suspended as a number of smartphone manufacturers removed 3.5 mm sockets from their mobile phones. However, we are currently modifying the ear jack insert and hope to reassess the viability of this product.

## REFERENCES

1. James Tysome, Rahul Kanegaonkar (Editors). Hearing: An Introduction & Practical Guide, 1st edition (Kindle Edition), CRC Press; 2015.
2. Kelly EA, Li B, Adams ME. Diagnostic accuracy of tuning fork tests for hearing loss: a systematic review. Otolaryngol Head Neck Surg. 2018 Aug;159(2):220–230. doi: 10.1177/0194599818770405. Epub 2018 Apr 17.
3. Bayoumy AB, de Ru JA. Sudden deafness and tuning fork tests: towards optimal utilisation. Pract Neurol. 2020 Feb;20(1):66–68. doi: 10.1136/practneurol-2019-002350. Epub 2019 Aug 23.

# 2

# The innovation process

RAHUL KANEGAONKAR

The innovation pathway is outlined in Figure 2.1. Navigating the stepwise process illustrated allows product progression and reduces the risk of the project failure by anticipating potential problems such as establishing intellectual property ownership early to satisfy potential investors later.

## CONCEPT

Successful projects arise from first identifying a clinical need and matching this with an appropriate solution.

If innovators pursue a project for which there is a limited clinical need or which addresses a rare pathology, this may result in an expensive and fruitless

DOI: 10.1201/9781003164609-3

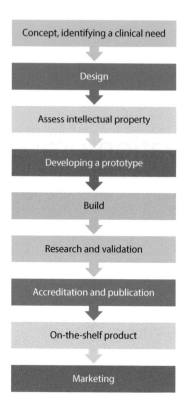

Figure 2.1 The innovation pathway.

project. Regardless of the potential product, if the innovator has limited clinical or industrial experience, professional advice should be sought. Those with clinical experience are often able to identify key devices that require improvement or substitution. It is, in fact, often the case that healthcare workers adapt their approach to individual patients and, on occasion, modify a particular instrument. If an item is regularly altered, this certainly has the potential to generate a medical innovation. Interestingly, it was often the case at the start of the 20th century that surgeons developed their own instruments (which are often named after the inventor), customised for a particular procedure and patient demographic.

Unfortunately, it is not uncommon for an innovator to generate a solution to a clinical problem but fail to act upon this. It may be the case that colleagues ridicule or dismiss ideas or question the medical problem and the need for a different approach: "Why would we need this?" Often innovators disregard an idea, thinking, quite rightly, that someone else must have thought of it first. This is very likely to be the case, but a determined inventor will act upon their idea.

What distinguishes an innovator from an entrepreneur? An entrepreneur is prepared to invest both time and their own money into an idea. Others may have failed to drive their projects for a variety of reasons, some of which are outlined in the section "Why Projects Fail".

Dizziness and vertigo are common symptoms, and patients are often required to undergo specialist testing to assess their balance pathways in order to establish a diagnosis. Testing includes pure tone audiometry, videonystagmography and sway testing. The latter is undertaken using a dynamic posturography machine or a force plate. Purchased new, a dynamic posturography machine may cost approximately £85,000 and a force plate approximately £30,000. Sway is measured by asking a subject to stand upright with their hands by their sides on a square metal plate. Patient movement is digitally recorded and presented to a technician.

As an otorhinolaryngologist with a specialist interest in balance disorders, I was disappointed to learn that our departmental dynamic posturography machine and force plate were beyond repair. With limitations on the departmental budget, we were unfortunately unable to replace either.

Consequently, Viv Austin, a digital architect, and I developed the iPhone application, *D+R Balance*, to measure sway (Figure 2.2). The app required appropriate validation and CE approval via the Medicines and Health Regulatory Authority (Whittaker 2014; Yvon, Najuko-Mafemera, and Kanegaonkar 2015). We were the recipients of an innovation award from the Chartered Society of Physiotherapists in the United Kingdom, and the app is now used internationally by both doctors and physiotherapists.

Tamsin Brown's *Hear Glue Ear* bone conductor and app are timely to address the delay in intervention for patients with hearing loss due to "glue ear" (middle

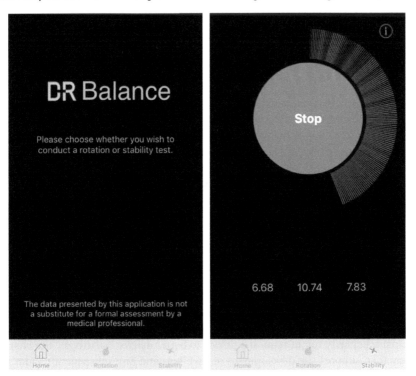

Figure 2.2 The D+R Balance application.

Figure 2.3 The Hear Glue Ear platform.

ear effusions). The system delivers sound directly to the inner ear, restoring hearing and allowing children to progress at school. Her platform was a deserved winner of "children's app of the year" at the UK App awards in November 2019 and the overall winner of Forward Healthcare awards by Leading1Health (note Figure 2.3).

## INSTITUTE OF MEDICAL SCIENCES INNOVATION ALLIANCE

The Institute of Medical Sciences Innovation Alliance (IMSIA) project is an initiative that aims to draw together the Academic Health Science Network, the National Institute of Health Research, and Medical Charities.

In a similar vein to the James Lind Alliance (identifying specific research needs determined by members of charities), IMSIA aims to generate a list of innovations required to assist groups of individuals. A published list allows potential innovators to develop specific solutions (e.g. members of a visually impaired charity might request a device to better deliver eye drops). The charity may then support the development of this item and any subsequent validation. With a potential stake in the equity of the device, the charity, members and innovation team benefit from the collaboration.

## DESIGN

A good design should be simple and clearly solve the clinical problem that it addresses. Complex designs or those that set out to solve multiple problems should be avoided if possible. This not only allows relative ease of manufacture but also validation of the final product for that specific use. A device that claims to address more than one problem may also be more difficult to market.

## ASSESS INTELLECTUAL PROPERTY (IP)

Is your idea truly novel? It is often worthwhile spending time researching patents, publications and the World Wide Web. It is often useful, although expensive, to hire a specialist in this field as some patents may be difficult to find as key terms and descriptors may be ambiguous. Guidance should be sought from an intellectual property rights lawyer if an innovator is considering legal protection for their idea (note Chapter 3).

## PROTOTYPE

This process may take some months, and new innovators are encouraged to fashion prototypes themselves. This allows them to gain an understanding of the materials that may be used and individual parts required to develop a working model. On occasion, components may be harvested or adapted from off-the-shelf products, but with the introduction of 3D printers unique shapes can be produced quickly, in a variety of materials and at relatively little cost.

A prototype also provides a tangible item that can be used to attract investment and a starting point for a manufacturing process. The object can also be altered and optimised, the prototype cycle, until a practical working model is developed (note Case Study A: D+R Hearing, in Chapter 1).

## BUILD

It is often the case that a physical build will require working with an established company. One should always seek a non-disclosure agreement (NDA) when approaching potential collaborators, and I would always encourage innovators to keep their ideas private and not to present them at meetings or publish them on the internet. Once in the public domain, it may not be possible to secure intellectual property rights, and the invention may even be taken on by another person.

Almost all projects need a good, determined team. For example, *Docbook.co.uk* was an online picture book series that Dr Aslan Mirza (a general practitioner with incredible IT skills), Dr Junaid Bajwa (now chief medical scientist for Microsoft) and I published in 2007. Each page displayed a video or series of static pictures followed by a number of increasingly difficult medical questions. Although the site included only ENT content, at its close in 2011, the platform had attracted over 3.2 million hits from over 150 countries.

Figure 2.4 D+R therapy platform.

More complex digital platforms require an understanding of security and regional protocols. We recently developed a remote physiotherapy platform, *Flexio*. A physiotherapist prescribes the exercises a patient is required to undertake on a website. This is linked to an app downloaded onto the patient's smartphone (note Figure 2.4). The app presents users with a video clip and text description of the exercises prescribed, but uniquely records and relays movement data back to the physiotherapist. This not only improves compliance but also reduces the potential need for weekly review (Vaish, Ahmed, and Shetty 2017; Saleh, Parkar, and Tolat 2018). The cost saving to the National Health Service (NHS) is potentially enormous. We were fortunate to secure a place on the Microsoft Accelerator programme and navigate the necessary compliance issues required.

## RESEARCH AND VALIDATION

Some but not all Innovation projects will require some form of validation. It is of benefit to have links with the Clinical Research Network as they are supportive of Innovation research, and the Research Design Service can assist with project design and delivery. It is also worth linking with a trust that has an interest in medical innovation. One should, however, have a clear understanding of the cost and time frame involved.

The *Cupris iPhone otoscope*, for example, developed by Mr Julian Hamann provides an elegant remote method for assessing and recording ear pathology. A simple lens attachment converts the smartphone into a digital otoscope that combined with a series of clinical questions can be used as a screening tool for potential referrals (note Figure 2.5).

The *Digital Ear Trainer* developed by Adam Rouilly was an interesting validation project. This teaching aid was tested by ENT surgeons and medical students from throughout the southeast of England, and the data was used to support this simulator's penetration into the market.

Figure 2.5 The Cupris iPhone otoscope.

## ACCREDITATION AND PUBLICATION

Clinicians are by nature risk averse. Many, myself included, would be more comfortable using a new innovation having assessed the evidence base first. Hence, research is an essential element when developing and validating a medical innovation. Proof of concept to product development for CE marking and the safety data that may be required for Medicines and Healthcare products Regulatory Agency (MHRA) approval requires careful planning, with funding often required at each stage. One may also need to satisfy regional or international standards (note Chapter 7).

On occasion, however, the publication or presentation of a study or clinical trial may be withheld if this information would be advantageous to a parallel developer or established competitor.

## ON-THE-SHELF PRODUCT AND MARKETING

Marketing of a novel innovation can require substantial investment. I have previously hired a stand at an ExCeL conference, but it can be difficult to attract potential customers despite high volume footfall. Advertising in medical journals and via specialist marketing companies may be essential to get the word out.

Platforms have been established that provide innovators to present to groups of potential buyers at specialist meetings. Although attractive, the cost of a brief oral presentation may run to thousands of pounds with no guarantee of product uptake. This outlay is somewhat perverse as many innovators may self-fund their projects, but it may need to be factored into the potential cost of developing a product.

## WHY PROJECTS FAIL

An inevitable part of the innovation process is failure. This may be difficult for enthusiastic innovators who have committed significant time, funds and their reputation. However, undergoing the process of innovation is of value, and many entrepreneurs will recognise this despite what may be deemed to be failure.

There are a variety of reasons why an innovation may fail to progress. These are listed in Table 2.1.

A common cause for demise is that the project is poorly defined, with no clear product. A useful text, applicable both to industry and academia is the *Seven Habits of Highly Effective People* by Stephen Covey. The second principle describes the need for a well-defined endpoint. Whilst in innovation, this is seldom inappropriate, the final product may be virtually unrecognisable to the initial basic science platform (c.f. Augustus Waller and the development of the electrocardiograph). A product may, with additional support, develop into a product that is superior to that originally envisaged.

In academia the second habit approach, "Begin with the end in mind", will define the target date and place for presentation at an academic meeting and publication in a specific journal.

Table 2.1  Reasons why a project may fail

| Product | Poorly defined scope of project |
| --- | --- |
| | Failure to identify needs of market (both local and global) |
| Temporal | Slow to market |
| | Competitor superiority |
| | Delay in early adoption |
| | Inaccurate time estimates |
| Leadership | Poor, ineffective or inexperienced project management |
| | Incomplete team |
| | Poor communication between members of team |
| | Disjointed team |
| | Failure to recognise and anticipate key steps |
| | Key staff turnover |
| Intellectual property | Failure to identify ownership |
| | Infringement of existing intellectual property |
| Pharmaceutical | Therapeutic advances that negate need |
| Regulatory | Lack of detailed formal documentation |
| | Inadequate risk management |
| | Change in assessment |
| | Change in regulations |
| Academic | Insufficient evidence for practical use |
| Financial | Insufficient funding stream |
| | Unanticipated costs |
| | Poor fee structure |
| | Cost of intervention replacement |

An inexperienced project manager or team may be unable to recognise the necessary steps required to progress an innovation which may then inhibit potential investors. Investors are also more likely to relinquish funds if they are aware that an appropriate team has been brought together to address the project needs (e.g. software development) or outsourced if required (e.g. branding).

The clinical need for the innovation is often overlooked. Factors that should be borne in mind include the clinical need, frequency of cases and relative cost of the novel intervention. In the case of the latter, this may also apply to a potential industrial partner who may prefer to maintain their current product as opposed to upgrading to an improved model (as the cost of retooling, marketing and validation may be significant). An innovator may hence be held in limbo awaiting a decision that prevents product development.

In some cases, a change in product or process may be perversely unattractive to a healthcare provider where the current or standard management pathway is of greater financial benefit as opposed to improving patient outcome (e.g. the cost of managing a complication versus reducing the rate of that complication).

A product that is slow to market may be preceded by another. Entry to the market is then likely to be more difficult but may also be aided as the concept and need for the intervention may have already been recognised. A subsequent product may need redevelopment in order to penetrate the market.

Inadequate leadership may also result in poor progression. Investors may expect a broad team who will drive a project. Occasionally this may require an innovator to leave their clinical post, a step that could inhibit further progression.

An additional issue may be staff turnover, whereby key members are attracted to competing or separate entities. Offering equity may provide a method of retaining staff, but commitment to the project must be stipulated.

Intellectual property ownership remains an issue that must be clearly defined early when developing a project. Potential investors are likely to avoid projects where this is ambiguous.

An employer, including an NHS trust, will expect an innovation to be registered with their research and innovation department. The trust should then assess the project and either relinquish all intellectual rights or provide appropriate support. In the case of the latter, this should be clearly defined: Will the trust offer the innovator time or financial support or perhaps both? A trust may, downstream, demand the majority of the net income of a financially profitable innovation, especially if argued that this was related to the innovator's workload.

The risk-averse nature of clinicians may also hinder the potential uptake of a medical innovation. Clinicians often expect a significant evidence base to support the implementation of a pathway or product. This can be forged by working with an independent assessor (e.g. academic or clinical unit).

Funding is likely to be an issue for many innovators. However, there are a number of avenues available within the United Kingdom (note Chapter 6). Innovators may need to invest their own funds initially to produce a tangible working model supported by their hospital trust if bursaries and prizes are also available.

Motivation is key to delivering a product. There are times during every project that phases appear insurmountable and team members may lose interest or wish to abandon the idea. Bearing in mind that the average time from concept to delivery of a medical innovation is approximately 12 years, it is essential to choose team members carefully and enlist those determined, and patient, to see the project to its conclusion.

## PLATFORMS

In recent years a number of platforms have been launched to aid medical innovators and accelerate their innovation journey. Some offer educational support and workshops guiding innovators in key areas such as raising capital, marketing and branding. Most arrange networking events that allow members to meet experienced innovators and industry leads.

Admission to these accelerator programmes is often through a competitive process (e.g. Microsoft). The level of support may, however, vary and one should fully understand what the platform will expect to gain by the innovator-platform association (e.g. equity, industry contact). This may not always be reflected in the subscription fees required by the platform. From a personal perspective, a productive innovation hub depends on the staff rather than the quality of the soft furnishings and broadband speed delivered within its space.

## THE CLINICAL ENTREPRENEUR TRAINING PROGRAMME

The Clinical Entrepreneur Programme (CEP) was launched by Professor Tony Young, National Clinical Director for Innovation at NHS England. To date the programme has fostered over 500 innovators including doctors, dentists, midwives and nursing staff.

At no cost to the innovator, the programme provides mentoring, exclusive networking and training to develop innovative ideas into products and businesses for patient benefit. Admission is via a competitive process.

The curriculum, delivered face to face or, more recently, online, is delivered as a series of educational events attended by industry leaders (note Table 2.2). Crucially, the programme allows entrepreneurs to pursue their innovation without having to leave the health service, providing a wider benefit to economic growth through inward investment in the health and life science sectors.

## THE FUTURE OF MEDICAL INNOVATION

During my journey through the medical innovation space, I have been truly humbled to work with some incredibly talented and determined medical innovators. Funding often remains a hurdle, but investors may see innovators who have injected their own funds into their project (perhaps then better described as *entrepreneurs*) as a sign of commitment.

I would encourage clinicians at all stages of their careers to consider developing their own medical innovation projects and support those hoping to develop theirs. Some projects may fail, and I often remind innovators that their first

Table 2.2 Key features of the clinical entrepreneurship programme

- One-to-one mentoring and coaching
- Networking opportunities and system introductions
- Placements and internships
- Bespoke advice and guidance on setting up and running a successful business
- Business planning support
- Educational "pit stop" events, topic-specific workshops and guest speakers
- Expert webinars, video content and e-learning
- Accredited curriculum
- Invitations to conferences and events
- Pitching opportunities
- News, communications and media
- Signposting to investment sources, sponsorship offers, funding opportunities, awards and prizes
- Time out for entrepreneurial activities
- Peer-to-peer support forum
- Badge of permission
- Professional development including assessing and improving entrepreneurial skills.

innovation may not be their best but that they understand the process and avoid pitfalls for future projects. A minority may prove lucrative, but they will all be interesting and challenging.

## REFERENCES

Kanegaonkar RG. Radial Bacterial/Viral Filter. UK Patent No. GB 2 233 904 B (1991).

Saleh A, Parkar F, Tolat A. The use of the D+R therapy physiotherapy iPhone application in the management of radial head fracture. Res Rev Orthop. 2018 March;2(1).

Vaish A, Ahmed S, Shetty A. Remote physiotherapy monitoring using the novel D+R therapy iPhone application. J Clin Orthop Trauma. 2017 Jan-Mar;8(1):21–24.

Whittaker M, Mathew A, Kanani R, Kanegaonkar RG. Assessing the Unterberger test: Introduction of a novel smartphone application. J Laryngol Otol. 2014 Nov;128(11):958–960.

Yvon C, Najuko-Mafemera A, Kanegaonkar R. The D+R balance application: A novel method of assessing postural sway. J Laryngol Otol. 2015 Aug;129(8):773–778.

## CASE STUDY B: GENERATION MEDICS

Generation Medics is an award-winning community of healthcare professionals providing up-to-date career information, advice, opportunities and networks for people from all backgrounds. They are champions of social mobility, equality and diversity and are recognised as leaders in the sector.

### THEIR STORY

Like many entrepreneurial stories, Generation Medics started when a group of likeminded people were catching up over coffee. Their conversation turned to a topic hot on all their minds: The worrying lack of useful information available to help students build a successful career in medicine and healthcare.

They discussed the difficulties facing students applying to university with no advice or support, Dr Rafique's experience of supporting students struggling at university, and the challenges navigating further career progression. They lamented the fact that certain socioeconomic groups were being dealt a worse hand within this competitive sector.

There and then, this bright-eyed group of health professionals came up with the initiative to extend opportunities to anyone who wanted to be a doctor, nurse, midwife, scientist or paramedic, etc. They sought to inspire folks who wanted to spend their career improving the public's health. Dr Rafique decided to formalise this opportunity and scribbled a plan and a logo on the back of a coffee shop napkin.

Seven years on and Generation Medics has helped thousands thrive in healthcare roles. Their eager alumni and volunteers have allowed students and professionals to innovate and give back. Together, they are building a pipeline of talent for the NHS.

## CASE STUDY C: THE I-GEL

Tens of thousands of patients worldwide require airway control each day. This is an essential requirement for general anaesthesia and in some trauma situations. Traditional devices include endotracheal tubes and laryngeal masks, but both have limitations. Laryngeal masks, for example, require a cuff to be inflated, are not always anatomically correct and may be bitten down on by a patient, which can result in airway obstruction.

Endotracheal intubation is technically challenging, requires two clinicians and necessitates cuff inflation to protect the lower airway and allow adequate ventilation.

The i-gel is a novel supraglottic airway device. Anatomically designed with a non-inflatable mask composed of a soft gel, the soft cuff fits snugly onto the peri-laryngeal framework, with its tip lying in the proximal opening of the oesophagus, isolating the oropharyngeal opening from the laryngeal opening. The device has a buccal cavity stabiliser which adapts to the oropharyngeal curvature of the patient. This stabiliser houses airway tubing in addition to a separate gastric channel [1-3].

The i-gel has several advantages over previously established airways:

1. Easy and fast insertion (less than 5 seconds) [4]
2. Reduced risk of trauma [5]
3. Superior seal pressure
4. Allows the gastric inlet to be separated, allowing stomach aspiration or insertion of a nasogastric tube
5. Has an incorporated bite block
6. A uniquely non-inflatable cuff

Development from concept to production required a decade of perseverance by Dr Muhammed Aslam Nasir. His initial plasticine models were superseded by a variety of materials, and designs altered in line with multiple cadaveric studies. The eventual material of choice was styrene ethylene butadiene styrene (SEBS), a soft, malleable yet robust enough material to perform efficiently in most testing clinical scenarios. It is this material that prompted the parent company Intersurgical to name the product, the i-gel.

The i-gel has now become the airway of choice for many elective surgical procedures requiring general anaesthesia and in most cases of airway control in trauma settings. This airway is available for both adult and paediatric anaesthesia and has also been adapted for veterinary use, the V-gel.

## REFERENCES

1. http://www.i-gel.com/products/theinventor/.
2. I-gel User-guide. Available from: http/www.i-gel.com/lib/docs/userguides/i-gel User Guide English.pdf.
3. I-gel supraglottic airway device with non inflatable cuff. Available from: http://www.i-gel.com/faq/i-gel.
4. An J, Nam SB, Lee JS, Lee J, Yoo H, Lee HM, Kim MS. Comparison of the i-gel and other supraglottic airways in adult manikin studies: systematic review and metaanalysis. Medicine (Baltimore). 2017 Jan; 96(1): e5801
5. Michalek P, Donaldson W, Vobrubova E, Hakl M. Complications associated with the use of supraglottic airway devices in perioperative medicine. Biomed Res Int. 2015;2015:746560. DOI: 10.1155/2015/746560.

## CASE STUDY D: THE GUY'S HOSPITAL MULTIDISCIPLINARY BALANCE SERVICE

Dizziness is a common problem, with an incidence of approximately 3% and a prevalence of 23% [1]. Although the majority of patients are managed in primary care, 12% are referred to secondary care [2]. One study found that balance patients endured, on average, 36 months of symptoms before a diagnosis was made, whilst another study concluded that patients regularly attended multiple outpatient hospital visits to a variety of specialties (e.g. otorhinolaryngology, neurology, general medicine, elderly care, cardiology and psychiatry) often undergoing unnecessary investigations before a diagnosis was made [3, 4]. This resulted in prolonged patient pathways, delays in care and inefficient use of clinic capacity (note Figure D.1).

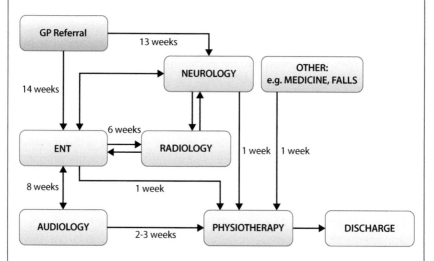

**Figure D.1 Example of general patient pathway and wait times.**

Dr Gareth Jones was responsible for developing the Guy's Multidisciplinary Balance Service. This specialist clinic, drawing from the expertise of otorhinolaryngologists, audiologists and vestibular physiotherapists provided a one-stop approach to the assessment and management of balance patients (note Figure D.2). An initial assessment by a specialist vestibular physiotherapist, and subsequent vestibular function testing, was followed by a discussion in a multidisciplinary setting and a personalised

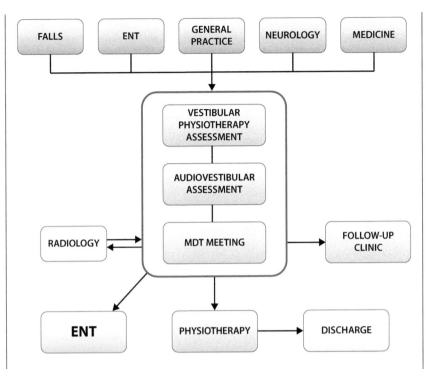

Figure D.2  The multidisciplinary balance clinic pathway.

management pathway forged. The service was both effective and efficient and showed the following benefits:

- A reduction in scanning rates from 75% to 14%.
- A reduction in the number of balance patients seen in general ear, nose and throat clinics from 25% to 5%.
- A simpler pathway avoiding a scattered, prolonged pathway.
- A significant decrease in follow-up appointments, up to five visits for some patients, and a reduction in cross-specialty referrals.
- Resulted in the formulation of a 100% management plan c.f. 25% in a general ear, nose and throat clinic.
- Investigations ordered in the balance clinic at 6% as opposed to 50% in the general clinic.
- Follow-up rates down from 40% to 8%.
- An opportunity to undertake research and innovation projects.

Similar successful models have been developed at Medway Maritime Hospital and is currently being developed at the Royal London Hospital.

## REFERENCES

1. Neuhauser HK, Radtke A, von Brevern M, Lezius F, Feldmann M, Lempert T. Burden of dizziness and vertigo in the community. Arch Intern Med. 2008 Oct 27;168(19):2118–2124.
2. Arya AK, Nunez DA. What proportion of patients referred to an otolaryngology vertigo clinic have an otological cause for their symptoms? J Laryngol Otol. 2008;122(2):145–149.
3. Swift A. Topics on Otorhinolaryngology, Head and Neck Surgery. 1st ed. London: Mark Allen Publisher; 2005.
4. Heaton JM, Barton J, Ranalli P, Tyndel F, Mai R, Rutka JA. Evaluation of the dizzy patient: Experience from a multidisciplinary neurotology clinic. J Laryngol Otol 1999;113(1):19–23.
5. Lee A, Jones G, Corcoran J, Premachandra P, Morrison GA. A UK hospital based multidisciplinary balance clinic run by allied health professionals: First year results. J Laryngol Otol. 2011 Jul;125(7):661–667.

# 3

# Intellectual property

EMMA HODGE

The term intellectual property (IP) covers a variety of rights that protect creations ranging from, for example, an artistic work to a technical invention. This chapter will focus on those intellectual property rights (IPRs) most relevant to innovations in the medical field: patents, design rights and know-how. Essentially, patents protect technical inventions and design rights protect the appearance of a product, while know-how is confidential, proprietary information and materials which may provide a competitive advantage.

It is often stated that it costs in excess of $1 billion to bring a new pharmaceutical product to the market, while a 2016 study of 106 newly launched drug products found the estimated average out-of-pocket cost per approved new compound was $1395 million.[1] For medical devices, the cost of development to market will depend on the regulatory pathway required, the cost being an estimated average of about $94 million if the premarket approval route is required by the FDA in the US, compared to an estimated $31 million for the less stringent process applied to devices deemed to be of less risk to the health, safety or welfare of the patient.[2]

Intellectual property rights, by protecting the product from copying, can provide a period of exclusivity and secure a period in which the large investment involved in developing such a medical innovation and successfully obtaining regulatory approval in one or more countries can be recouped.

## PATENTS

Patents protect technical inventions in any field: a product or a process, a new way of doing something, or a new technical solution to a problem. It should be noted that in Europe, patents cannot be granted for "methods for treatment of

DOI: 10.1201/9781003164609-4

the human or animal body by surgery or therapy and diagnostic methods practised on the human or animal body".[3] However, claims for "products, in particular substances or compositions, for use in any of these methods"[4] are allowed so that in practice patents can be granted for medical devices, pharmaceutical products, etc. For example, patents are granted with claims to the active drug compound itself, to combinations of active ingredients and to the device, such as inhalers, etc. Additionally, since patents are a national right and laws do differ from country to country, it is possible to obtain a granted patent for a method of treatment in some other countries, such as in the US.

To be patentable, an invention must be novel (i.e. must not been disclosed to the public before the filing date of the patent application). This is a global requirement and covers all written publications, anywhere in the world, however obscure, in any language, as well as any non-written disclosures such as an oral presentation at a conference, public use of an invention, or disclosure to a third party in the absence of a confidentiality agreement.

This novelty requirement means it is vitally important to ensure that any invention remains strictly confidential before a patent application is filed, or it will not be possible to get a patent granted. Confidentiality agreements should always be in place before discussing a project with any third party prior to filing a patent application, and preferably also after an application has been filed since there may also be know-how that should be protected. The UK Intellectual Patent Office (IPO) states that "the most common mistake made by inventors is to reveal their invention before applying for a patent". Since this mistake could result in the loss of a patent, everyone involved in an innovation project should be made aware of the important of confidentiality.

The invention must also have an inventive step. This means that the invention must not be considered an obvious modification of the existing body of knowledge by a person of ordinary skill in the relevant technical area.

Patent protection provides a monopoly right for 20 years from the filing date (provided the required renewal fees are paid), which right is granted by the state in return for a full disclosure of the invention in the patent specification. It is, therefore, another requirement of patent law that the patent application provides sufficient details that a person skilled in the relevant technical field would be able to put the invention into practice, for example, synthesise the claimed pharmaceutical active ingredient, or manufacture the claimed medical device.

A typical timeline for a patent application is presented in Figure 3.1, starting with an initial filing at the UK IPO and progressing through a Patent Cooperation Treaty (International) application.

The patent application expires 20 years from the filing date (which may be 21 years from the initial claimed priority date). However, in certain jurisdictions such as US, Europe and Japan, it is possible to extend the patent term for pharmaceutical and veterinary products for a limited time to compensate for the delays caused by the requirements to obtain regulatory marketing approval.

While obtaining a granted patent gives you the right to exclude others from using your invention, it does not give you the right to make and market your invention yourself. It is, therefore, important to consider not just whether

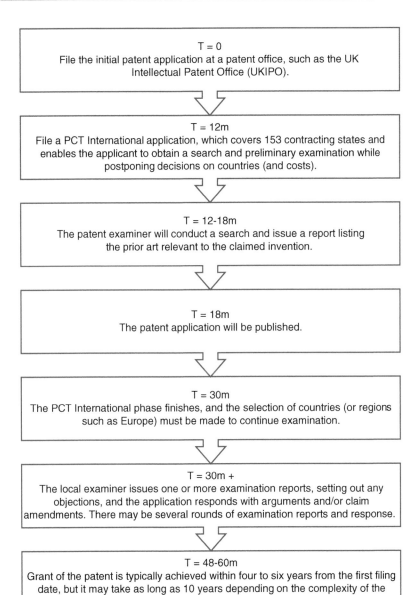

Figure 3.1 The timeline for a patent application.

your invention is patentable but also whether you have "freedom to oper-ate", that is, whether anyone else owns a patent that could prevent you from marketing your own invention. The claims of granted patents can, and do, overlap so that it is possible to have your own granted patent yet not have freedom to operate.

As an example, Edwards Lifesciences and Boston Scientific spent several years litigating patents covering their respective transcatheter valve prod-ucts in mainly the US, UK and Germany, each company alleging infringe-ment, before finally reaching an agreed settlement in 2019. However, this was not before injunctions banning the sale of Edwards devices were granted in Germany and in the UK, although some measures to protect patients were ordered by the UK court.

Freedom-to-operate searches may be required at regular stages throughout a research and development programme, particularly if the direction of the pro-gramme changes. Conducting searches for freedom-to-operate clearance is a specialised task, and it would be prudent to use someone experienced in this, whether internally or an external search firm. Since the searches will likely need updating as the programme develops, a member of the project team should take responsibility for keeping oversight of this.

Should any conflicting rights be identified as a result of the searches, these should be discussed at an early point with your patent attorney to work out the best options for you to overcome the conflict: you may decide to watch and wait or to oppose the granted right; you may want to design round the issue; or you may decide you need to obtain a licence from the earlier rights holder if a design round is not possible.

## DESIGN RIGHTS

In the UK, "unregistered" design right automatically exists to protect the shape or configuration of an object for 15 years after it was created, or for 10 years after it was first sold, whichever is the earliest date. However, this is not a monopoly right and you can use it only to stop someone copying your design, not from independently creating the same design. It is recommended to keep proof of when you created a design, for example, by getting signed and dated copies of your design drawings or photos certified and kept by a legal professional.

In contrast, registered design right protects both the product's shape and dec-oration and provides protection for up to 25 years, provided the renewal fees are paid every five years. To be eligible for protection as a registered design right, the design must be new and have individual character.

"New" in this sense means that no identical design, or no design whose fea-tures differ only in immaterial details, can have been published or otherwise publicly disclosed anywhere in the world. Although a so-called "grace period" exists which allows the applicant to register a design in the UK up to 12 months after the first disclosure by the designer, this should be treated with caution. Third parties can acquire rights of prior use if they independently and in good faith develop an identical or similar design during that grace period. It should also be noted that some other jurisdictions do not have such a grace-period, so reliance on the grace period could result in loss of design rights overseas. For these reasons, the grace period should not be used as a matter of routine but only if strictly necessary.

Individual character means that the design produces a different overall impression on the informed user (i.e. a person who is familiar with the type of product in question) in comparison with known designs. When assessing individual character, the degree of freedom available to the designer is taken into consideration.

The UKIPO examines applications only for compliance with formal requirements. The design is published in the *Registered Designs Journal* around three weeks after the application is filed, although deferred publication can be requested, for up to twelve months in the event that there is an interest in keeping the registration confidential initially, and applications will typically be registered around two months after filing, unless objections are raised.

If design protection is required in other countries, there is a system for claiming priority, similar to that for patents. However, for registered designs, the relevant period is six months. Separate applications can be made in individual countries; or a Registered Community Design (RCD) covers the whole of the European Union (EU); or the Hague System can be used to apply to a number of different jurisdictions via a single application. In each case, the priority period is six months from the date of the application for the UK-registered design.

Registered Community Designs are examined by the European Union Intellectual Property Office (EUIPO) in Alicante, while the Hague System is administered by the World Intellectual Property Office (WIPO) in Geneva. As with the UK designs, the examination by both EUIPO and WIPO is limited mainly to checking for formalities. If the application is found to meet the formal requirements, the design is then registered and published, although again, both before EUIPO and WIPO, deferment of publication may be requested of up to 30 months from the filing date or from the priority date.

## KNOW-HOW

Not all proprietary information can be protected by registered IPRs, for example, patents or registered design rights. However, such know-how (also referred to as trade-secrets) can be an important part of the overall protection around a medical innovation and can also be licensed along with patent rights. It is very important to retain the confidentiality in this know-how, and care must be taken to mark relevant documents as confidential, with access restricted.

A product may be protected simultaneously by one or more patents, design rights and know-how. For example, for an inhaler, the shape may be protected by Registered Design Right; technical details of the inhaler's workings may be protected by patents, together with the drug product; and the formulation may be retained as know-how.

## NOTES

1. DiMasi et al., *Journal of Health Economics*, Volume 47, May 2016, pp. 20–33
2. Source: Drugwatch.com
3. Article 53, European Patent Convention
4. Article 53, European Patent Convention

# 4

# Establishing a company

JANE OLLIS

## BEFORE YOU START

Before you think about setting up a business to take your idea through to a clinically validated and accepted product or service, draw a deep breath. The journey you are about to choose is hard, a rollercoaster ride, where you will experience the biggest highs precipitously followed by the lowest of lows. Failures will prevail over successes, and your resilience and ability to pick yourself up will be crucial to your survival as an entrepreneur. You will need to raise money, work a huge number of hours and maintain at all times the absolute belief in what you are doing.

If this sounds like you, read on.

So you have an idea. Before you get started ask yourself the following three questions.

1. Am I totally confident there is an unmet need for my product or service, and if I ask lots of people whose opinions I respect, will they give me the same answer? Your aim should always be to fix problems where you

DOI: 10.1201/9781003164609-5

can see a really clever way to make something more convenient, easier, better or affordable for your patients or customers.

2. Is this the right time for my innovation? If you look back for patterns in successful businesses, you might expect that the most common ingredients for success were the founder, the ideas and the investment. Actually, it's all about being in the right place at the right time, a bit of good luck and knowing when the market is ready for you. The creator of photocopiers, Chester Carlton, started presenting his designs in 1939 to big companies, including IBM, but five years later was still unsuccessful as people could not see past carbon copies. Chester did not give up; he refined his process and eventually, in 1949, was approached by a small New York manufacturer of photographic paper and together Xerox was born. Whilst his idea needed developing, it was essentially just 10 years too early.

3. Aside from the fact that you are now considered an artist and sculptor of the business world, I need to let you know that the position of founder comes with some less glamorous activities. In the early days, you will need to guard your pennies very closely and will find yourself chief washer-upper, bookkeeper and website creator. Multiple skill requirements, low or no pay and working all hours are your new reality. Does this fit with your family and financial needs?

## GETTING GOING

If the answer to the above is yes to all questions, then start thinking about how you can prove your concept quickly and cheaply whilst building a clear route map to get from idea creation to market, with some very clear go/no go points along the way.

Step 1 is to prove your concept. This means building something as cheaply as possible that will allow you to validate your idea with a clear but small set of results to show that it works. Either you will need to dig deep into your own pockets for this or use grant funding, working with an academic or research institution (in which case, read very carefully any contract you enter into, to ensure you keep any intellectual property that emerges).

If this is successful, you can move to a prototyping phase where you can build and test a full replica of your innovation. In this phase, take good advice around patent protection, which will be one of the first things that any early-stage investor will want to see, and decide if you have enough technical information to support an application and the claims that you want to make. Funding your prototype will require either securing further grant funding or reaching out to friends, family or angel investors. As it is hard to value the company in these early days, convertible notes, a form of short-term debt, are often used and converted to equity at a later stage when there are more data points on which to base a valuation.

When you are in this stage and busy securing funding and building, the biggest mistake you could make is to forget about your end user. Involve patients right from the beginning; ask them about the design and all the features that will make it really easy and attractive for them to use. Put the user at the centre of everything you do.

Start thinking about the team you need around you, unless you have started with a co-founder to share the journey. Investors will want to know that you have the combined skill set and competency to build the company out. If you cannot afford to hire people full-time on the payroll, when you lay out your share allocations (use either SeedLegals, a one-stop platform for all the legal matters, or a lawyer you know and trust), reserve a pool for those whose time you can buy with shares rather than cash in hand.

Think about your board as well and people who bring shared wisdom, influence and networks.

## DEFINING YOUR VALUE PROPOSITION

A value proposition is quite simply the promise of the value you will bring. So rather than thinking about the features of your product, it is the statement of why someone should buy something from you, why it is unique and how it will make their life so much better.

To help you craft it, try using these three easy steps:

1. Think about all the benefits you offer and why this is valuable.
2. Identify your customer's main problem.
3. Connect your value to this problem, and then differentiate yourself as the only player in town who can deliver this value.

## WRITING THE BUSINESS PLAN AND DOING THE FINANCIALS

The time will come when you need to commit to writing your business plan and putting together all your best assumptions and turning them into a financial forecast.

A good business plan will help you determine if your business has a chance of making a profit and give you clarity on all your start-up costs and how much finance you will need to raise.

It will also force you to answer questions around your revenue model, marketing strategies and pricing. Use your network for help as chances are there will be unknowns: What are subscription models for an app? How do I calculate life time value for customers? What is my pricing once I know the cost of acquisition and expected lifespan? Will this deliver my required level of profit?

To be successful, you will need to have a thorough understanding and plan for every aspect of the innovation process and be able to talk with complete confidence. There is no shortcut.

Here are some headings

1. **Executive Summary** – include your vision, mission and values and the problem you are solving

2. **Your solution** – What makes your product or service unique in relation to solving the problem and the benefits? Define your long-term road map and the industry in which you operate. What is the IP status, and how will you protect this?

3. **Your market** – Describe the market in which you sell. Highlight the segments of the market, the key characteristics of customers in each segment and what influences their purchasing decisions. How large is each market segment? What is your planned market share? What are the important trends, such as market growth or changing environment? Explain the reasons behind the trend. Do you have any confirmed orders, and who are your best prospective customers?

4. **The competition** – What are the competing products or services? What are their advantages and disadvantages compared to you? For example, price, quality, distribution. Why will customers buy your product or service over others?

5. **Your marketing and sales strategy** – Where do you position your product or service in the market? What is your pricing policy? How do you promote your product or service? What sales channels do you use to reach your target customers? How will you sell your product or service?

6. **The team structure** – Set out the structure and key skills of the management team and the staff. Clarify how you cover the key areas of production, sales, marketing, finance and administration. Address any areas of deficiency and your plans to cover this weakness. Explain your recruitment and training plans, including timescales and costs.

7. **Your business operations** – What production facilities do you need, and if out-sourcing, who will be your key suppliers and your relationship with them. What management and IT information systems are in place? What quality or regulatory standards will the business need to conform to?

8. **Business model, financials and exit strategy** – How will the company make profits – via a direct sale, subscription (Netflix), franchise or platform (e.g. Facebook, Uber)? Will you be selling to business or consumer? Provide forecasts for the next three (or even five) years. Do the forecasts allow for the possibility of problems and delays in getting to market that could affect cash flow? Use the cash flow forecast to predict any financing requirements. Describe your exit plans and give comparative exit prices using relevant examples. If necessary, get help with this section.

9. **Risks** – Set out a one-page analysis of strengths, weaknesses, opportunities and threats. Be honest about your weaknesses and the threats you face and how you will mitigate any risks.

## CHOOSING THE RIGHT LEGAL STRUCTURE

There are a number of legal structures to consider summarised in Table 4.1.

The likely structure for your medical innovation, given that you are going to generate intellectual property and likely to raise funds for this, is going to be a private company that is incorporated and limited by shares. This means that the

Table 4.1  Types of business structures

|  | Summary | Pros | Cons |
| --- | --- | --- | --- |
| Sole trader | Good if you are just wanting to be self-employed | Easy to set up Low cost of running | Full liability for any debt |
| Partnership | Between two or more individuals who share management and profits | Easy to form, manage and run and more potential to raise finance | Full liability, affecting all partners and risk of partnership disagreements |
| Private limited liability company (Ltd) | Owners legally responsible for debts only to the extent of the amount of capital they invested | Good for raising finance, protecting IP and less personal financial exposure with limited liability protection | Involves set up costs; annual accounts and financial reports must be placed in public domain |

company has shareholders, and the liability of the shareholders to creditors of the company is limited to any money they originally invested. A shareholder's personal assets are also protected in the event of company insolvency, but money invested in the company may be lost.

Limited companies must pay an application fee and be incorporated with Companies House. You can register online and will need

- The company's name and registered address
- At least one director
- At least one shareholder
- Details of the company's shares
- Rules about how the company is run – known as "articles of association"

## GETTING INVESTMENT READY

Depending on your innovation, it is likely that to get to market you are going to need to raise funds and grant income to get to the end of your R&D pathway. Many founders find that their time gets preoccupied with fund raising and ensuring that the company's cash reserves give them sufficient runway to get to market.

There are a number of investment strategies to consider, but they generally start with pre-seed funding, the first time you will officially give away some of your company in return for funds. It is rather like planting a tree. Typically, investors will put in small amounts, say £300–£500K in return for 10%–20%, whilst you are still pre-market and therefore high risk. With your first round you may be able to offer a convertible note, a form of short-term debt that converts into equity when you are in a stronger position to value the business.

There are a number of angel networks around the UK, and getting through and pitching to these takes determination. Preparing your pitch deck is an art unto itself, and then delivering a timed presentation followed by a grilling is an experience you will need to get used to.

The pitch deck should comprise some highly visual slides; don't even think of bullet points. Everyone has a slant on what they like to see, but as a guide you will need to cover the following:

- Your vision and value proposition
- The problem you are solving
- Your target market and opportunity
- Your solution
- Your amazing team and partnership
- Your revenue model
- Your roadmap to get to market, showing how funding rounds link to value creation in the business
- Your marketing and sales strategy
- Your exit plan and returns investors can expect, based on comparisons with other relevant sales

Once you have generated interest, investors might propose a term sheet, a non-binding agreement that sets out the basic terms and conditions under which the investment will be made. When you get to this point you will need to take a view on the value of the business (always tricky at this stage, as stated earlier). How many shares you are willing to give away and for how much? Once the terms are agreed upon, the investor will commence their due diligence on your business, so make sure all your company documentation is organised and can be shared. This whole process invariably takes three times longer than you think, so be prepared and don't get stressed.

## ENJOYING THE JOURNEY

The entrepreneur's journey up the mountain is a long one, and so it is really important to enjoy it and celebrate each time you reach a little plateau. Enjoy the view, the people who you meet on the way, the little things you can do that make a difference to people's lives around you. Remember, perseverance is key. By knowing and planning your route, sharing each step with people who you care about and as a combined team, you can make the world a better place with your innovation.

## CASE STUDY E: ORGANA

Currently $120 billion is spent annually on developing new medical devices and assessing these technologies through clinical trials. More than 90% of these innovations fail to reach the market, on occasion, because they may be unsafe or ineffective.

This may be due to a lack of accurate, pre-clinical testing methods; the industry is dependent on methods that do not always accurately represent the human system. Cadaveric, animal, silicone and machine-model testing can be unethical or physiologically and anatomically inaccurate.

The ultimate goal in this environment is to provide human-like testing before clinical trials, achieved by providing artificial organ models that contain the physical, anatomical and biological properties of real organs. This will de-risk the R&D of cutting-edge medical devices, saving valuable time and money.

Organa has developed synthetic organs that look, feel and behave like real organs (Figure E.1). These human-like products provide testing capabilities far earlier in the development cycle of new medical devices and treatments. This will allow companies to iterate their innovations safe in the knowledge that the performance of their innovation will translate with

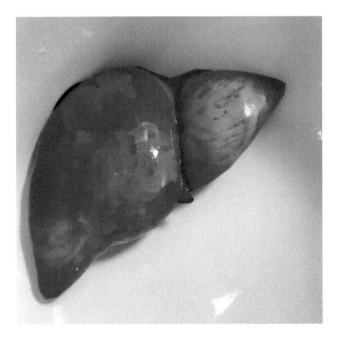

Figure E.1  Synthetic liver model with tissue-mimicking properties.

a high degree of certainty to real human use. The technology can also be applied in surgical training, a field which has seen a rapid decrease in the number of hands-on training hours that surgical trainees are provided. This has led to lower proficiency and poorer patient outcomes. Introduction of a hyper-real training opportunity will provide the much-needed ability for trainees to freely practise their skills.

To create this, Organa has developed a novel biomaterial that can be formulated to accurately represent the behaviour of human organs. They have already obtained evidence to support their materials' ability to mimic the mechanical response of real brain, lung and liver tissue during surgical procedures to 95% accuracy, unachieved by any commercially available material [1]. The mechanical response of their synthetic material mimics that of real tissue through three independent mechanical parameters; the stress-strain response, surgical needle insertion force and friction force at the needle–tissue interface. Additionally, the material is compatible with common surgical techniques such as ultrasound, MRI, diathermy and other energy methods.

Organa fabricates artificial organs using both advanced cast-moulding methods and novel 3D-printing methods. Their cast-moulding method allows them to easily achieve high product volumes. Additionally, they have developed a bespoke 3D-printing technique that can replicate complex biological architecture, such as patient-specific anatomy and rare disease cases (Figure E.2). Their novel 3D cryogenic printing method is able to produce stable 3D structures by utilising the liquid to solid phase change of their printing ink. Using their formulation as the printing ink, the setup is able to successfully create 3D complex geometrical structures with the required physical properties, and therefore, mimics the mechanical properties of required organs. Their material also has the potential to impact the

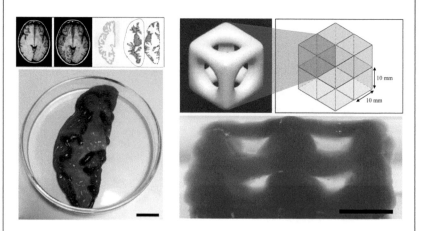

Figure E.2 3D-printed patient-specific brain slice and tissue scaffold.

pharmaceutical industry as it is a viable substrate for 3D cell culture. Cutting-edge research in the field of cancer biology and mechanobiology is providing evidence that cellular response depends on the mechanical properties of the culture substrate. The drug discovery process could, therefore, be enhanced if experimental therapies are tested via high throughput cell cultures seeded on substrates that are akin to their native microenvironment. They have evidenced the cell viability of their 3D-printed material constructs by seeding human dermal fibroblasts. The cells showed good attachment and >97% viability on the collagen-coated 3D printed structures [2].

Organa envisions transforming the medical device industry by providing a synthetic organ platform from which all devices and treatments can be developed.

## REFERENCES

1. Tan, Z., Dini, D., Rodriguez y Baena, F. & Forte, A. E. *Mater. Des.* 160, 886–894 (2018).
2. Tan, Z., Parisi, C., Di Silvio, L., Dini, D. & Forte, A. E. *Sci. Rep.* 7, (2017).

## CASE STUDY F: RHINAMITE

Rhinamite, a device designed to stop nosebleeds in a pinch, conceived within the healthcare setting, sits at the bleeding edge of modern product design and innovation

The majority of people experience self-limiting nosebleeds. For 15% of the global population though, these are recurrent [1], and many require hospital attention. Nosebleed admissions to A&E constitute the most common ENT presentation, at 30% [2]. They comprise 0.5– 1% of admissions to A&E overall [3]. Nosebleeds continue to cause death worldwide.

Most nosebleeds stop with a 10-minute pinch to the nose. A&E staff and distressed patients, however, struggle to sustain this. This frequently leads to the extremely uncomfortable process of nasal packing, requiring admission for an average of three nights [4]. Whereas packs are required for persistent and posterior bleeds, concerns exist that some cases undergo unnecessary packing.

*Rhinamite* works by applying cooling pressure over the sides of the nose in a comfortable self-holding manner. Patients should obtain a *Rhinamite* over the counter for home use – thus preventing hospital visits. *Rhinamite*

Figure F.1 **Rhinamite.**

can also be used in A&E to prevent admission and may allow an ENT specialist to cauterise the vessel [5]. In short, this simple device can greatly reduce visits to A&E as well as hospital admissions.

In sport, *Rhinamite* can be placed on the nose to stop a bleed or address swelling, acting as a cool compress. Nosebleeds in the international contact sports sector incur cross-infection risk and a cost of player downtime. Blood loss during contact sport can be frightening – particularly in schools. Demand for improved safety in the field exists.

Nosebleeds predominantly affect children and the elderly. As the ageing anticoagulated population grows, the scale of the problem increases. The effects on patients and their networks are far-reaching, including overnight ambulance calls, emergencies in sports, distressed teaching staff in schools and unnecessary hospital admissions. Treating the condition in hospitals allowed for in-depth insight into the problem, and the scale seemed unbelievable – surely a simple solution should exist.

I set about asking questions of users and researching existing products to ascertain features required in a device solution, completing detailed lean canvassing. The solution required a self-holding mechanism with ease of fit to empower the user to self-treat and allow them to relax during treatment. It should be comfortable and look appealing, especially to younger users. The device gradually took shape and improved over many iterations of prototyping.

When clinicians adopt a design mindset, solutions to the most frustrating medical problems can be just out of the reach of our fingertips. A novel way of treating patients can be established through a perspective which cannot be learned from a textbook, vastly improving patient experience. Understanding device innovation provides the clinician with a far-reaching opportunity to impact their patients' lives positively, by design.

## REFERENCES

1. Rainsbury JW, Molony NC. Clopidogrel versus low-dose aspirin as risk factors for epistaxis. *Clinical Otolaryngology* 2009; https://doi.org/10.1111/j.1749-4486.2009.01926.x.
2. Tomkinson A, Roblin DG, Flanagan P et al. Patterns of hospital attendance with epistaxis. *Rhinology* 1997;35:129–131.
3. Pallin DJ, Chng YM, McKay MP et al. The epidemiology of ED visits for epistaxis. *Annals of Emergency Medicine* 2005 Jul;46(1):77–81.
4. Goljo E et al. Cost of management in epistaxis admission: Impact of patient and hospital characteristics. *Laryngoscope* 2015 Dec;125(12):2642–2647.
5. Mehta N, Stevens K et al. National prospective observational study of inpatient management of adults with epistaxis – a National Trainee Research Collaborative delivered investigation. *Rhinology* 2019 Jun 1;57(3):180–189. doi: 10.4193/Rhin18.239.

# 5

# Prototyping

## GERAINT GREEN

## INTRODUCTION

Prototyping is an essential stage of product development. A working prototype allows an innovator to assess their design, test and, if necessary, remodel the product to optimise its function and appearance. One should always remember that the prototype does not necessarily represent the final product but allows industry collaborators to understand, through a tangible model, the components required, the functionality of the product and design of the final manufacturing process.

## TYPES OF PROTOTYPES

The process of prototyping may be classified into tangible (i.e. physical) product and intangible (e.g. software) modelling. These require different approaches and industry support.

## TANGIBLE PRODUCTS

### Proof of concept

A proof-of-concept prototype may be constructed using off-the-shelf materials. Many inventors have started their innovation journey by exploiting components harvested from off-the-shelf objects from hardware stores and general household

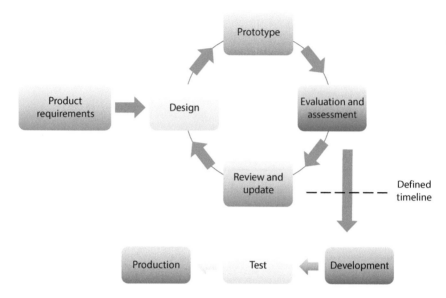

Figure 5.1 The prototype cycle.

items. This process not only allows the construction of a working model that can be tested and remodelled but also allows an innovator to understand the number of components required and their assembly. The prototype cycle is illustrated in Figure 5.1. It should be borne in mind that the cycle cannot continue indefinitely or a tangible product may never actually come to market. A timeline should be set and the product generated for market.

## Visual prototype

A visual prototype is a model that demonstrates the overall appearance, size and dimensions of the product. It may be used to present to early investors and potential collaborators. Whilst this prototype was formerly constructed from cardboard, foam, wood and even plasticine, many innovators have now turned to 3D printing to create realistic, elegant models of their proposed products. This form of printing may now be performed at home with commercially available 3D printers. Materials that may be used include plastics, powders, resin, metal and carbon fibre.

## Functioning prototype

A fully functioning prototype is used by a team for pitching, testing and market research. Although this model is often closely aligned to the pre-production phase prototype, it is often remodelled according to feedback gained and testing of the design.

## Pre-production prototype or factory sample

This form of prototype is provided by a manufacturer prior to full production to ensure quality and functionality. Although one may source an established company working within that field, the proposed product may come into direct competition and hence the product may not progress. An industry leader may not wish to invest in a proposed product that may come into direct competition with their own existing manufactured item. One should always seek a non-disclosure agreement (NDA) when approaching potential collaborators and industry partners.

A factory prototype is used to market the product and present to retailers and chain stores. Also known as production samples, these may be produced in small volumes to identify manufacturing problems.

Although the process of manufacturing is beyond the scope of this book, it is useful for an innovator to understand the potential methods of production. These are illustrated in Table 5.1.

Table 5.1  Manufacturing methods

| | |
|---|---|
| Casting | Casting involves pouring a liquid material into a mould. A hollow cavity within the mould defines the desired shape, which can be ejected once the material has solidified. Materials include metals, plastic and glass. See Figure 5.2a. |
| Laser sintering | Laser sintering is a manufacturing process that uses a high-powered laser beam to melt and fuse layers of metallic powder. This is a useful and rapid method of producing metal prototypes and early production parts. See Figure 5.2b. |
| Vacuum forming | Vacuum forming is a manufacturing process in which a sheet of heated plastic is moulded into a three-dimensional shape by applying a vacuum or compressed air. See Figure 5.2c. |
| Injection moulding | Injection moulding is commonly used in the manufacture of plastic products and components. The process involves injecting melted plastic into a defined mould cavity. The mould separates once the plastic has solidified, ejecting the required shape, and the process is repeated. See Figure 5.2d. |
| Extrusion | This manufacturing process produces an object of a specific cross-sectional shape and is often used to produce tubular structures. Molten plastic or metal is forced under pressure through a die. The lumen dictates the shape of the structure, which solidifies on leaving the container. See Figure 5.2e. |

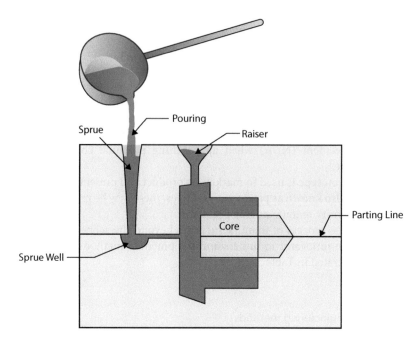

Figure 5.2a Casting.

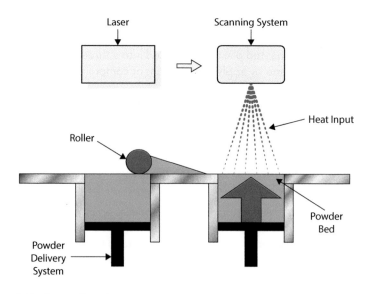

Figure 5.2b Laser sintering.

Step 1: Sheet is heated and brought over to a male mold

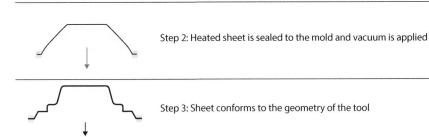

Step 2: Heated sheet is sealed to the mold and vacuum is applied

Step 3: Sheet conforms to the geometry of the tool

Figure 5.2c  Vacuum moulding.

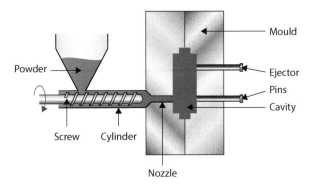

Figure 5.2d  Injection moulding.

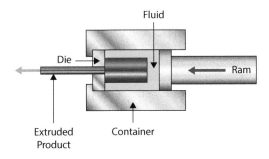

Figure 5.2e  Hydrostatic extrusion.

## SOFTWARE PROTOTYPES

In many respects software prototypes serve the same purpose as physical proto-types – i.e. they are intended to demonstrate the function and benefit of a product without expending the time and effort required to produce the finished article. However, as there is no manufacturing process involved in software develop-ment, the distinction between the finished production software and a prototype can be blurred. In fact, modern, agile software development processes focus on the production of a Minimum Viable Product (MVP) – a prototype implement-ing the least amount of functionality necessary for the user community to assess the function and usability of the software – before iteratively adding functional-ity to meet user requirements. In modern, web-focused, software development, this iterative development may continue indefinitely.

## HORIZONTAL AND VERTICAL SOFTWARE PROTOTYPING

A horizontal prototype is focussed on demonstrating the operation of the soft-ware from the user's perspective. This essentially means producing a user inter-face which allows the prototype user to interact with the software in a manner indicative of the way a user would with the production software. In a hori-zontal prototype, the majority of effort is focussed on the user interface, and therefore, typically, the back-end data processing functionality is sacrificed, with the user interface displaying sample or synthetic data as necessary. A vertical prototype, in contrast, focuses on demonstrating the data-processing functionality of the proposed software whilst keeping the effort expended on developing the user interface to a minimum. In reality, any software prototype is going to need to be able to demonstrate its potential to the stakeholders to whom it is presented. This will require sufficient data-processing functional-ity to allow the stakeholders to understand the value of the proposal and a sufficiently developed user interface to understand how users will use it. The proportional amount of effort spent in developing the user interface as opposed to the back end will depend on the relative importance placed on the usabil-ity of the platform versus the data-processing functionality, and therefore, on the nature of the product being prototyped and the stakeholders to whom it is being presented.

## DATA PRIVACY AND SECURITY

The purpose of prototype software is to demonstrate the minimum set of func-tionality to allow stakeholders to understand the value of the proposed product. In selecting the minimum set of functionality, the non-functional requirements of the software are typically ignored. This is to be expected, and a significant proportion of the work required to move software from prototype to produc-tion readiness is focused on addressing these non-functional requirements, for example, performance, resilience and security. However, it is this last item which requires at least some consideration during the prototyping phase.

Software applications operate on data, and in order for a prototype to demonstrate the function of the proposed product, it will be necessary to provide a representative data set for the software to process. Such a data set may be generated, or an existing dataset may be used. In the event that an existing data set is procured, it should be used only with the permission of the data owner, and where it contains identifiable personal information it will be subject to data privacy legislation such as the General Data Protection Regulation (GDPR). GDPR requires that any personal data is used only for specific and explicit purposes, must be used only in a manner directly relevant to the purposes for which it was originally collected and must be adequately protected. The financial penalties for breaching GDPR can be severe; fines in the UK are capped at £17.5 million or 4% of annual global turnover, whichever is greater. Therefore, before using an extant data set for the purposes of prototyping a product, it is essential that it is established that such activities can be said to be relevant to the purpose for which the data was originally collected and that sufficient safeguards are in place to protect the data. The security measures put in place to protect any real personal data used in a prototype will need to be equivalent to those used in production software and will need to extend beyond cyber security measures to physical and procedural measures, such as physically securing IT equipment to prevent theft and ensuring that only those with a legitimate requirement to view the data are granted access to the prototype. Given the overheads incurred in meeting such extreme security requirements, the constraints imposed on demonstrating the prototype to interested parties, and the severe ramifications should data be compromised, it is almost always preferable to ensure that any data used for prototyping data is synthetic, i.e. generated using random or arbitrary data; however, this can have consequences as discussed in the following section.

## MOVING TO PRODUCTION

Having demonstrated a working prototype of a software product which seems to incorporate all the features and functions required, it can be natural for stakeholders to assume that minimal work will be necessary to develop the final product: the fixing of a few bugs and maybe some tweaks to the user interface. Software development is expensive and time-consuming, and it is this type of assumption which has led to the great number of budget and schedule overruns for which the industry is notorious. Assuming that a prototype has fully implemented all the functions and features of the finished product, it will still be necessary, in addition to fixing all the bugs and making all the tweaks to the user interface, to meet all the non-functional requirements necessary to run software in production, such as the following:

- **Security.** Security architecture will need to be put in place to protect data, infrastructure and intellectual property.

- **Scalability.** Whilst a single user account may be used to demonstrate a prototype, modern web applications may need to handle hundreds or thousands of users simultaneously.
- **Performance.** Whilst a prototype may perform adequately with a small set of test data, the production platform may have to deal with vastly greater volumes. This can be compounded where the test data, particularly synthetic data, are not properly representative of the production data.
- **Stability.** Typically, a software prototype will be required to operate only for the duration of a demonstration or test. Production software may need to be available 24 hours a day, 365 days a year, with "five-nines" (99.999%) availability.
- **Maintainability.** In order to provide "five-nines" availability a support team will need to be able to manage, maintain and diagnose faults in the production software platform.

The effort and time typically required to meet such non-functional requirements are significant and almost always unrecognised or underestimated until the product development is over budget and behind schedule. In this respect, the limitations of a software prototype are almost as significant and may have as great an impact as the features and functions it demonstrates, and therefore, must be understood.

## CASE STUDY G: DOCBOOK.CO.UK

Medical education is delivered through a variety of platforms. These include lectures, tutorials, small group discussions and published literature. Of the latter, self-assessment picture books are a common method of revision and education, of particular benefit to those sitting oral examinations. Each book, in general, consists of approximately 50 scenarios, each depicted by a single image such as a photograph, table or chart. Each is followed by a series of questions with answers listed on the following page. Books are currently marketed at approximately £40–50 pounds.

*Docbook.co.uk* was developed by Dr Aslan Mirza (a general practitioner with incredible IT skills), Dr Junaid Bajwa (now Chief Medical Scientist for Microsoft) and me in 2007 (note Figure G.1). The website consisted of 80 pages illustrating ear, nose and throat pathology. A static illustration was replaced by a video clip, audio or photograph series. Eight questions, of increasing difficulty, were posed to the reader. Answers were presented when the cursor was placed over a corresponding "answer" box.

Docbook is a free online medical resource, which aims to support Healthcare Professionals at all stages of their careers from student to specialist.

All our modules are written by experts in their fields.

☑ I accept Docbook's terms and conditions

Continue onto Docbook Questions

Figure G.1  Docbook.co.uk

At no charge to the user, this altruistic platform provided a unique method of self-assessment and education. At its close in 2011 the platform had attracted over 3.2 million hits from over 150 countries. Although attracting significant footfall, the platform was closed as the server costs outweighed the income obtained.

The platform is soon to be republished with a wider range of surgical and medical specialties.

# 6

# Raising capital

## *How innovators raise funding to drive medical innovation*

IAN M. NEWINGTON

## INTRODUCTION

You have a great idea and positive feedback from friends and colleagues and maybe clinicians and patients. Having invested a lot of time, effort and possibly some hard-earned savings, you now have confidence that what you have – be it on paper, a mock-up or even a crude prototype you made in the workshop or laboratory – could be the basis of a business. You may have already set up a company.[1] As you look into the next steps on the innovation journey,[2] the realisation hits you that you are going to need more capital even to file a patent,[3] let alone to get this over the finish line. So how do you finance the journey from your great idea to a product that clinicians can use and patients benefit from?

This book aims to help you along that journey, and this chapter provides a description of the different sources of capital for each stage and things to consider in accessing them. It's worth saying at the outset that you should not underestimate the amount of time and energy you will need to invest just to fund your technology from concept to product.

DOI: 10.1201/9781003164609-7

It's tough for all start-ups, and healthcare technology development comes with the additional challenges of regulatory compliance[4] to certify safety and the need to generate sufficient evidence of clinical utility[5] and cost-effectiveness[6] if you are going to convince someone to buy the product.[7] Moreover, unlike in biotechnology and drug development, medtech products are rarely bought out or licensed by big companies until they are generating revenue. So, if acquisition or licensing is your exit strategy, you still have a long road to finance.

Assuming you have decided to establish a company,[1] the rest of this chapter will describe the various sources of funding available and how and when to access them.

# FIRST THINGS FIRST

## Business plan

Make sure you have the best business plan you can construct. Ideally, you will have done this before you set up your company.[1] If not, **do it now** – there are plenty of templates out there, or take a look at a few from other entrepreneurs in your network. It makes clear to everyone, yourself included, what the opportunity is and the trajectory over the next few years to revenue generation, including capital requirements, timing and market access. (Remember, UK is only 2% of worldwide healthcare.) It is something that you can share with potential investors and you can use to guide your activities and measure progress. It is a living document and forms the basis of your "pitch deck", which is the set of visuals you will be using to describe to investors why they should invest in your company.

## Valuation

You need to have a realistic idea of the value of your company and how much you are prepared to exchange for the investment you need – there are a number of ways to do this, and it would be a whole chapter in itself to explore.[8] It is also not an exact science and will depend on current market conditions, the size of recent exits in the sector, the strength of your team and your desperation for finance. Here are some simple approaches that work in most cases:

- Base value on your three-year cash forecast (be realistic)
- Use the book value of the business (assets minus liabilities)
- $3 \times$ EBIT (earnings before interest and tax); income less expenses
- Business expert valuation – e.g. use an angel network
- What you think it's worth – be prepared to be challenged!

For example, if your valuation is £1m and you need £250,000 to reach the next step, which should see a significant jump in value, you need to have to be prepared to exchange 25% of the share value of your company (or more) for that investment.

# SOURCES OF INVESTMENT CAPITAL

## Smart capital

A recent report[9] highlights some trends in UK investing and summarises the available types of investors to approach for capital. You should look for "smart" capital – investors who will bring their knowledge, network and active advice can really help accelerate your growth and avoid common pitfalls. Accelerators provide the opportunity to learn skills and access additional resources (e.g. Digital Health London; and see Corporate Venturing section). A wide network who may be able to advise, help in accessing expertise and resources, and perhaps even invest at the next stage of growth, means networking and getting to know potential investors. This is critical to your success in raising capital.

## Available funds

**University seed funds** – funds are available to academic researchers and supported by government; these can allow academic researchers to develop their ideas further before a company is spun out, giving the company a statistically better chance of survival. If this is you, you are also in a position to apply for grant funding (see Grants section) and, as they do not require you to give up any equity in your company, can help you de-risk your technology further before venturing out of the shelter of your institution. However, your terms of employment may mean that your employing organisation will own any IP you develop, and so you should understand the terms on which they would allow you to take this into a company and exploit it before choosing this route.

**Business Angels** – these are typically high-net-worth individuals, often belonging to a larger network (e.g. Cambridge Angels); usually you will need several angels to invest to reach your target; also they typically bring business and possibly sector expertise alongside the capital. Make sure you identify angels who invest in the healthcare technology sector.

**Venture Capital (VC) Funds** – VC funds manage a pool of money from investors seeking private equity stakes in startups and small- to medium-sized enterprises with strong growth potential; they are generally characterised as very high-risk/high-return investments. VC funding may come with the requirement of directorship, which is a way for the fund to reduce its risk by providing management expertise and to oversee the investment.

**Corporate Venturing** – many large corporates run their own venture funds to invest in smaller companies in their sectors, where this is mutually beneficial. Often this will come as incubators or accelerators (e.g. J&J's JLabs), where the early-stage company can be nurtured before moving on to seeking commercial investment, or possibly as a further investment from the corporate themselves. Increasingly, these accelerators are awarded on the basis of competition and come with no commitment on either side (e.g. Philips Accelerator), but the access to facilities and skills enhancement plus the networking benefits make them extremely valuable.

**Crowdfunding** – there are a number of platforms that allow a large number of small investors to invest through a nominee company (e.g. Syndicateroom or Crowdcube). Often, a keystone investor needs to be on board, bringing a minimum proportion of the investment round before such a platform will consider raising funding for you.

**Grants** – there are a number of sources of grant funding for many stages of developing your product, generating evidence of safety, efficacy and cost-effectiveness, through to scaling up for the market; generally these come without you giving up equity. (More details in the section below.)

**Debt** – this is rarely available until the company has grown and has revenue to repay the loan and has sufficient assets to back it, so it is more useful for the growth stage of the company. The British Business Bank is a government mechanism to provide support to grow and sustain businesses, often requiring other investments to match the loan. Most banks can provide loans for this stage of the company's life.

## Other sources not to ignore

These may make the difference between business survival and failure and can reduce the amount of equity you need to give up early on when your company is least valuable.

**LEP and other local or regional support** – often small amounts (£1,000–10,000) available as grants to support new businesses.

**SEIS/EIS**[10] – Eligibility for Seed Enterprise Investment Scheme allows investors to invest up to £100,000 per year with 50% tax break, and a single enterprise can receive up to £150k in SEIS funding. Enterprise Investment Scheme allows investors to commit up to £1M per tax year with a 30% tax break, and companies can receive up to £12M in EIS funding. There are rules for investors, in particular a minimum three-year investment. A similar scheme, called Social Investment Tax Relief (SITR), exists for non-profits and CiCs. Check out the HMRC Venture Capital Schemes Manual for more detail.[11]

**R&D Tax credit**[12] – this is definitely something you should check out. HMRC will reduce liability to tax or even pay you cash back towards your R&D expenditures. Of course, there are rules for eligible expenses, but this is one not to be missed.

**Patent Box**[13] – this is another under-claimed tax relief on profits from exploiting IP you own or have licensed exclusively.

## More on grant funding

Given the particularly high risks involved in healthcare technology and the relatively risk-averse nature of investors in the UK, publicly funded grants and awards should definitely be in your plan. These require as much effort as pitching to investors, with sometimes complex and demanding application forms with rigorous assessment by experts. You also may be required to attend a panel interview. Schemes can have single or two-stage application processes (expression of interest followed by full details). They are generally quite competitive but often less so for more specific challenges.

The main sources of such public funding for medical technologies are as follows:

- Innovate UK[14] – who have a number of schemes to fund UK companies
- The National Institute for Health and Care Research (NIHR)[15] – funding for primarily translational and clinical projects
- NHS England – SBRI Healthcare[16]

Some tips for grant application:

- Read the guidance and all material provided – this may sound obvious but many do not and miss useful information that can help avoid silly mistakes. Offline versions of the application form can be downloaded.
- Check out the Ts&Cs to know what you are signing up to – e.g. download a copy of the NIHR contract you will need to sign.
- Understand the subsidy or state aid requirements – Innovate UK grants are registered for State Aid,[17] and match funding is required. (Only 70% of eligible costs is payable for small companies doing industrial research or feasibility studies.)
- Register on the application portal early – almost every application is online.
- Check that you know the deadline – day and hour.
- Don't leave everything to the last minute; funders make few, if any, exceptions for late applications (only if their system has a problem).
- Take advantage of the free support and advice available to you from organisations like KTN[18] (particularly for Innovate UK grants) and the RDS[19] (NIHR). It is especially helpful to contact them well in advance of competitions.
- Don't be afraid to contact the grant team – the contact details are available. The people running the scheme do not make the funding decisions, so they can advise you (within limits).
- Do treat the application as seriously as you would if you were writing your pitch to an investor.
- Have a plan B – check success rates.

## THE INVESTMENT JOURNEY

There is a range of types of investment that map onto the product development journey (Figure 6.1). You may not need or want to use all the stages, but of all the reasons for start-ups to fail, running out of capital is second on the list at 29% of failures.[20] Your business plan should indicate how much you will need to raise and when. One of the goals is to increase the value of the company significantly at each stage, so a) you keep your investors happy and b) you do not need to give up so much equity at each round.

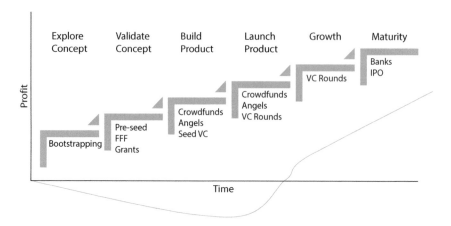

Figure 6.1 Product development stages and capital sources.

## Stages of investment

Table 6.1 describes the investment *vs* value as you go through the journey:

- **Bootstrapping** is using your own money, often personal savings. According to Investopedia[21] a bootstrap business is "built from the ground up on personal savings and luck and pays its way with sales". Further investment may be raised by selling your services. You are likely to entirely bootstrap a business in healthcare technology only with non-regulated digital products. It's important to decide how much you are prepared to raid your piggy bank.
- **Pre-seed** funding is early investment to develop your MVP (minimum viable product). It technically includes bootstrapping but is here defined as the first externally raised capital. Traditionally such funding comes from friends, family and fools (FFF),[22] but increasingly early angel and venture capital investors are putting money into this stage, usually with a lot of handholding. Crowdsourcing can also be useful at this stage, although perhaps less so in medical technology businesses. Ideally, look for investments without exchange for equity at pre-seed stage.
- **Seed** funding is a critical stage of company development and represents a large risk for investors, who require equity in exchange. This is where you get your product or service to market.
- **Venture Capital – Series A** is about showing your business model can scale. High growth is expected (two to five times revenue over 18 months). If lack of cash is slowing growth, then Series A is appropriate, but if slow market adoption is the problem, you may have difficulty convincing investors. **Series B** is usually for growing companies that are probably starting to generate profit and need cash to take full advantage of the opportunity. **Series C** is for companies that are growing large and usually to prepare for buyout or listing (IPO).

## Approaching investors

When approaching investors and making your pitch, there are a few things to remember:

- Find organisations that support investor events
- Know your investors before you ask them for money
- Take opportunities to refine your pitch – many pitch events require you to go through their training
- Practise your pitch – pitch when you don't need money; get feedback to improve

## SUMMARY

Your business plan describes your company and the journey you are on. Raising the capital to make it happen will take probably more effort than you think if you are to avoid failing because the cash runs out.

Always remember, start-up investors are in it for high reward to offset the high risk, but some bring more than just cash. Time your capital raising for when your company value has risen significantly; take advantage of all the help that is available and you increase the chances that you will be one of the successful ones and that patients will benefit from your innovation.

Table 6.1 Sources of capital, with typical amounts and company value

| Investment | Amount | Source | Company Valuation |
|---|---|---|---|
| Bootstrapping | £50k | Self – savings and/or other revenue | £10–100k |
| Pre-seed | | Family and friends; early angels or (micro) VC funds, e.g. Forward Partners (https://forwardpartners.com/); maybe Crowdfunding | |
| Seed | Up to £3M | Family and friends, angels and early-stage (micro) VC funds and crowdfunding | £3–6M |
| Series A | Up to £10M | VCs and angels | £10–30M |
| Series B | Up to £30M | VCs | £30–60M |
| Series C | Up to £50M | Late VCs and private equity funds, hedge funds, banks | £100–120M |
| Exit | £50–500M | IPO, PE, large company | £100M in revenue |

## NOTES

1. Establishing a Company – Chapter 4
2. The Innovation Process – Chapter 2
3. Intellectual Property – Chapter 3
4. The Regulatory Landscape – Chapter 7
5. Research and Validation – Chapter 9
6. The Guidelines Manual, NICE – https://www.nice.org.uk/process/pmg6/chapter/assessing-cost-effectiveness
7. Penetrating the NHS – chapter 11
8. For a good summary see McKinsey "Valuing High-Tech Companies" https://www.mckinsey.com/business-functions/strategy-and-corporate-finance/our-insights/valuing-high-tech-companies#
9. https://uk.practicallaw.thomsonreuters.com/0-500-8350?transitionType=Default&contextData=(sc.Default)&firstPage=true
10. Governmentguidance:https://www.gov.uk/guidance/venture-capital-schemes-tax-relief-for-investors
11. Venture Capital Schemes Manual: https://www.gov.uk/hmrc-internal-manuals/venture-capital-schemes-manual
12. R&D Tax Credits for SMEs: https://www.gov.uk/guidance/corporation-tax-research-and-development-tax-relief-for-small-and-medium-sized-enterprises
13. Forausefuloverviewsee:https://smithandwilliamson.com/en/insights/patent-box-what-you-need-to-know/
14. https://www.gov.uk/government/organisations/innovate-uk
15. https://www.nihr.ac.uk/
16. https://sbrihealthcare.co.uk/
17. https://eur-lex.europa.eu/legal-content/GA/TXT/?uri=CELEX:52014XC0627(01)#ntr41-C_2014198EN.01000101-E0041 - note this may change after January 2021 if the UK Government subsidy diverges from EU State Aid Rules
18. Knowledge Transfer Network – https://ktn-uk.org/
19. Research Design Service – https://www.nihr.ac.uk/explore-nihr/support/research-design-service.htm
20. Reasons for startup failure – see: https://www.cbinsights.com/research/startup-failure-reasons-top/
21. Investopedia "Bootstrapping" https://www.investopedia.com/terms/b/bootstrap.asp
22. Avoiding the pitfalls of FFF: https://pando.com/2013/11/28/avoiding-the-pitfalls-of-raising-money-from-friends-and-family/

# 7

# The regulatory landscape for medical devices in the UK and EU

JACQUES DU PREEZ

## INTRODUCTION

Medical devices are instruments, apparatuses, appliances, software, implants, reagents, materials or other articles intended by the manufacturer to be used, alone or in combination, for human beings for diagnosis, prevention, monitoring, prediction, prognosis, treatment or alleviation of disease and which does not achieve its principal intended action by pharmacological, immunological or metabolic means.

DOI: 10.1201/9781003164609-8

All medical devices are required to meet regulatory requirements in order to be legally made available on the market they are entering. The purpose of regulations is to ensure that safe devices that perform effectively are placed on the market. To achieve this, regulations provide a framework whereby a manufacturer may show compliance to a set of safety and performance requirements.

The United Kingdom and the European Union (EU) separated and, from 1 January 2021, applied different regulatory requirements and compliance marks to show that medical devices comply with regulatory requirements. The EU uses the "CE" mark and the UK introduced the "UKCA" (United Kingdom Conformity Assessment) mark.

In order to apply the CE mark, medical devices must conform with the Medical Device Regulations EU 2017/745 (MDR). In order to apply the UKCA mark medical devices must comply with the Medical Devices regulations 2002 (SI 2002 No 618), the UK law equivalent of the Medical Device Directive (MDD)

CE marking provides access to the European Single Market comprising 27 member states, the European Economic Area (Iceland, Liechtenstein, and Norway) and, through bilateral treaties, Switzerland and Turkey. These 32 markets mostly comprise a wealthy, ageing population of over 450 million consumers. In addition to the above markets, CE marking can be leveraged to access other markets such as the Middle East, Asia and South America, adding further to its importance.

UKCA marking provides access to England, Scotland and Wales which also mostly comprise a wealthy, ageing population of over 60 million consumers[i] and is currently requirement from 1 July 2024, though this is expected to change with the inclusion of a transition period.

This chapter sets out the broad requirements for CE and UKCA marking. It is strongly recommended that medical device technology developers put in place a regulatory strategy against which they execute their plan to ensure they are legal, comply with the requirements and optimise the route to market from a timing, resource and effort perspective.

## CE AND UKCA MARKING

Most medical device regulatory framework requirements can be broken down into two broad areas, and the CE and UKCA marks are no different.

The first is quality management system (QMS), or good manufacturing practice (GMP), which applies to the manufacturing organisation. A QMS ensures that devices are developed appropriately, that every device that is produced meets the standard required to be placed on the market, is traceable and that the manufacturer monitors the device once on the market and provides a feedback mechanism for improvement and reporting to regulatory authorities.

The second aspect of medical device regulations covers the medical device itself, and the clinical evidence supporting the benefit and effectiveness of the device. This is captured in a technical file, or design history file, and is the recipe for how to make the device, as well as evidencing its safety and effectiveness.

The specific requirements for a medical device are determined when a regulatory strategy is put in place.

## REGULATORY STRATEGY

A regulatory strategy assesses whether a medical technology falls under the medical device regulations, sets out the conformity assessment paths available for a device based on its classification, and includes the quality management system requirements, technical file requirements and clinical evidence requirements.

The regulatory strategy will add key delivery milestones to the technology development plan, such as certification of the QMS, first in human studies, completion of a clinical investigation or clinical evaluation report, and certification of the device.

## DEVICE CLASSIFICATION

The starting point for classification is setting out the device's *intended use,* from which it can be determined whether it is a *medical device* and, if it is, what the *classification* is.

Medical devices are classified into four product risk groups. Classification of devices within the product risk groups is determined by applying the classification rules that are based on the vulnerability of the human body and take into account the potential risks associated with the technical design and manufacture of the devices. The special rules are considered before the product group rules, and the highest classification takes precedence. In classifying a device the following considerations are taken into account:

- Where will the device be used, e.g. central nervous system, cardiovascular system?
- Is it invasive?
- How long will it be in contact with the patient?
    - Transient – less than 60 minutes
    - Short term – less than 30 days
    - Long term – more than 30 days
- Is it an implantable?
- Is it an active device?

Device classifications are:

- Class I (low risk)
- Class IIa (medium risk)
- Class IIb (medium to high risk)
- Class III (high risk)

In addition to these classes, Class I devices have three further sub categories; Class I **s**terile, I **m**easuring and I **r**eusable (reusable is CE only).

Classification is determined using the following rules, which are divided into four groups:

| Product groups | UKCA | CE | EXAMPLES |
|---|---|---|---|
| Non-invasive devices | Rules 1–4 | Rules 1–4 | Walking aids, wound dressings |
| Invasive devices | Rules 5–8 | Rules 5–8 | Stents, catheter, hip replacement |
| Active devices | Rules 9–12 | Rules 9–13 | Software, lasers, MRI |
| Special rules | Rules 13–18 | Rules 14–22 | Biological heart valves |

Many medical devices will have the same classification under both UKCA and CE regulations. Where it differs, it is likely that the device will have a higher classification under the CE regulations. Examples of where classifications differ are around software as a medical device (SAMD); where the CE regulations have a dedicated rule covering software (Rule 11); surgical mesh, spinal disc replacement, implantable devices which are Class IIb under UKCA and III under CE regulations; and substance-based devices that are Class I to IIa under UKCA but are Class IIb or III under CE marking regulations, depending on where they are placed for absorption e.g. stomach, skin, etc.

## CONFORMITY ASSESSEMENT

The conformity assessment routes are set out in the regulations. *Conformity assessment* is the process whereby the manufacturer demonstrates that they have fulfilled the requirements of the regulations. There are nuances about which route to use, as in some cases a device developer may have more than one option. As a general guide, all devices require a technical file and all or part of a quality management system; however, Class I devices (Figure 7.1) self-certify that they have met these requirements, whereas every other class (Figure 7.2) – from a Class I

Figure 7.1 Class I devices – self certification.

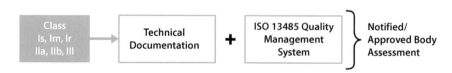

Figure 7.2 All other classes – third-party certification.

measuring device through to a Class III device – requires a notified body (CE mark) or an approved body (UKCA mark) to certify that the legal manufacturer of the device has met the regulatory requirements.

## QUALITY MANAGEMENT SYSTEMS

Quality management system requirements are set out within the regulations. Class I devices do not require a certified quality management system but do need to comply with the quality management system requirements that are set out for them.

All classes above Class I require an ISO 13485 certified quality management system plus any additional requirements set out in the regulations. It is important that organisations learn to work on a daily basis within a quality management system.

The starting point for all quality systems is document control and then identifying those areas that require a process. The QMS can then build as the organisation grows. For new technologies the design and development standard operating process is one of the cornerstone processes to implement and use.

## TECHNICAL FILE REQUIREMENTS

Technical documentation provides evidence of conformity. For UKCA marking there is flexibility in how they are compiled, whereas the CE marking regulations provide a framework which can be used for UKCA marking as well. Table 7.1 sets this out in more detail.

In addition to these six areas, manufacturers are required to implement a post-market surveillance (PMS) system which collects and utilises all available information about their device including publicly available information for other comparable devices.

For post-market surveillance, the manufacturer is required to proactively collect and evaluate clinical data with the aim of confirming the safety and performance throughout the expected lifetime of the device and of ensuring the continued acceptability of identified risks and of detecting emerging risks on the basis of factual evidence.

## CLINICAL EVIDENCE REQUIREMENTS

All conformity assessment routes require clinical evidence to demonstrate safety and effectiveness. The clinical evidence must be of a sufficient amount and quality to allow a qualified assessment of whether the device achieves intended clinical benefits and safety when used as intended.

Clinical evidence comes from clinical data and a clinical evaluation. The clinical evaluation of a device is a systematic and planned process to continuously generate, collect, analyse and assess the pre- and post-market clinical data relating to the device. The whole process is documented in a clinical evaluation report which continues to be updated throughout the life cycle of the device.

Table 7.1 Technical file requirements

| | |
|---|---|
| 1. Device description and specification including variants and accessories | Intended use, how it works, product specification, materials, classification, conformity assessment route, EC Declaration of Conformity |
| 2. Information supplied by the manufacturer | Labels, instructions for use, promotional material, language requirements |
| 3. Design and manufacturing information | Design stages and further detail, manufacturing process, critical suppliers, product release process, address of manufacturing and subcontractor sites and certificates |
| 4. General safety and performance requirements (GSPRs) for CE or essential requirements checklist (ERC) for UKCA | Completed general safety and performance requirements document, list of applied standards<br>or<br>Completed essential requirements checklist, list of applied standards. |
| 5. Benefit-risk analysis and risk management | Risk analysis and control: ISO 14971- Summary of the risks identified, analysis of how the risks have been controlled and reduced, risk management plan. Importantly needs to incorporate PMS. |
| 6. Product verification and validation | Summary of the results of verification and validation activities, e.g. engineering tests, laboratory tests, biocompatibility data, medicinal substances, animal or human cells, tissues or their derivatives, sterilisation, software verification and validation. Clinical evaluation, transportation and shelf life reports |

Evidence developed while undertaking research is supportive but not equivalent to a clinical investigation and, in most cases, is not sufficient. All clinical investigations are registered with a competent authority such as the Medicines and Healthcare products Regulatory Agency (MHRA), obtain ethics approval from an ethics committee and are allocated a clinical investigation number.

## KEY STANDARDS AND GUIDANCE

There are hundreds of standards covering the many thousands of medical devices. However, there is a core set of standards that are applicable to many devices. These are listed below and are in addition to any specific standards applicable to your device. When completing your Essential Requirements Checklist or General Safety and Performance Standards the device manufacturer will point to the use of these standards and their outputs as evidence of addressing the requirements.

| | | | |
|---|---|---|---|
| **Quality management:** | ISO 13485 | **Software:** | EN 62304 |
| **Risk management:** | ISO 14971 | **Medical equipment:** | EN 60601 |
| **Clinical investigations:** | ISO 14155 | **Usability:** | EN 62366 |
| **Biocompatibility:** | ISO 10993 | **Symbols:** | ISO 15223 |

## TEN STEPS TO UKCA/CE MARKING YOUR DEVICE

In summary below are ten steps to getting your device UKCA/CE marked:

1. Determine intended purpose.
2. Determine classification – Class I to III.
3. Determine conformity assessment route.
4. Implement required quality management system or processes.
5. Compile technical documentation.
6. Complete a clinical evaluation.
7. For devices above Class I, undertake an assessment by a notified or approved body.
8. Prepare and sign a Declaration of Conformity.
9. For a device above Class I, obtain QMS and CE certificates from your notified or approved body; for a Class I device register with a competent authority such as MHRA.
10. Place CE marking on device and make it available on the market.

## FIVE STEPS TO KEEPING IT ON THE MARKET

Once your device is on the market there are a number of ongoing activities that need to be undertaken to keep it in conformity with the regulations. These include the following:

1. Post market surveillance
2. Maintaining the device technical files
3. Using and maintaining the quality management system
4. Managing device changes
5. Successfully completing annual notified or approved body audits and recertifications as necessary

## OTHER MEDICAL TECHNOLOGIES

Medical technologies sometimes may not be classified as a medical device, and therefore, different regulations and legislation may apply. Below is a list of some of the alternatives.

## Medicinal products (pharma)

A substance or combination of substances that is intended to treat, prevent or diagnose a disease, or to restore, correct or modify physiological functions by exerting a pharmacological, immunological or metabolic action. Readers should look at EU Directive 2001/83/EC and in the UK, The Human Medicines Regulations 2012.

## Advance therapy medicinal products (ATMP)

A medicine for human use that is based on gene therapy, cell therapy or tissue engineering. Readers should look at EU Directive 2001/83/EC and the ATMP Regulations 1394/2007 and in the UK, The Human Tissue (Quality and Safety for Human Application) Regulations 2007.

## In vitro diagnostic medical devices (IVDs)

The technology is a reagent, reagent product, calibrator, control material, kit, instrument, apparatus, piece of equipment, software or system, whether used alone or in combination, intended by the manufacturer to be used in vitro for the examination of specimens, including blood and tissue donations, derived from the human body, solely or principally for the purpose of providing information. Though this chapter does not specifically cover IVDs there are many similarities, and similar principles apply regarding quality management systems and technical files.

## Combination products

It is also becoming increasingly common to see combination devices that include different types of technologies such as medicinal and medical device, e.g. drug-eluting stent. These technologies require individual assessment before determining the appropriate regulatory strategy and pathway.

## SUMMARY

Developing a medical device is more than proving the technology. Medical device regulations require that good practice, and the safety and effectiveness of the device are demonstrated throughout the life cycle of the device from development through to retirement.

A starting point is to determine whether the technology is a medical device and if it is, the intended use of the device, its classification and subsequently the regulatory requirements. A good regulatory strategy will cover this and set out an action plan to achieve conformity. Your regulatory strategy is a dynamic document and will need to evolve as regulations and standards are updated.

## NOTE

i https://www.ons.gov.uk/peoplepopulationandcommunity/population-andmigration/populationestimates/bulletins/annualmidyearpopulation estimates/mid2019estimates

# CASE STUDY H: D+R BALANCE

Normal human balance depends on sensory information from the visual, peripheral vestibular, proprioceptive and auditory systems [1]. This information is integrated and interpreted within the central nervous system. Interpretation requires comparing this sensory information with preformed vestibular templates. The absence of a suitable template due to a change in sensory function in one or more pathways, or the inability to compare relayed information with central templates due to central pathology, results in symptoms of dizziness, vertigo or unsteadiness [2].

The clinical assessment of dizzy patients involves taking a detailed history and performing a thorough clinical examination. A number of clinical tests form the test battery undertaken and in combination will allow an accurate diagnosis to be made.

Romberg's test is performed by asking a subject to stand upright for 30 seconds with their hands by their sides and their eyes closed. A variety of methods have been developed to assess the extent of postural sway during this clinical investigation. These have included attaching a belt–pencil assembly to a patient's waist that could plot movement on a small table placed behind a patient, or by using a force plate or computerised dynamic posturography machine. The latter involve standing on a metal plate that records a change of the centre of gravity. These are immobile and cost several tens of thousands of pounds.

D+R Balance is an iPhone application that was developed to improve clinical testing of balance patients (note Figure H.1). Once attached to the subject and initiated, the device is able to calculate the extent of movement and present this as the volume of an ellipsoid. This application is inexpensive and is used internationally to assess balance patients [3].

The Unterberger and Fukuda step tests are commonly used to assess balance function. Subjects are asked to march on the spot, and the extent of rotation is recorded. After 50 steps, rotation of 30 degrees or greater is suggestive of reduced function in the inner ear balance organ that the patient has rotated towards (i.e. a peripheral vestibular deficit). However, accurately assessing the extent of rotation is difficult. Estimating rotation has been shown to be poor, and drawing floor grid lines is often not possible.

The second function of D+R Balance iPhone application was developed to accurately record the extent of rotation by exploiting the compass function of the smartphone. Once attached to the subject, the iPhone accurately recorded the extent of rotation, allowing this clinical test to be undertaken in a meaningful manner [4].

Narinder Sharma, a specialist vestibular physiotherapist in North Kent, was the recipient of an Innovation Award by the Chartered Society of

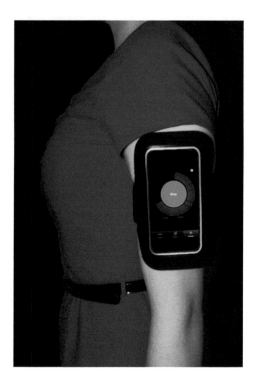

Figure H.1 The D+R Balance iPhone application.

Physiotherapists. The application was used to both assess and motivate patients to comply with their balance exercises as it provided an objective outcome for patients performing their exercises with improved outcomes.

## REFERENCES

1. Kanegaonkar RG, Amin K, Clarke M. The contribution of hearing to normal balance. *The Journal of Laryngology and Otology* 2012; 126(10): 984–8.
2. Hansson EE, Beckman A, Hakansson A. Effect of vision, proprioception, and the position of the vestibular organ on postural sway. *Acta Oto-laryngologica* 2010; 130(12): 1358–63.
3. Yvon C, Najuko-Mafemera A, Kanegaonkar R. The D+R Balance application: a novel method of assessing postural sway. *The Journal of Laryngology and Otology* 2015 Aug; 129(8): 773–8.
4. Whittaker M, Mathew A, Kanani R, Kanegaonkar RG. Assessing the Unterberger test: introduction of a novel smartphone application. *The Journal of Laryngology and Otology* 2014 Nov; 128(11): 958–60.

# 8

# Responsible business conduct

*Why and how healthcare companies should incorporate environmental sustainability, social responsibility, and business integrity into their practice*

MAHMOOD F. BHUTTA AND CHIRANTAN CHATERJEE

In recent years there has been increasing recognition that free market economics, in combination with an expanding human population and a heightened demand for goods, has cultivated unsustainable models of consumption and failed to protect planetary health, social value, and, in some cases, business integrity. The market economy is built on consumption, and if monetary gain is placed foremost, this can lead to environmental harm from the continual extraction of raw materials, production of goods, or disposal of waste and can perpetuate global value chains: the production of goods across international borders often

DOI: 10.1201/9781003164609-9

in low-resource settings, where risks of labour rights infringement may be high. With some corporations putting monetary gain truly foremost, we have also seen instances of corruption, fraud, and tax evasion. This is an important consideration for those innovating in the healthcare sector, particularly when considering environmental harms: at least 50 countries have committed to developing low-carbon health systems,[1] with an acknowledgement that such strategy must include those who supply the health system. The majority of healthcare associated carbon emissions arise in the supply chain.[2]

Responsible business conduct is a growing ideology that recognises and encourages positive contributions from business towards environmental as well as economic and social progress, sometimes termed the triple bottom line of "people, planet, profit". Responsible business conduct should be differentiated from allied initiatives that organisations may undertake under the broader umbrella of "corporate social responsibility", such as donating to charitable causes. Charitable giving is worthwhile but should not be used to excuse or window-dress poor business practice.

The Organisation for Economic Co-operation and Development (OECD) recognises eight components of responsible business conduct (Table 8.1).[3] The growing importance of this topic is reflected not only by the increasing adoption of such practice amongst companies and corporations[4] but also in international regulation, policy, and law.

## AN EVOLVING REGULATORY LANDSCAPE

In recent years regulations have increasingly signalled an expectation for business to be conducted responsibly. In 2020 a survey including respondents from 28 countries from the OECD[3] found that in the public procurement of goods, all 28 nations had developed a regulatory framework to protect the environment. Most also had a framework to protect labour rights and to ensure business integrity (Figure 8.1). However, to date there has been varied and inconsistent implementation of these frameworks in practice.

Many of these regulations are relevant to the healthcare market. For example, for those supplying goods, and particularly those with components manufactured using overseas labour, several countries have now enacted laws requiring evaluation and reporting of the risk of forced labour in supply chains.[5] (In the UK that is currently mandatory only for companies with a turnover above GBP £36 million, but the fine for non-compliance is unlimited.[6]) Furthermore, recent policy on UK government procurement, including supply to the National Health Service (NHS), requires companies with a contract valued at over £5 million per annum to document how they are reducing greenhouse gas emissions in their operations,[7] and the NHS has a pledge to reduce plastic use in healthcare.[8] And these types of requirements are set to expand: concerns about environmental pollution by manufacturers of pharmaceuticals in low-resource settings (such as Hyderabad, India[9]) have led to calls for the European Union to strengthen their regulations around environmental and human rights protection in the

Table 8.1 Components of responsible business conduct recognised by the Organisation for Economic Co-operation and Development (OECD). Adapted from the OECD report of 2020.[3]

| Component | Definition |
| --- | --- |
| Environment | Any activity to maintain or restore the quality of the environment through preventing emission of pollutants or reducing presence of polluting substances in the environment. Can relate to pollution, carbon footprint, water footprint or use, biodiversity, micro-plastics, climate change, deforestation, chemicals, waste reduction (water, packaging), fossil fuels, land use or tenure, energy and renewable energy, circular economy. |
| Labour rights | Includes principles in the ILO 1998 Declaration on Fundamental Principles and Rights at Work as well as the ILO Tripartite Declaration of Principles concerning Multinational Enterprises (ILO MNE Declaration). The 1998 Declaration includes freedom of association and the right to collective bargaining, effective abolition of child labour, elimination of all forms of forced or compulsory labour, and non-discrimination in employment and occupation. |
| Human rights | As expressed in the International Bill of Human Rights, consisting of the Universal Declaration of Human Rights and the main instruments through which it is codified: the International Covenant on Civil and Political Rights and the International Covenant on Economic, Social and Cultural Rights and other core international human rights treaties |
| Minority rights | Refer to rights in society of cultural, ethnic, religious and linguistic minorities. |
| Disability rights | Refer to inclusion of those who have a physical, mental or sensory impairment that has a substantial and long-term adverse effect on their ability to carry out normal day-to-day activities. |
| Unemployed rights | Refer to rights of people who have been unemployed for 12 months or more. |
| Gender rights | Refer to equal rights, responsibilities and opportunities of people of all genders |
| Integrity | Consistent alignment and adherence to shared ethical values, principles and norms for upholding and prioritising the public interest over private interests in the public sector. Integrity breaches include corruption, fraud, bribery and tax evasion. |

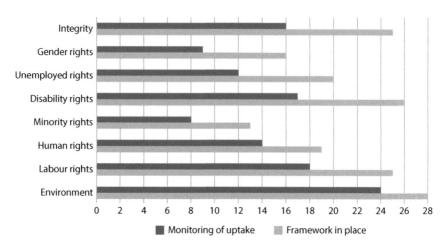

Figure 8.1 Results of 28 countries responding to a survey of members by the Organisation for Economic Co-operation and Development (OECD) on whether they have a framework in place to evaluate organisations contracted to supply the public sector against the eight components of responsible business conduct and whether they have mechanisms in place to monitor uptake of such requirements. Data extracted and adapted from the OECD report of 2020.[3]

procurement of pharmaceutical products,[10] and a ban by Germany on azo dyes has forced innovation in the Indian textile and chemical industries.[11]

Aligned to this there has been increasing action and sanctions. In 2019 persistent protests by a local community in Chicago, USA, against toxic atmospheric levels of ethylene oxide released from a local medical sterilisation company generated new regulations that led to the closure of the company's 25-year-old plant.[12] In 2021 the UK Competition and Markets Authority issued fines of over GBP £260 million to several pharmaceutical firms that had colluded to over-charge the NHS for hydrocortisone tablets[13] and £100 million to another firm that over-charged for liothyronine tablets.[12] In the USA a manufacturer of endoscopes was fined US $646 million for bribing physicians to use their products,[14] which was one of 67 fines totalling US $1.9 billion issued to medtech companies in the USA between 2014 and 2019.[15] Between 2019 and 2021, the presence of forced labour in factories[16] led to successive import bans by the US Customs and Border Agency on five major Malaysian glove manufacturers[17], including Top Glove, the largest manufacturer of gloves in the world – with demonstrable effects to their share price and revenue.

There is still debate about how effective bans and regulation are in creating change. For example, in the pharmaceutical sector in India there is evidence that firms facing price regulation repositioned their products at increased prices in the unregulated submarket,[18] and sales data show that medicines banned for being substandard continue to be sold in large quantities even after a ban.[19]

So, is there a carrot for responsible conduct as well as a stick?

## BUSINESS BENEFITS OF RESPONSIBLE CONDUCT

Whereas it is important to be aware of the changing regulatory landscape, in fact, the growth in recent years of responsible business conduct precedes, and often goes beyond, what is mandated. Many corporations have adopted and maintained the principles of responsible business conduct not because of fear of regulation but because these principles help to build efficient and resilient businesses.

Firstly, for those supplying goods or services, the process of responsible business necessitates greater transparency and scrutiny of company structure and operations and associated vulnerabilities. For example, to quantify environmental footprint a company may conduct a detailed evaluation of where and how staff travel or how products are cargoed, which could identify opportunities for efficiency in transport infrastructure. To understand labour rights risk associated with a product requires transparency of where each major component of the product is manufactured and how, which can highlight places to collapse the supply chain, as well as lead to a closer relationship with suppliers and manufacturers, in turn enhancing security of supply and enabling greater quality assurance.[20,21]

It is true that to pursue responsible business often requires an upfront investment, but where efficiencies are identified and realised, such changes may reduce costs. For example, UK supermarkets like Co-op, Sainsburys, and Waitrose sell only Fairtrade bananas without any increase in price to the customer.[22] Hotels that ask guests to reuse towels and sheets typically save a quarter of their energy bill.[23] And PepsiCo saved over US $375 million in the first five years following implementation of its water, energy, waste-reduction, and green packaging initiatives.[24]

The adoption of responsible business conduct also creates a culture and ethos that is valued by others. For example, recent reports of consumer values found that 66% intended to make more sustainable purchases in the next six months, and 74% believed that ethical corporate practices are an important reason to choose a brand.[25]

Business values also attract current and future employees. When people are employed by an organisation that behaves ethically, they are likely to reciprocate by engaging, supporting, and furthering the organisation. A study in 2020 of over 1,000 employees in US corporations found that 88% believed that corporations must behave responsibly, that 69% would not work for a company without a clear purpose, and that if they knew they were working for a responsible company, 60% would accept less pay and 92% would be more likely to recommend their employer to others.[26] Similarly, a survey conducted in 2020 in 45 countries and comprising 23,000 people aged under 40 found that less than half thought that businesses have a positive impact on society, and in the preceding two years over 40% of them had made choices based on personal ethics over the type of work they were prepared to do or organisations they would work for.[27]

## FINANCIAL BENEFITS OF RESPONSIBLE CONDUCT

In summary, responsible business conduct not only supports legal and regulatory compliance but can also create cost efficiency, better quality products, security of supply, company reputation, and employee recruitment, retention, and

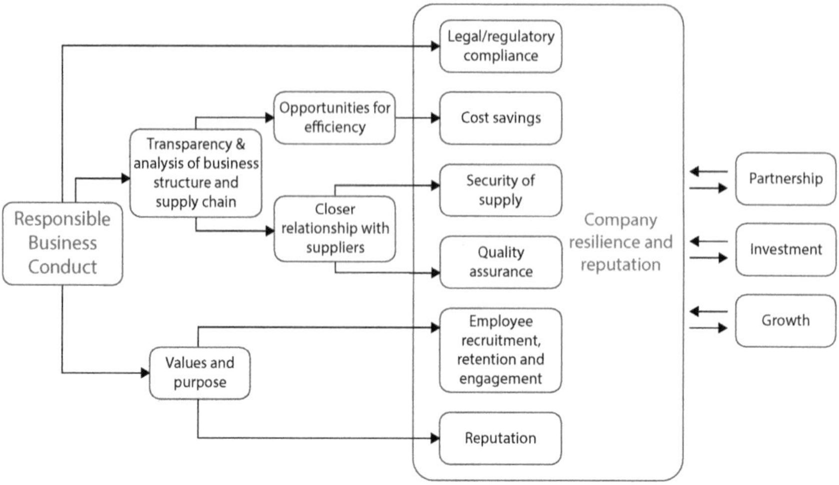

Figure 8.2 How responsible business conduct contributes to company resilience and reputation.

engagement (Figure 8.2). Responsible business helps build resilient and reputable companies. Responsible business is good business.

There is also compelling evidence that responsible business is "good business" in terms of financial stability and growth. Analysis undertaken in 2021 found that, despite the Covid-19 global pandemic, 81% of global sustainable financial indexes outperformed their parent benchmarks.[28] And amongst 4,000 companies, those ranked in the top quartile for sustainability had 21% higher financial margins that those ranked in the lowest quartile.[25] This financial growth is also reflected in investment: the organisation Principles for Responsible Investment has grown from 63 signatories and US $6.5 trillion in its portfolio in 2006 to 3,626 signatories and $121.3 trillion in 2021.[29] Being a responsible company makes it more likely that people will invest and partner with you.

## RESPONSIBLE BUSINESS CONDUCT IN PRACTICE

So, what are some of the practical steps to becoming a responsible business?

The first is to ensure that the values of environmental sustainability, social responsibility, and business integrity are voiced and made public through company policy. But of course such a statement must not be hollow, and it is important to stick to those values and support them with meaningful action. You should identify a person to take the lead for responsible business conduct – at first that may be the CEO, but as the company grows, you may appoint a person dedicated to this work, or even a team.

What actions a company takes on depend upon what the company does. For example, if you are selling a service, do you recruit staff locally? If you are marketing a digital platform, is that service inclusive: accessible to minority groups or those with disabilities? For those marketing a product, it is likely that some or all components of the product are manufactured overseas, and so your responsibilities need to extend wider. Visiting manufacturing sites and speaking to those in your supply chain may give you a lot of insight into potential issues and risk, but it is important to see beyond your supplier's management office, which could be a façade covering serious labour abuse or environmental degradation in a manufacturing plant. Where finances allow and/or supply chains are complex, enlisting the support of external auditors can help to evaluate risks of labour abuse (e.g., using SA-8000, Sedex) or environmental harm (e.g., using ISO 14000, IEMA) as a basis for following up with a programme of change and continual improvement: it is the programme of change that is important, not the audit findings. And then there is the product itself: an ethical product will be manufactured with minimal environmental harm, pay workers a living wage, be designed to last and reused many times, and be easily repairable.[30,31] This idea can be at odds with historical notions of repeated sales of products as the basis for business growth, but many businesses have moved to revenue generation from subscription to a service, whether that service is or is not aligned to a product.

Perhaps the most important thing here is to maintain integrity, honesty, and self-regulation. There are multiple examples of where audits have failed to identify serious breaches of labour rights abuse,[32] perhaps because everybody (except those who are being abused) would prefer to see a report that shows no problems, incentivising an approach of superficial or false auditing. And on the environmental side we have seen a proliferation of "greenwashing" – the act of misleading consumers regarding environmental practices of an organisation on the benefits of a product or service, typically through making claims on environmental performance that are vague, contain important omissions, or are plain false.[33]

A roadmap of honesty and continual improvement is what defines responsible business conduct, not a fake report.

It is wise to remember that your suppliers or partners may avoid enforcement or adopt strategic behaviour to evade short-term losses, even if this has an effect on the long-term reputation of their brand or yours. Globalisation of supply chains enhances possibilities for affordable innovation, but the gains come at a cost of risky supply chains, which may look the other way on quality concerns, human rights abuse, or environmental degradation, or may trust self-regulation by firms without co-regulation or external regulation. Should those risks become apparent, they can seriously damage your brand reputation or the security of day-to-day conduct of your business. That could prove highly detrimental or even fatal to a start-up company operating in a competitive market.

If your product or service is good, you will likely succeed. But if you also run your business responsibly, the added benefits to company resilience and reputation should not be underestimated.

## OPPORTUNITIES AND EXAMPLES OF INNOVATION IN GREEN HEALTH

Innovation in green healthcare has historically lagged behind other sectors[34] but is a growing field. In 2021 and 2022 new funding streams for research and innovation to reduce environmental impacts of healthcare were announced by several UK funding bodies, including the Small Business Research Initiative (SBRI),[35] several programs of the National Institute for Health Research (NIHR),[36] and the Medical Research Council (MRC).[37]

Some notable innovations in healthcare process include the following:

- Reusing water used for haemodialysis[38] was projected to save Ashford Hospital (UK) over £10,000 per year and 1,240 kg of $CO_2$e.
- Using efficient systems and reuse of equipment for cataract surgery in India was associated with a 30-fold lower carbon footprint than the same operation performed in the UK[31].
- Moving to long-acting injections for treating psychosis[39] was estimated to save the NHS in England £300,000 per year and 170,000 tonnes of $CO_2$e.
- Using a gasless approach to laparoscopic appendix surgery in Leeds teaching hospitals was predicted to save 107 tonnes of $CO_2$e per year and £78,000 in procurement costs.[40]
- Several studies have reported lower carbon emissions from remote consultation, due to reduced patient transport.[41] For example, a study from Ireland of over 1,000 consultations in urology over a three-month period found that 77% were conducted remotely, saving six tonnes of $CO_2$e and over 1,200 hours of patient time.[42] It is important in such analyses to carbon footprint the entire pathway: if a greater proportion of those having remote rather than face-to-face consultation undergo review or investigation, the carbon savings may be over-estimated.
- Barts Hospital (UK) partnered with the company Recomed to recycle PVC medical products, and in its first year it averted 450 kg of PVC from clinical waste streams.[43]

Some notable innovations in healthcare products include the following:

- Medclair, based in Sweden, has created units that can break down nitrous oxide, a potent greenhouse gas used in anaesthesia,[42] into the harmless gases nitrogen and oxygen.[44]
- Elemental Healthcare,[45] based in the UK, has produced modular instruments for laparoscopic surgery that have a quarter of the carbon footprint of the equivalent entirely disposable unit.[46]
- Several companies are innovating in reuseable personal protective equipment in healthcare, such as masks[47] or gowns,[48] and such reuse could significantly reduce associated environmental harms.[49]
- There is increasing interest in medical device reprocessing, where single use or limited use medical products are reprocessed and certified for use again,

typically at 30–40% of the new purchase cost. In 2020 this was used by over 10,000 hospitals globally, saving them over US$400 million.[50] For an electrophysiology catheter, reprocessing halves global warming potential compared to the virgin product.[51] Of course, a product designed to last a long time is still better than one that needs repair or reprocessing.

## CONCLUSION

Responsible business conduct includes the triple bottom line of people, planet, and profit. Although this ideology is nascent in the field of healthcare, it is set to be the future model, and one that carries benefits to your business beyond just "doing good". Innovators in healthcare would be well advised to integrate such concepts into their company ethos and operations.

## REFERENCES

1. Wise J. COP26: Fifty countries commit to climate resilient and low carbon health systems. BMJ 2021; 375: n2734.
2. Tennison I, Roschnik S, Ashby B, Boyd R, Hamilton I, Oreszczyn T, Owen A, Romanello M, Ruyssevelt P, Sherman JD, Smith AZP, Steele K, Watts N, Eckelman MJ. Health care's response to climate change: A carbon footprint assessment of the NHS in England. Lancet Planet Health 2021; 5(2): e84–e92.
3. OECD (2020). Integrating Responsible Business Conduct in Public Procurement, OECD Publishing, Paris. www.oecd.org/gov/integrating-responsible-business-conduct-in-public-procurement-02682b01-en.htm
4. www.reutersevents.com/sustainability/why-all-mba-graduates-need-be-part-sustainability-revolution
5. globalnaps.org/issue/forced-labour-modern-slavery/
6. www.legislation.gov.uk/ukpga/2015/30/contents/enacted
7. www.gov.uk/government/publications/procurement-policy-note-0621-taking-account-of-carbon-reduction-plans-in-the-procurement-of-major-government-contracts#history
8. https://www.supplychain.nhs.uk/sustainability/plastics/
9. Lübbert C, Baars C, Dayakar A, Lippmann N, Rodloff AC, Kinzig M, Sörgel F. Environmental pollution with antimicrobial agents from bulk drug manufacturing industries in Hyderabad, South India, is associated with dissemination of extended-spectrum beta-lactamase and carbapenemase-producing pathogens. Infection 2017; 45(4): 479–491.
10. Swedwatch (2020). The Health Paradox: Environmental and human rights impacts from pharmaceutical production in India and the need for supply chain transparency. Report 96. ISBN: 978-91-88141-29-3. swedwatch.org/wp-content/uploads/2020/02/96_Pharma-report.pdf
11. Chakraborty P, Chatterjee C. Does environmental regulation indirectly induce upstream innovation? New evidence from India. Research Policy 2017; 46(5): 939–955.

12. www.chicagotribune.com/news/environment/ct-sterigenics-ends-ethylene-oxide-operation-willowbrook-20190930-nkelcjshkbawdhxx2snjk3oaxe-story.html
13. www.gov.uk/government/news/cma-finds-drug-companies-overcharged-nhs
14. www.gov.uk/government/news/cma-fines-pharma-firm-over-pricing-of-crucial-thyroid-drug
15. www.skadden.com/insights/publications/2020/04/us-prosecutors-continue-to-target-medical-tech
16. www.bsms.ac.uk/_pdf/about/forced-labour-in-the-malaysian-medical-gloves-supply-chain-full-report-july-2nd-2.pdf
17. www.reuters.com/legal/government/us-customs-bans-malaysian-glove-maker-brightway-over-alleged-labour-abuses-2021-12-20/
18. Chatterjee C, Mohapatra DP, Estay M. From courts to markets: New evidence on enforcement of pharmaceutical bans in India. Social Science & Medicine 2019; 237: 112480.
19. Bhaskarabhatla A, Anurag P, Chatterjee C, Pennings E. How Does Regulation Impact Strategic Repositioning by Firms Across Submarkets? Evidence from the Indian Pharmaceutical Industry. Strategy Science. 2021; 6(3):209–227.
20. Alliance for Logistics Innovation through Collaboration in Europe (2021). Sustainable, safe and secure supply chains. www.etp-logistics.eu/wp-content/uploads/2015/07/W16mayo-kopie.pdf
21. The Joint Ethical Trading Initiatives (2017). Guide to buying responsibly. www.ethicaltrade.org/sites/default/files/shared_resources/guide_to_buying_responsibly.pdf
22. www.fairtrade.org.uk/media-centre/blog/are-fairtrade-products-really-more-expensive/
23. www.latimes.com/business/story/2019-09-20/how-businesses-profit-from-environmentalism
24. onlinemba.wsu.edu/blog/3-reasons-an-ethical-business-leads-to-profits
25. Accenture (2021). Shaping the Sustainable Organization. www.accenture.com/_acnmedia/Thought-Leadership-Assets/PDF-5/Accenture-Shaping-the-Sustainable-Organization-Report.pdf
26. Porter Novelli (2020). Employee Perspectives on Responsible Leadership During Crisis. www.porternovelli.com/wp-content/uploads/2021/01/02_Porter-Novelli-Tracker-Wave-X-Employee-Perspectives-on-Responsible-Leadership-During-Crisis.pdf
27. Deloitte (2021). The Deloitte Global 2021 Millennial and Gen Z Survey. www2.deloitte.com/content/dam/Deloitte/global/Documents/2021-deloitte-global-millennial-survey-report.pdf
28. www.blackrock.com/corporate/investor-relations/larry-fink-ceo-letter
29. www.unpri.org/pri/about-the-pri

30. MacNeill AJ, Hopf H, Khamuia A, Alzamir S, Bilec M, Eckelman MJ, Hernandex L, McGain F, Simonsen K, Thiel C, Young S, Lagasse R, Sherman JD. Transforming the medical device industry: Road map to a circular economy. Health Affairs 2020: 39(12): 2088–2097.

31. Bhutta MF. Our over-reliance on single-use equipment in the operating theatre is misguided, irrational and harming our planet. Annals of The Royal College of Surgeons of England 2021: 103(10): 709–712.

32. Clean Clothes Campaign (2019). Fig Leaf for Fashion. cleanclothes.org/file-repository/figleaf-for-fashion.pdf/view

33. Netto SV, Sobral MFF, Ribeiro ARB, Soares GR. Concepts and forms of greenwashing: A systematic review. Environmental Sciences Europe 2020: 32, 19.

34. World Health Organisation Regional Office for Europe (2018). Circular Economy for Health: Opportunities and Risks. https://www.euro.who.int/—data/assets/pdf_file/0004/374917/Circular-Economy_EN_WHO_web_august-2018.pdf

35. https://sbrihealthcare.co.uk/

36. https://www.nihr.ac.uk/researchers/funding-opportunities/

37. https://www.ukri.org/councils/mrc/guidance-for-applicants/types-of-funding-we-offer/

38. Connor A, Milne S, Owen A, Boyle G, Mortimer F, Stevens P. Toward greener dialysis: A case study to illustrate and encourage the salvage of reject water. Journal of Renal Care 201; 36(2): 68–72.

39. Maughan DL, Lillywhite R, Cooke M. Cost and carbon burden of long-acting injections: economic evaluation. BJPsych Bulletin 2016; 40(3): 132–136

40. https://sustainablehealthcare.org.uk/news/2021/10/introducing-team-2-green-surgery-challenge

41. Purohit A, Smith J, Hibble A. Does telemedicine reduce the carbon footprint of healthcare? A systematic review. Future Healthcare Journal 2021; 8(1): e85–e91.

42. Croghan SM, Rohan P, Considine S, Salloum A, Smyth L, Ahmad I, Lynch TH, Manecksha RP. Time, cost and carbon-efficiency: A silver lining of COVID era virtual urology clinics? Annals of The Royal College of Surgeons of England 2021; 103(8): 599–603

43. https://recomed.co.uk/case-study/barts-health-divert-450kg-of-used-pvc-devices-from-clinical-waste-in-first-year-with-recomed/

44. https://www.medclair.com/en/products

45. https://www.elementalhealthcare.co.uk/

46. Rizan C, Bhutta MF. Environmental impact and life cycle financial cost of hybrid (reusable/single-use) instruments versus single-use equivalents in laparoscopic cholecystectomy. Surgical Endoscopy. doi: 10.1007/s00464-021-08728-z. In Press.

47. https://www.revolution-zero.com/

48. https://nthsolutions.co.uk/services/the-reusable-gown-service/

49. Rizan C, Reed M, Bhutta MF. Environmental impact of personal protective equipment distributed for use by health and social care services in England in the first six months of the COVID-19 pandemic. Journal of the Royal Society of Medicine 2021; 114(5): 250–263.
50. http://amdr.org/reprocessing-by-the-numbers/
51. Schulte A, Maga D, Thonemann N. Combining life cycle assessment and circularity assessment to analyze environmental impacts of the medical remanufacturing of electrophysiology catheters. Sustainability 2021; 13: 898.

# 9

# Research and validation

JAMES TYSOME

## INTRODUCTION

Research is the key to developing and validating medical innovation, from proof of concept to product development for CE marking and post-market research. Careful planning is needed at each stage in order to ensure that the correct methodology is used to determine safety and efficacy. The most effective innovations are usually the product of partnership between different academic disciplines together with industry partners. It is by working together that expertise is shared and innovations accelerated to market. Funding is required at each stage and comes from a variety of sources, including investors and competitive research grants. Research provides safety and performance data required to satisfy regulatory bodies such as the Medicines and Healthcare products Regulatory Agency (MHRA) and to be successful in gaining CE marking for trade within the European Economic Area or Food and Drug Agency (FDA) approval for trade within the USA.

This chapter will explore research methodology used at each stage of medical innovation, identifying the funding streams and support available for research and innovation in the UK as examples; similar funding bodies exist within most other countries.

## EARLY-STAGE DEVELOPMENT

Clear aims and a succinct research question form the starting point. When considering medical devices, initial ideas and concepts are developed and evaluated by the design team and clinicians in partnership in order to shortlist the most promising concepts. Basic demonstrators of these concepts can then be built to facilitate further development and evaluation to allow the best concept to be identified to take forward for construction. This is an iterative process and may need several rounds before a final decision is made. A qualitative evaluation is often used, with feedback from the potential end users important in helping choose the best design concept.

The device concept is then refined through a similar iterative development process to deliver a prototype that can be tested on representative models; cadaveric work may be appropriate at this stage. This will inevitably result in further evaluation and refinement to allow the production of a device that can be used in a pilot proof of concept clinical trial.

The process for drug development is similar, with drug discovery and development taking place in a laboratory environment. In some cases, drug libraries can be searched for specific molecular characteristics or potential panels of drugs tested in cell-based models in vitro. Once candidate drugs have been identified, preclinical research may involve testing drugs in animal models where appropriate.

Examples of research funding at this stage include seed funds from charity, industry or universities as well as early-stage academic grants such as the Engineering and Physical Sciences Council or the National Institute for Health Research (NIHR) Invention for Innovation programme for devices and the Medical Research Council for drugs. UK Research and Innovation is a public body established in 2018 that brings together the seven disciplinary research councils, Research England (responsible for supporting research in higher education institutions in England) and Innovate UK (UK innovation agency) to coordinate the research and innovation landscape in the UK and provide funding opportunities to researcher, businesses, universities, NHS organisations, charities and non-governmental organisations.

## CLINICAL TRIALS

Clinical trials are required to demonstrate safety and efficacy of new devices and drugs. They require careful planning to ensure that the correct methodology is used in order to give the data required to support further development of the innovation. There is a lot of support available for clinical trial development within the UK. The NIHR is the United Kingdom's largest funder of health and care research and has 15 local clinical research networks (CRNs) within England that provide support and coordinate research within the NHS and social care. A research design service is available within each CRN to guide the development of clinical trials and applications for NIHR funding, working in partnership with the NHS, universities, local government and industry.

In terms of medical devices, clinical trials are either pre- or post-market. Pre-market studies are primarily to establish safety data, with some efficacy data, and are needed to demonstrate compliance with the requirements for CE marking, allowing the device to be sold within the European market, and/or FDA approval for access to the US market. Post-market clinical trials take place after CE marking and/or FDA approval and focus specifically on efficacy data to demonstrate that the device works effectively in line with its intended use.

## Building a research team

Planning the clinical trial is the most critical stage as it ensures that the study is likely to result in the data required to support the product. A research team needs to be assembled, involving stakeholders from different areas in order to ensure that the correct expertise is available. This usually includes subject matter experts from industry, clinical medicine and academia as well as those with specific knowledge of trial design and running clinical trials such as a clinical trials co-ordinator and a statistician. In some post-market trials, a health economist will need to be involved where cost-effectiveness is to be demonstrated. Patient and public involvement (PPI) is also essential to ensure that the research question is relevant to the end user and is a requirement of most bodies that fund clinical trials. For larger or multi-centre clinical trials, the involvement of a clinical trial unit is essential, not only to aid in the design process but importantly to guide the trial through the correct regulatory pathways, determine costs and co-ordinate data handling, monitoring and analysis of a clinical trial.

## Research question

A good research question is simple, specific and succinct. It is based on the aspects of your innovation that you need to demonstrate, which are usually safety and efficacy. It is formulated based on your proposed innovation but also with the benefit of any initial background literature review and searches for previous products on the market that may have a similar use. The research question should be formulated by the clinical trial team to ensure that it is clear to all stakeholders. The PICO process is a helpful framework in formulating a research question for a clinical trial:

P – Patient, problem or population
I – Intervention
C – Comparator or control
O – Outcome measures

Consultation with relevant public and patient groups will ensure that the research question is worth asking.

## Trial design

The trial design should be the most appropriate to answer the research question (Table 9.1). While a pre-market clinical trial may simply be a case series without a control group, post-market clinical trials usually benefit from the inclusion of a control group where other similar devices or drugs exist for the same purpose in order to demonstrate the efficacy of the product compared to those already available on the market. Randomised controlled trials are usually necessary for drug therapies but are often not appropriate for medical devices. The background and rationale for the study justify the need for the clinical trial and allow definition of

Table 9.1 Levels of clinical evidence: Oxford Centre for Evidence-Based Medicine and Study

| Strength | Level | Design | Randomisation | Control |
|---|---|---|---|---|
| High | IA | Systematic review of randomised control trials (RCT) | Yes | Yes |
| | IB | Randomised clinical trial (RCT) | | |
| | IIA | Systematic review of cohort studies | No | Yes |
| | IIB | Cohort study | | |
| | IIIA | Systematic review of case controlled studies | No | Yes |
| | IIIB | Case-controlled study | | |
| | IV | Cross-sectional studies Case series | No | No |
| Low | V | Expert opinion | No | No |

the aims of the study as well as the objectives. The primary objective will usually be to answer the main research question, such as the efficacy of an innovation. There may be several secondary objectives, such as safety data and a health economic assessment.

The study protocol should be able to justify the choice of methodology as the most effective approach, define comparators where appropriate, determine sample size, define primary and secondary outcome measures, include blinding where possible and other methods of reducing bias, determine how safety and efficacy will be monitored in the trial and how the results will be published.

## Study participants

The inclusion and exclusion criteria clearly define the study participants that will be eligible to take part in your study. This must be representative of the entire population to ensure that the results of the trial are relevant to your entire market. It is, therefore, important not to exclude study participants that are likely to benefit from your innovation. This can be addressed through an equality impact assessment. This takes into consideration geographical location, age, disability gender, ethnicity, socioeconomic status, religion/belief and sexual orientation or potential study participants as well as access to health or social care.

## Outcome measures

The primary outcome measure is the main or primary endpoint of the clinical trial that answers the research question. Like the research question, it should be simple, specific and succinct. This could be a safety outcome in pre-market trials or an efficacy outcome in post-market trials and must include a specific time frame, e.g. change in X at three months after treatment. This is important as it is also the outcome measure for which the sample size calculation is usually based to ensure that the study is powered to answer the research question. A clinical study can have many secondary outcome measures. These are still important in the clinical trial and relevant to the research question, although the study may not necessarily be adequately powered to demonstrate these.

Where a control group or comparator is used, the trial can be designed to show that the treatment is superior to (superiority), at least as good as (non-inferiority) or not worse than (equivalence) the comparator. Although subtly different in implication, the trial design often has a significant impact on the sample size and should be justified. In a superiority trial, the trial must be powered to demonstrate the clinically important difference. While the clinically important difference should be evidence based, it should also be clinically reasonable and therefore pragmatic. PPI at this stage is also essential to determine what difference is important to patients as this may be different to that considered important to clinicians. Non-inferiority and equivalence trials require definition of a clinically unimportant difference. In a non-inferiority trial, the treatment could be either no better or no worse than the comparator, whereas in an equivalence trial, the treatment should be both no better and no worse than the comparator.

## Sample size and statistical analysis

The sample size used should also be justified based on the primary outcome measure and the trial design, particularly when a comparator is used. It is important to be realistic about the treatment difference that the trial is looking to determine. Any assumptions should be based on previous data in the literature on the primarily outcome measure, in particular to define the standard deviation of the primary outcome measure, with the clinically important or unimportant difference based on this data in combination with experience from the study design team and feedback from PPI. There is little point going to the time, effort and expense of setting up and running a clinical trial if it is not powered to determine the answer to your research question and demonstrate safety and or efficacy of your innovation. The sample size should allow for anticipated study participant dropout. Again, this should be a realistic estimate based on clinical experience of managing the condition that your innovation is designed to treat and will allow the final sample size to be determined. A statistician should be involved to calculate sample size but also to advise on the most appropriate statistical tests planned for data analysis, taking into account the type of data (parametric or non-parametric), the likely distribution (normal or other) and sample allocation (e.g. randomisation).

## Recruitment plan

A plan on how study participants are to be recruited can be very simple for small pre-clinical pilot studies of medical devices, but it is critical for larger, multi-centre studies, particularly in rare diseases where it can be challenging.

An internal pilot phase is often used to assess the ability to open sites, recruit participants, adhere to randomisation if appropriate and retain them in the study. A traffic light system is usually used to assess the progression from an internal pilot to the main phase of the clinical trial. This ensures that studies progress if they are achieving recruitment, adherence to the protocol and low dropout rates (green) but that any problems with recruitment are identified early and either remedied where possible (amber), often by opening additional sites, or in some circumstances result in the study being stopped if it is unlikely to recruit enough participants in an agreed time frame (red).

## Adverse events

Management and reporting of adverse events should be planned, both for medical devices and drug trials. An adverse event is an event that causes, or has the potential to cause, unexpected or unwanted effects involving the safety of the device users or study participants, whether related or not to the medical device or drug. In terms of medical devices, this can include a patient or healthcare professional being injured as a result of device failure or misuse, misdiagnosis or interruption of treatment due to device failure. Adverse events must be documented during the clinical trial and, if classed as serious or drug/device related, reported to the regulatory authorities (MHRA in the UK) and research ethics committee.

## Ethics, notification and monitoring

All clinical trials are subject to approval by an ethics committee. These issues should be considered when designing the trial, particularly in terms of potential clinical benefit from the innovation, informed consent, any blinding in the study, equality and diversity, data protection and conflicts of interest. The competent authority in each country where the study is to be conducted should be notified if the study involves a non-CE–marked device or a CE-marked device not being used for its intended purpose. For medical devices, this includes an investigator's brochure containing the background literature review, any pre-clinical data and instructions for use, a case report form that contains the information to be recorded during the study, patient information sheets and consent form.

A data monitoring committee (DMC) is required for larger clinical trials. This committee is an independent group of experts that are not involved with running the study; they review data at pre-determined time points during the trial primarily to assess for safety issues but also any important efficacy endpoints. A trial steering committee (TSC) provides overall supervision of a clinical trial and ideally is independent of the investigators, funders and sponsors. The committee monitors the progress of the trial, including its recruitment and conduct, such as protocol compliance, and acts on the recommendations of the DMC to decide whether a trial needs to be stopped early due to poor recruitment and retention or safety and efficacy issues. It is the TSC that would decide whether a trial with an internal pilot phase should progress to the full study with advice from the DMC.

## Publication and dissemination

At the end of a study, each site is closed and all CRFs checked along, with the investigator files, to allow a final study report to be written. Effective dissemination of the results of your trial should be planned from the beginning. This may be as simple as submission of the results to a notified body for CE marking for pre-market trials or much wider dissemination to clinicians and the public in post-market clinical trials. Publications in academic journals and presentation at academic meetings along with a social media or other marketing campaign to potential users may be appropriate depending on the device or drug. This will ensure that the end users are kept informed of the development of your innovation.

## CONCLUSIONS

Clinical trials are essential to demonstrate safety and efficacy of any medical device or drug. They require involvement of a team with relevant expertise and careful planning to ensure that the trial is asking the right question, is able to recruit enough patients, runs smoothly and records the outcomes required to support the development of the medical innovation.

# 10

# Marketing

## RICHARD ANDERSON

## PREPARATION – IT'S A STATE OF MIND

Marketing your product or service will make the difference between success and failure: it is that simple. Inferior products can succeed at the expense of better ones if they are supported by a stronger marketing programme, and you should not let yourself be on the wrong side of that equation if you are developing a medical innovation; it is simply too important.

Marketing should really start early in its development. The sooner you start to explore what your potential customers think, want and (with caution) think they want, the better your chances of success. You will need to get out of the lab and go to visit people once you have enough of a working prototype to show them and before you spend too much time refining it. While this is a vital step in product development, this type of research is also the beginning of your marketing strategy. Carefully listening to people who could one day be users of your product will tell you if you are going in the right direction and help you to shape

DOI: 10.1201/9781003164609-11

it to their needs. As well as helping you to develop a working product, it will also ensure that your innovation is commercially viable and competitive. Market research is something that should be a continuous part of the development of your marketing plan, and later on we will look at how you can apply it to test your ideas.

Perhaps the most important lesson for medical innovators is that you should keep an open mind – do not let yourself be tied down by preconceptions. In fact, it is highly likely that wherever you start and mean to finish is not where you will end up. It is important to listen to feedback and adapt.

## WHO ARE YOU TALKING TO?

Whether you are engaged in desk research or discussing your innovation with people who can help you to shape your ideas, it is vital to build a picture of who your customer will ultimately be. In particular, there are two elements that you will need to work hard on.

Firstly, the process of identifying your customer (your primary audience) should conclude with a precise definition of who they are; where they fit in the organisations that employs them; their role, influence and budget; their professional and organisational needs. If your marketing strategy is to work effectively, then an in-depth knowledge of these people is essential. If the product is going to be used by professional people in a healthcare environment, then it should be fairly straightforward to identify who they are – for example, clinicians, research scientists or administrators – but you will need to go much further to develop a full understanding of them in relation to your innovation.

If your product is going to be recommended or prescribed by healthcare professionals but used by patients, then you will need to work out the balance of this relationship to understand the needs of the clinicians and the patients. Finally, if your product will be used by consumers without any intervention from healthcare professionals (for example, a simple home pregnancy test) then you will need to work even harder as this is a much larger and more complex population to understand.

As well as developing your insights about customer needs, you will need some understanding of the personal demographics of your target group as well. For example, are they predominantly female or male? What age group (if any) is the most common for your customers? What socioeconomic group do they fit in? Where do they source their news and social feeds, both personally and professionally? These insights are vital for developing your brand and your marketing plan. You will really need to have a good sense of who you are talking to.

## AND THEN THERE IS EVERYONE ELSE

Although your customer is your primary audience, you will also need to be aware of the wider ecosystem of influencers who will have an impact on purchasing decisions. For medical products this could include scientific and medical peers, industry regulators, charities, patient groups, hospital procurement managers, university funders and many more. Mapping these influencers and understanding their role in the buying decisions of your customers is an essential next step as you will need to use your marketing activities to create a supportive environment amongst these secondary groups.

## DEVELOPING A BRAND FOR YOUR PRODUCT

Branding is something that is often thought of as being associated to a much greater extent with consumer products than with medical innovations, but branding is about more than a name and a logo. Your brand is really your promise to customers, it is the sum of all the associations that you want to make in people's minds when they think of your innovation. Your brand is a way of distinguishing your product from its rivals in the eyes of your customers. Developing a strong brand will enable you to command and maintain market share, create loyalty and trust and weather unforeseen storms to overcome market and product issues.

## TAKE THE TIME TO GET IT RIGHT

Brands take time to develop, and they need constant nurturing, so it is important to begin by developing an initial brand position from which to build.

In the case of a medical innovation, there are really three elements that you will need to consider: i) the scientific evidence base that underpins your invention, ii) the product's commercial viability and its potential to succeed in a competitive environment and iii) your 'corporate' credibility (initially based largely on your reputation and behaviour in the earliest pre-company formation stages). These three elements will form the basis for your brand platform. Simply put, your product will have to be built on a strong basis of medical or scientific evidence, fit a customer need, be affordable and competitive, and you or any company that you form will need to have the credibility to take the product forward to the market.

## NAVEL GAZING AND HORIZON SCANNING

Carry out what is commonly known as a SWOT analysis – Strengths, Weaknesses, Opportunities and Threats. It is an honest appraisal of your own invention. Begin with the inward-looking part of the exercise to analyse the strengths and weaknesses of your idea, product or service. Now assess your product in relation to the world around you, both now and as far into the future as it is possible to anticipate; what are the future opportunities that you see and the threats that you face from competitors, other approaches or changing needs? Involve others who are familiar with what you are doing to help make your assessment as objective as possible. Map it all out and keep it as a working document. As you move forward with your idea and you learn more about the environment you will be working in, keep updating it so it is always fresh.

## BE ABSOLUTELY CLEAR ABOUT WHAT
## EVERYONE ELSE IS DOING

Before you develop a brand position for your own product, you are going to need to study what everyone else is doing. How do they position themselves? What is their marketing saying? Are they cheaper, faster, smarter, more convenient, more accurate? There are many ways of capturing and analysing this data that are freely available, and you will be able to find one that suits you. It is important that you complete this exercise to give you context for developing your brand. If you are looking for external investment, then every potential investor will expect you to have this information at the front of your mind when you are asking for funding. You will need to explain how you can beat them all.

## BE CLEAR ABOUT YOUR AMBITION

However, early you are in the conception and development of your idea, your marketing will need to capture people's imagination, rationally and emotionally. Your ambition for the difference that your innovation can make to people's lives should shine through the way you present your innovation. Take some time to imagine what things will look like in three to five years' time. How do you want to be seen, and what do you want people to say about you at that time? Write down some short descriptive phrases and adjectives that capture this. Be realistic; whatever you say will need to be evidence-based, so rein in too much excitement and distil your plans into some inspiring words that are grounded in reality. It is not an easy exercise, so work with others to challenge you and check that you can defend the language and image that you arrive at.

## DEVELOP A BRAND POSITION

Your brand position is the strategic ambition for your idea. It is the touchstone for all activities, strategies and decisions within the business, from the staff you recruit to the message on your website. While a tremendous amount of time and resources need to go into securing a brand position once the product has been launched; planning for it beforehand is crucial. If you are developing a medical innovation, you may think that launching your product is far into the future so this aspect can wait until later. The reality is that before you launch your product, your company is the brand; and before you start your company, you are the brand. If you are talking to business partners, scientific collaborators, future investors or even just friends and family, you will need to establish a compelling position for your idea in their minds. Everyone has to believe in it, because if you cannot convince those closest to you, then what hope do you have of persuading people from professional life to commit time, funds or their reputations to what you are doing?

A brand position is not what you do to a product or service, it is what you do to the mind of your customer or, earlier on, to your collaborators and investors. Your aim should be to position your product in the minds of the people who will buy it so that you can overcome the problem of being heard above the noise, creating impact and achieving differentiation.

Imagine that brands are positioned in ladders in people's minds. The top brand on each ladder will be the 'brand of choice' in that category, and any position or 'rung' can be held by only one brand at a time. We are all familiar with the consequences of this type of laddering through the choices that we make when we buy something, although most of the time it operates only at a subconscious level. Generally, the first person/product/company with the loudest voice and most compelling vision will establish the desired position. The fact that someone else could come along and try and take it does not mean they will be successful. If you have done a good job, it will be almost impossible for them to take over your position. From the consumer world there are thousands of examples. Look at Coke and Pepsi. Coke has the position of the established leader in the market. Pepsi is the 'choice of a new generation'. There is nothing stopping either of them trying to pretend that they are the other by attempting to usurp the other's position – there is nothing intrinsic in the black fizzy drinks to stop them. But would Coke customers suddenly believe Pepsi was 'the real thing'?

A strong brand position, especially one based on a scientific or medical advance, needs to be built on four pillars:

**Sustainability** – You need to be able to maintain your position over time. Your ambition must be reflected in your brand position, but only if you have the evidence to give you the confidence that it will be sustainable.
**Uniqueness** – No two brands can successfully hold the same position – customers will believe only one of the brands. It will be the first with the best brand to claim the position.
**Credibility** – Your position can be backed up with the messages you give the customer. These are called reasons to believe, and they will need the evidence base with, ideally, published data to back them up.
**Competitive** – It needs to gain you something versus your competitors.

## THE POSITIONING STATEMENT

The positioning statement is, initially, an internal statement to capture the essence of your brand. Do not imagine that your early drafts will be the public-facing, fully polished phrasing. Start with something you are comfortable with, no matter how long and unwieldy; it just needs to get to the truth, the 'why', and then you can hone it down to make it as concise as possible. You will get a much better result if you work with others to develop this, ideally in a workshop format with an independent (unbiased) facilitator who can test your ideas, push back where needed and help you to work your way to the best possible result.

Keep it simple and use a format such as 'to, is, that, because'.

**To** – This will be your primary audience, the one you established as your target customer, for example, 'GPs with a specialisation in asthma' or 'diagnostic laboratory managers who need to increase the throughput of Covid-19 tests'. Try to be as specific as possible.

**Is** – Describe your innovation in as concise a way as possible so that you include the market space where you will be operating, such as an 'inhaler for asthma sufferers' or a 'rapid Covid-19 lab test'.

**That** – Identify the highest ownable benefit that you can claim for your product or service. This can be quite a challenging exercise and also works well as a workshop exercise. Your innovation will offer many benefits, but some will be more powerful and significant than others, so try to build a benefits ladder with each benefit higher than the one below it in terms of the positive difference it will make. For example, at the bottom of a benefits ladder for a new Covid-19 test you might write 'faster result'. Now consider whether that is the best you can do. Apply the 'so what' test. Faster result – so what? Your answer might be that it is more efficient and increases lab throughput. Again, so what? Answer: patients get their results more quickly. So what? Answer: if they are positive then they can self-isolate sooner and reduce the risk of infecting more people. So what? And so it goes on until you establish the highest ownable benefit. This is what you should write into you positioning statement.

## BECAUSE

'Because' is the reason to believe. It is the brand's most competitive key feature – the simple truth that justifies the brand benefit, the proof of what you are saying. When you have established the full 'to, is, that, because', you will have your positioning statement.

## BUILDING THE MESSAGE MATRIX

Establishing a simple message matrix will give you the basis for all the content that you need to create, including your website, product information, presentations and press releases (Figure 10.1). The idea is known as a message house, in which your brand positioning statement is supported by core messages and supporting messages that provide the evidence that back up the core messages.

Figure 10.1 The message house.

Draft your messages and then check them by

- Asking what the relevance is to the target customers of each of these messages.
- Asking what other key messages could be communicated.
- Evaluating key messages.
  - Ensure that all elements of your position are covered.
  - Eliminate duplicate ideas.
  - Identify sub-messages of other messages.
- Ranking key messages.
  - Rank messaging according to priority in supporting statement.
  - Identify timing of message release (now/later).
  - Capture action relating to generation of new messaging.
  - Review key messages to ensure maximum impact.

## TIME TO GET GOING

When you are ready to launch your company or your innovation, you will need a website and a communications plan. This is usually beyond the experience of most medical innovators and trying to do it yourself will most likely be sub-optimal in terms of quality of outcome and inefficient for you when you should be focusing on the core business.

Write a brief that outlines what you want to achieve and include the work that you have done so far based on what we have outlined in this chapter. You can send this to a specialist marketing communications agency that operates in the scientific and medical fields. When you have chosen one to work with, they will be able to advise you, create your marketing materials and execute an effective plan. This may include speaking at conferences, advertising, sending news to journalists, networking, direct marketing, or other tactics depending on your needs. Whatever the plan, it is vital to measure the success of the implementation at every step to maximise your return on investment. Done well, this will help to drive customers or investors to your door and put you in control of your success.

# 11

# Penetrating the National Health Service and private sectors

NIGEL SANSOM

## A RECENT HISTORY OF INNOVATION MANAGEMENT IN THE NHS

The National Health Service (NHS) is an enormous entity and is very expensive to run, with almost as many staff as the Chinese army has soldiers. Yet it is actually a great place for innovation. For anyone, wherever they are based, successfully innovating in the NHS is seen as a stamp of approval from one of the most respected healthcare systems in the world.

However, navigating the NHS innovation landscape is not so much hard as complicated. It is populated by numerous organisations, many of which sound like they should probably do the same thing, and some that do the same thing but sound like they shouldn't. One of the things that new entrants absolutely hate, but the NHS adores, is the fact that everything – absolutely everything – has an abbreviation. It is common practice to change abbreviations just as everyone has become used to them.

For example, NHSE is now NHSE&I; STPs are now ICSs; CCGs are now comprised of numerous PCNs (see glossary for terms). With support from the NIHR, MHRA, ABHI, BIVDA, AMRC, BIA, NICE, BEIS, and the DH, the AAC now sponsors the AHSNs, the NIA, SBRI for Healthcare, EAMS, and the ITP programme. NHSx is a thing, and definitely not NHS Digital! But GPs are still GPs…

To best understand the NHS innovation landscape, a potted history of its innovation management approach is needed. Whilst this area does not have a lengthy history, there have been a great many casualties along the road that has led to the system we now have, as those involved have persevered to get it right.

Very early in the new millennium it was decided that it would be a good idea for the NHS in England to have a system to manage innovation. Up until that time, a surgeon (for example) might make some kind of working prototype in her garage and then go and license it to a big medical device company before laughing all the way to the bank and driving off in a shiny new Porsche. The big realisation was that whilst an individual clinician may have become significantly richer, and a US device company may have both enhanced their product portfolio and pleased their shareholders, a multi-million-pound revenue stream may have been lost forever. An additional worry was 'How many times has this happened, and how much poorer are NHS trusts as a result?' 'Not many' was the likely answer, but it was clear that innovation was happening, and the NHS, NHS trusts, NHS departments and 'UK plc' were not getting a slice of the action, and patients were not benefitting. Up to that point, less than 20 years ago, there was no 'IP policy' and there had been no clear thinking about how the NHS should manage innovations, at all.

Initially there were ten regional 'NHS innovations hubs', which were to some extent coordinated by the NHS National Innovation Centre (NIC), which was itself 'hosted' by the NHS Institute for Innovation and Improvement, a 'special health authority'. The hubs and the NIC were all about finding, developing and ultimately deploying technological innovation into the NHS, whilst the NHS Institute was mostly about helping 'develop a culture for innovation', leadership and 'thinking differently'. For too many reasons to recount here, in less than ten years, most of the initial innovation landscape inhabitants were consigned to history, but new initiatives have given rise to the NHS innovation ecosystem we see today. However, whilst in existence, the various players helped develop and deploy a framework for managing innovation in the NHS, including IP policies.

The past ten years have seen the Department of Health (DH) roll out the Academic Health Science Networks (AHSNs), which forms the interface between the NHS, academia and industry. There are 15 AHSNs, which form the AHSN Network. If you are a UK-based innovator with some technology innovation you feel is destined for the NHS, your local AHSN is most definitely your first port of call. Also, following the Accelerated Access Review, we now have the Accelerated Access Collaborative which should 'accelerate the access' of proven innovations into clinical practice. There is a new organisation called NHSx, which should facilitate adoption of digital health technology in that space and will hopefully refine the evidence standards framework. Lastly, the current NHS 'National Clinical Champion for Innovation', has developed the Clinical Entrepreneur Programme, which aims to help NHS staff (including non-clinicians) to develop innovative ideas. These are all worth a look.

## WHAT IS INNOVATION?

Here are a few popular definitions of innovation:

- The future delivered
- Anything that is new, useful and exciting
- Introduction of new products and services that add value to the organisation
- The application of ideas that are novel and useful

The two main categories of innovation important for the NHS are service innovation and technology innovation. The former generally involves reconfiguring existing structures, processes that are aimed at changing aspects that are at the root of resource integration, for example, deployment of a new service which can be rolled out locally, that has positive impact for a particular patient group. Innovation that happens in the NHS is mostly of this type. Technology innovation – from medicines management, through capacity monitoring systems, to surgical robots – is less common and more difficult to deploy. At their core, technology innovations in healthcare usually have three things in common: intellectual property that is in some way protectable, the capability to generate revenue and most importantly capacity to improve health.

Innovations may also be either 'sustaining' or 'disruptive'. The former are the sort of thing we expect from large companies: the incremental year-on-year improvements that do not create new markets but sustain, and in some cases develop, an existing one. The main reason large companies are good at sustaining innovation is because they are executing a business plan, with the approval of current shareholders, within approved budgets. Smaller companies, often formed around the emergence of an idea, are more agile. They are not executing a business plan but searching for one that works. Disruptive innovation occurs when new entrants identify a need that is not served by other suppliers and successfully establish what becomes a new market.

Many advances in healthcare are achieved by bringing together other innovations in disparate fields. A good example is cataract surgery. The original approach, known as 'couching', involved use of a thorn or pointy stick to push the opaque lens down so that light could be admitted and the patient issued a powerful positive lens. However, thanks to the convergence of advances in microsurgery, ultrasound, materials science, optics, the femtosecond laser and many other innovations, we now have modern cataract surgery which has enabled a quicker recovery and more predictable refractive outcome. Regardless of whether the medical innovation is sustaining or disruptive, the road ahead is long and multi-factorial.

## ACCESSING THE NHS

If you are on the outside of the NHS, the process can be disheartening. Whilst a particular arm of the NHS set up to deal with, for example, digital innovations, has provided you their direct email address during an innovation webinar, do not expect a quick response. They have a backlog in their inbox due to thousands of 'great ideas' being emailed to them, and there is no intelligent mechanism to sift through them. It is a sad reality that the vast majority of ideas presented to government-sponsored innovation agencies do not include an amazing innovation. Despite innovators' claims, their innovation probably isn't particularly innovative, may not address a clinical need and more than likely will not save the NHS many millions of pounds. Sometimes all these things are true, but they may not see this. It is hard to communicate this to innovators, but it is even harder to spot the absolute gems that exist within the detritus.

You have a technological innovation and, having successfully engaged relevant clinicians, you are now sure that there is a clinical need. Having researched the technical area and taken some professional advice, you are sure you have freedom to operate in the space and may even have applied for a patent. Your path towards successful uptake of your innovation partially lies in your ability to get the NHS to recognise its importance. This is a challenging task, but there are some well-defined steps that can make life easier.

You really need a clinical champion, a sufficiently well-respected clinician whom you can get access to, who will effectively champion your cause. Your local Academic Health Science Network can help with this. They have contacts that stretch across their region, within both primary and secondary care. Get on their radar early, and they can be very effective in helping you build the right relationships that you will need.

If you are an NHS insider, do look at the Clinical Entrepreneurship scheme. If you are on the outside and a bit more advanced, it is worth looking at the National Innovation Accelerator, which is sponsored by the Accelerated Access Collaborative, a fully mentored programme that can be very helpful indeed in building relationships with commissioners, procurement professionals, access to senior decision makers and forming collaborations with right-sized clinical teams to help develop and deploy your innovation more rapidly.

## COST EFFECTIVENESS AND THE GENERATION OF EVIDENCE

Once you have convinced potential users that your innovation meets their clinical needs, to have any chance of adoption, your innovation must be cost effective and will need evidence to support this.

Your novel invention may be more expensive than the current intervention, and if it is, then it really does need to be more effective. Establishing cost effectiveness is complicated and requires the assistance of a health economist. They will use the evidence you have generated and any metrics available for the standard clinical pathway.

When you speak to clinicians about your innovation, they will always ask what evidence you have that it works. If your innovation will save x number of lives and y number of pounds in z number of years, be prepared to back it up with evidence. However, what if you don't have any evidence that the innovation works and you are unsure how to get it. This is where a good relationship with your AHSN and/or an NIHR-MIC may prove useful. You can get help, support and advice in establishing what sort of evidence is required and what a study design should look like. Hopefully your new clinical champion will also be keen to help generate evidence by finding a way to actively engage with your innovation. A research study will generally require ethics approval, which is made via the Integrated Research Application System. An alternative to a research study for an innovation that is CE marked may be a service evaluation, which is in many ways easier and cheaper. Research and innovation officers should be able to advise on what the best course of action might be.

Most small- and medium-sized enterprises (SMEs) count money, specifically lack thereof, as a severely limiting factor. You need to generate evidence, but doing so costs money. Teaching hospitals love research; they love money too, and a full-blown randomised controlled trial (RCT) brings in money. When an NHS partner insists on such a programme of research, the outputs may well be fantastic evidence, but it will also cost your company a lot of money. Many SMEs have considerable agility, an enviable ability to pivot rapidly, and can readily design a tangible clinical plan that, if executed at the speed they're used to moving at, will see them through the next inflection point and permit them to raise more funds. However, the NHS doesn't move that quickly; just getting a data sharing agreement signed off can take a trust six months The NHS receives no end of small companies claiming to have the next best thing, and if during a research programme you come to the end of your financial runway, do not expect your NHS partner to mourn your death; another SME partner will come knocking on their door very soon. To survive you need your company to be able to raise sufficient finance to cover the stages of development required on the way to generating a satisfactory level of evidence. A satisfactory level of evidence that is twinned with proof of cost effectiveness and defined clinical utility should ideally be met with a commissioning decision and actual reimbursement, but of course this often is not the case. Think about what you need in terms of evidence, and take advice if unsure. Establish the minimum evidence standard sufficient to get to the next stage in your development pathway. A large randomised, double-blind, cross-over trial, while ideal, is expensive and probably unnecessary.

## GETTING REIMBURSED

So, you have developed working relationships with clinical teams to demonstrate clinical validity and utility and have published the evidence. A credible health economics team has had the chance to analyse your evidence and is publishing a paper in a peer-reviewed journal, which illustrates cost effectiveness of your innovation, QALY gains, and any other ways in which the healthcare system benefits. You have cleared the regulatory hurdles and gained a CE mark for your technology. You have done all the systems integration, and information governance is 'happy'. Is now the time to start talking to NHS commissioners and/or finance professionals in the hope they will start paying you? In short, no!

You need to start talking to these important people really early on. Use your local AHSN and find the right person there to help you both understand the complexities involved and to facilitate the right discussions at the right time. You should be developing an idea of price early and, in concert with a health economist, determining whether it's too high or too low and adjusting as necessary. As you're developing metrics on the impacts of the adoption of your innovation, keep commissioners in the loop. Having these conversations early will pay off in the long run.

An NHS trust will likely need to develop a business case to get sign-off for the acquisition of your innovation. Be ready for this as it's no small feat. NHS business cases are based on the HM Treasury 'Green Book' and are serious documents. Whilst there will be an NHS trust person who takes responsibility for writing and presenting the business case, they can't possibly be expected to compile all the necessary technical detail. It's your job to work with that person and help them state your case accurately.

Find out what the commissioning cycle is, and when you need to have your technology innovation in the frame. It's no good deciding you're finally 'good to go' and approaching the commissioner after the deadline for new proposals has passed. This can add a year to your development plans. Better to develop a working relationship early, keep them abreast of developments, ensure they're excited by the prospect of your technology being available, and make them feel like a partner in the process. There are a lot of balls in the air at once, it's true, but hopefully if your innovation ticks all the right boxes (clinically valid with proven utility and cost effectiveness) and you have had all the right conversations with the right people, have all the correct documents signed off and have regulatory clearance/approval, hopefully, you'll have your technology both deployed AND reimbursed.

What you need now is initial clinical users to become regional clinical champions. Get these people to sing the praises of your innovation for you. It's priceless! Co-author papers during development and beyond. Make sure that your message is getting spread across other regions, and for this, yet again, you must use the AHSN network. There is a machine out there which is underutilised by innovators. You have to use that machine to make sure you get your innovation on the radar of as many trusts or commissioners as possible. As more and more evidence accrues, it is possible that your innovation may have a NICE-led favourable Healthcare Technology Assessment and national 'guidance' issued. This doesn't necessarily mean that NHS England will mandate use of your tech, but it's on the way...

## GLOSSARY OF TERMS

**AAC** Accelerated Access Collaborative

**ABHI** Association of British Healthcare Industries

**AMRC** Association of Medical Research Charities

**BEIS** Business, Energy & and Industrial Strategy (a government department)

**BIA** Bio Industry Association

**BIVDA** British in vitro Diagnostics Association

**CCG** Clinical Commissioning Groups

**DH** Department of Health (set policy for the NHS)

**EAMS** Early Access to Medicines Scheme

**ICS** Integrated Care System

**ITP** Innovation Technology Payment

**MHRA** Medicines & and Health Regulatory Agency

**NHS Digital** The national provider of information, data and IT systems for commissioners, analysts, and clinicians in the NHS

**NHSE** NHS England (deliver/execute policy handed down from DH)

**NHSE&I** NHS England & and Improvement (their new name after NHS Improvement was subsumed into NHSE)

**NHSx** The x doesn't mean anything, but the unit develops best practice for NHS technology, digital, and data (including data sharing and transparency)

**NIA** National Innovation Accelerator

**NIHR** National Institute of Health Research

**PCN** Primary Care Network

**STP** Sustainability and Transformation Partnerships

**\*NHSx became subsumed into NHS Digital in 2022, which in turn has been subsumed into NHS Transformation.**

---

## CASE STUDY I: KENT AND MEDWAY PREHAB – TELEHEALTH-DELIVERED HOME-BASED PATIENT OPTIMISATION

### BACKGROUND

Prehabilitation ('prehab') is a relatively new concept rapidly gaining acceptance across the global medical community. Prehabilitation involves identifying and promoting health-optimising behaviours to mitigate the unwanted consequences of cancer treatment, often in the pre-treatment setting to improve post-operative outcomes. The benefits of prehabilitation for patients with cancer have been well documented. Accepted benefits of prehabilitation include improvements in functional capacity, clinical outcomes and adoption of healthy lifestyles. Much of the evidence in support for prehabilitation has studied the effects of in-person supervised programmes.

The Kent and Medway Prehab service started out as a single site-based pilot and then received funding to expand into the community. Dr Tara Rampal is the founder and director of the service. A firm believer in the triple aim of healthcare, she believes that services should offer not only improved clinical outcomes but patient experience and return on investment. Prior to the pandemic, the service was able to provide cancer patients centre-based, or face-to-face, prehabilitation interventions. There had been little attention given to telehealth-delivered and/or home-based programmes. In response to the pandemic, following the UK government's announcement of the national lockdown, Kent and Medway Prehab programme used digital technologies and telecommunication methods to continue the benefits of prehabilitation and to mitigate the consequences of shielding.

## SERVICE FLOW

Eligible patients are referred from multiple centres (NHS Acute Trusts and GP practices) to a regional prehabilitation unit providing telehealth-delivered home-based prehabilitation. Referrals are made via a webpage. Local hospital patient flow software now also includes teleprompts for referral to the service. Enrolled patients perform telehealth-delivered prehabilitation prior to surgery and/or during non-surgical cancer treatment.

Patients are stratified and streamlined based on an initial questionnaire-based screening tool. Remote consultations with a prehabilitation specialist and counsellors enable development of a supervised, targeted plan based on baseline functional capacity and clinical need.

## OUTCOMES

At the end of its first year, a review of the service revealed a positive relationship of the programme on patient-reported outcomes and has been through rigorous and published in peer reviewed journals. The digital service is capable of delivery of a personalised service, adding to self-efficacy and improved outcomes. It allows stratification of patients based on clinical need and offers flexibility and cost efficiency. There are individual and group sessions available along with psychological support on demand, which are greatly appreciated by the patients. Patient focus groups consistently provide feedback that the model promotes compliance, sets targets and reinforces positive messaging to improve patient confidence and self-efficacy. It allows supported self-management of holistic needs and removes opportunity costs for the users.

Key learning points: Like all innovative healthcare providers, the service reviews, adapts and evolves. The COVID-19 pandemic resulted in a number of unexpected challenges. However, the pandemic and the lockdown accelerated greater acceptability of telehealth, a sector that has traditionally lagged behind many others in adopting digital transformation.

Key figures/quotes: Tara Rampal, founder of Kent and Medway Prehab: 'Telehealth has the potential to enable accessibility, flexibility and sustainability for the providers and our population group. It does so whilst lowering delivery costs for healthcare providers and opportunity costs for our patients and we are absolutely delighted they have an overwhelmingly positive experience. Keeping our patients at the heart of all innovation, from conception to delivery and review, has been the guiding force responsible for our success.

'What we have learnt over the last few months is the value of being pragmatic and agile. There needs to be a strong focus on rapid adaptability of systems within organisations delivering programme. Robust governance structures to support implementation of ideas and clarity in communication'. (www.kentandmedwayprehab.org)

Additional useful resources:

- https://pubmed.ncbi.nlm.nih.gov/34204531/
- https://pubmed.ncbi.nlm.nih.gov/34376302/
- https://www.kentandmedwayccg.nhs.uk/news-and-events/news/virtual-prehabilitation-programme-launches-kent-and-medway-cancer-patients

Figure I.1 Kent and Medway Prehab- Digital Prehabilitation solutions.

Key contact:

- Webpage: www.kentandmedwayprehab.org
- Service: Tara.rampal@phb.community
- Twitter: @TaraRampal
- @KM_Prehab

# SECTION 2

# Horizon Scanning and the Emergency Technologies

# 12

# An innovator's journey

CHRIS COULSON

This is a good time to start dealing with some hard truths of innovation. You need to be very interested in money – it has to be at the forefront of your mind constantly, and you need to be singularly focused on making it. Sounds uncomfortable? Let me explain.

Many of you reading this book will be in a healthcare field. I was (and still am) a consultant ENT surgeon when we conceived our first product. In my mind, patient benefit trumped money by some distance. I found it hard to talk about prices, and indeed selling products initially felt a bit dirty. It's not what we innovate for, is it? We want to deliver improved patient care, no?

You'll need to get over this mindset fast if you are going to get a product to market! It is highly unlikely you possess all the skills required to complete the journey alone, so you are going to need external help – and that will come at a price. And these people may well become employees over time; then you'll have the monthly salary bill, in addition to legal fees, regulatory fees, further R+D fees, hardware, software, fulfilment centres, pensions, etc., etc. constantly in your mind. So, you need to be critically focused on money to ensure that you can complete the journey and protect the livelihoods of your employees.

DOI: 10.1201/9781003164609-14

I know what you are thinking: my idea is so good that as soon as I tell an investor/funding body about this amazing innovation, money will come pouring in (although maybe I would argue at this stage that the only thing you have found is a problem without a decent solution).

Unfortunately, the reality is that this does not happen. The principal reasons for this are twofold. Firstly, it is likely that your innovation is not mature enough in its lifecycle, coupled with the absence of a rudimentary business plan, leading to potential investors being unable to accurately assess the viability of your innovation. Secondly, if you are going down the venture capitalist funding route, depending on where you are in your medical career, you may be relatively uninvestable. 'What!!' I hear you cry. 'I am a consultant surgeon, I know what I'm talking about!' Typically venture capitalists are after people (and their products) who are keen to commit 110% of their life towards making their product a success – are you prepared to skip the family holiday when you are at a critical phase in the project? Do you want every day to be a work day? Yes, that does include weekends. If you are a practising clinician with a good income, it is (incorrectly) assumed that you will not have the drive to push your project forward to fruition.

## OK, SO HOW MUCH MONEY DO I NEED?

First up, you need to consider what the money is for, as you will want to avoid asking for money then realising that this is no way enough, putting you in the position where you need to ask for more or not deliver on what you promised.

There are many steps in taking a product from concept to market, and it is very likely that you have no desire to achieve all of these yourself. Although, be warned, in my experience you always need to take products further than you want to – unless you want to run the risk of the products not making it to market. Endoscope-I's first product, the endoscope-I adapter, was a case in point on this topic. We performed all the design work, prototyping and user trials in house. We then thought that medical device companies would be falling over themselves to take this (amazing!) product off our hands. We received a number of offers, but having spent a few years getting to this point, the offer of 1.5% of the net sale price of each item was far lower than we expected. This led us to regulate, manufacture, sell and distribute the device ourselves. Something we had no desire to undertake at the outset.

So knowing your planned exit point is necessary in deciding how much funding you require.

Once you've decided what steps need to be completing, you can start pricing these up. As flippant as it sounds, when you have your grand total, you can do far worse than doubling it to arrive at the actual amount! If this is your first time through the process, you will be extremely surprised at how quick you can burn through money.

## WHO OWNS THE INNOVATION?

A key part of the How much money do I need to achieve this? question is Where does the ownership lie? If you have conceived the innovation on your own, then you may naturally presume that you 'own' the IP. This impacts the money question

Table 12.1 Typical share distribution

| Cumulative Net Income | Trust | Directorate | Lead Inventor(s) |
|---|---|---|---|
| First £5,000 | n/a | n/a | 100% |
| Next £200,000 | 35% | 25% | 40% |
| Next £795,000 | 40% | 20% | 40% |

as you may well work for free on your product, safe in the knowledge that when it hits the big time, your reward will then arrive. But do you own the product? If you are a practising clinician or healthcare worker – does your employer own the product? This is a question that is worth bottoming out very early on, prior to any money being made, as money skews the negotiation and lots of people want their (perceived) cut of it.

If you are Mr Coulson approaching the hospital IP office with an idea that you are going to fund the development yourself, then they may give you most of the spoils. The alternative is naturally for the hospital to fund and then own it. However, as most ideas come to nothing, the hospital will rarely want to invest, so it seems reasonable that if all the risk (and capital) is yours, then you own it.

If you are Mr Smith informing the hospital that you have just agreed a sale of your innovation for £10,000,000, they will almost certainly take a different view.

The generality of an NHS trusts view on IP is as follows (paraphrased from a number of trusts' IP policies):

1. The trust legally owns all IP (copyright, designs and patents) arising from the delivery of patient care, the education and training of employees, and research and development programmes undertaken by its employees in the course of work for the trust, unless such IP is subject to a separate written agreement with an external funding realisation, or agreed otherwise.
2. Typical shares are shown in Table 12.1.
3. In the event of a cumulative net income greater than £1m revenue sharing will be dealt with on a case by case basis.

## RIGHT, SO WE HAVE WORKED OUT WHETHER WE OWN IT, HAVE DECIDED WHAT STAGE WE WANT TO GET TO PRIOR TO SELLING IT, AND SO HAVE WORKED OUT HOW MUCH MONEY WE NEED. WHAT'S NEXT?

Once you have bottomed out your business plan and understand all the steps that will take your concept to a global success, you will need to work out how to access money for the different stages of the project. Almost certainly any initial money will be for maturing prototypes of your idea, which in the grand scheme will be relatively cheap, compared to running trials of your 'thing'.

So, given you can't afford to fund this yourself, what are your options and what is the best route? (An upfront spoiler, there is no correct answer for this!)

## MAJOR HEALTHCARE GRANT-AWARDING BODIES

It is unlikely that this is a feasible option initially. Not unreasonably, major grant-awarding bodies are pretty keen that their money is spent on projects which look like they are going to be successful. So your concept needs to be realised and ideally have undergone a small trial of use prior to you being considered. This would certainly de-risk your project for them. If you are still at the concept phase, then it is very unlikely that this is a feasible option. This is worth bearing in mind for formal trials.

## LOCAL FUNDING POTS

Many hospitals and universities have small pots of money available for employees/students. These provide an ideal starter for your project. Both in terms of acquiring the skills of applying for funding and hopefully giving you the funds to jump to the next stage of development. You also get the opportunity to receive unbiased feedback. This can be invaluable. A word of caution: they are not always keen to give money to a private company.

## SELF FUNDING

Clearly this option is available only to those with money in the bank. There are certainly some major advantages and disadvantages that this option delivers. Let's start with the disadvantages first:

- It is only really relevant to small projects.
- You need to accept the fact that the money you spend may well never come back.

However, the advantages are large (on the presumption you have clarified ownership with your employer first):

- You own all the spoils.
- You have complete control to follow your nose and lead the project, however, you see fit.

## STRAIGHT TO MANUFACTURER

This can be a pragmatic choice and avoid many of the difficulties of producing your innovation yourself. Manufacturers are typically very happy to hear of new ideas. (Always discuss these under the cover of a non-disclosure agreement.) However, they are unlikely to offer a large split of the purchase price (1–2% net). The more mature your idea, the better negotiating position you put yourself in.

## UNIVERSITY RESOURCES

Universities are packed full of technical and creative people with all the skills necessary to solve your problems. These are often undergraduates who can take on some of the work required as part of a project within their course, which often makes the work performed free. When I say free, I mean in cash terms; you don't pay for it, but there will often be a split of any potential IP required.

## INNOVATION/BUSINESS GRANTS

Many countries have innovation/business grants whose principal aim is to increase the UK PLC GDP. These are often much easier to get than formal research funding but are often matched funding: if you can find £50,000, we'll give you £50,000. They are certainly worth investigating as they typically do not come with any strings attached in terms of ownership.

## VENTURE CAPITALIST INVESTMENT

This is a great way to generate money, but you need to be aware of the game you are getting into. Venture capital (VC) funds work by investing into hundreds of companies with the hope that a small number will make it big. If it becomes clear yours is not one of that number, then expect funding and support to end. You will be on a short (-ish) path to either major success or, more likely, closing. This may or may not represent the ideal solution for you.

Overall, the general principal of funding your project is to get as much money as possible, with as few strings attached, as possible whilst retaining as much ownership as possible.

# 13

# Digital health

ADITYA DESAI AND GEORGE KAROUS

In 1947, the invention of the transistor represented the human race's tentative first steps into the digital revolution, and this began the shift away from mechanical and analogue technologies to digital ones. This process picked up momentum with the introduction of the internet and home computers, and the invention of the World Wide Web triggered the proliferation of digital technologies. Novel computation and communication methods have continued to penetrate more aspects of our day-to-day lives in the form of smartphones, social media platforms and wearables to name a few. This includes healthcare, and these technologies (Table 13.1) offer new and improved ways of delivering healthcare, conducting health promotion activities and monitoring public health.[1,2]

To begin the discussion of digital health, we provide an overview of what *digital* means and give an explanation of several fundamental technologies that provide the foundation and architecture for most of the innovations that come under the umbrella of digital health. The technologies presented are then contextualised by exploring their applications to healthcare. We explore electronic health records (EHRs), as the digitisation of medical data is the basis of the many branches of digital health, making the discussion of EHRs relevant to the broader field of digital technology applications.

Following the analysis of contemporary digital technologies, we discuss cutting-edge digital health applications and their implications on the future before summarising what was covered with the aid of a case study of Flexio, a remote physiotherapy platform bringing together the various elements discussed throughout the chapter.

DOI: 10.1201/9781003164609-15

Table 13.1 Subdomains of digital health[1]

| Category | Example(s) |
|---|---|
| Telemedicine and telehealth | Remote healthcare delivery via digital technologies |
| Medical education | Training of healthcare providers using digital technologies |
| Health informatics | Electronic patient records |
| Digitised medicine delivery devices | Cochlear implants, insulin pumps, cardiac monitors |
| Digital epidemiology | Tracking disease outbreaks and spread |
| Digital health games | Online games/applications used for fitness, health promotion and education |
| Digital diagnostic technologies | Software/apps used to aid diagnostic processes |

## FUNDAMENTAL DIGITAL TECHNOLOGIES

Several core technologies play a significant role in enabling the function of most healthcare innovations. Whilst their ubiquity may make them inconspicuous, understanding how these technologies work helps to appreciate their impact on healthcare systems.

Let us begin by delving into what digital technology is. As these letters are typed on a computer keyboard, a digital signal is sent to the computer to register each keystroke. The language used to communicate to machines is different to the language humans use to communicate, as all information is stored as a series of the numbers 1 and 0, known as binary. A binary digit, or bit, is the smallest unit of data in computing. Although this may seem simple, the right combinations of 1s and 0s can be used to store pretty much any data imaginable.

To make use of digital data, an architecture is needed that enables the easy transfer and storage of this information. A good way to explore this notion is to think about the biggest global system of interconnected computer networks: the internet. How is it that the digital data that we type into an email can be transferred across the world in seconds? To understand this journey, let us follow the path of an email from a laptop in the UK to a smartphone in Australia.

Assuming that the laptop is connected to a router via an Ethernet cable, the stream of 1s and 0s representing the email is transferred along the wire using pulses of electricity. These cables are convenient for covering short distances as they are relatively inexpensive. However, over longer distances they are prone to signal loss. Instead, when it comes to the email's intercontinental crossing, the data continues its journey as pulses of light bouncing along fibre-optic cables spanning the ocean floor. This is a fantastically fast way for the email to travel, and it suffers no signal loss, meaning that the entirety of the email data completes its journey. A combination of copper and fibre-optic cables take the message all the way to Australia, but it still needs to be transferred to the smartphone. For the smartphone to wirelessly receive the digital data, it must be converted into a radio signal which the phone can pick up and convert back into the original email format.

This radio signal is better known as Wi-Fi, one of the most prevalent ways for data to be transferred wirelessly over short distances. This is an example of a communication between a router and a smartphone, and tens if not hundreds of such messages can be exchanged between the pair every minute. It is the state of active communication between the two devices that represents the smartphone being 'connected to the internet'.

Cloud computing makes use of this interconnected network and supports the rapid growth of digital technologies. On a basic level, cloud computing is the facility for the computer hardware and software that someone uses to be provided via the internet. The name comes from the visual metaphor that was used originally to describe the internet and its services in the 1960s: a cloud symbol. Cloud computing can mean different things for different sectors, but the overall structure enables users to access data and applications anytime and anywhere with an internet connection. This technology is enabled by dedicated cloud computing servers, which are remote computers used to store data and can host EHRs, patient portals, mobile apps and 'big data' analytics.

There are also scenarios where means of transferring data that do not involve the internet and Wi-Fi are preferred. A notable example is Bluetooth, a communications technology that is provided as standard in the majority of consumer electronics, such as smartphones, wireless mice and portable speakers. Bluetooth is an example of a technology which acts independently from the internet 'cloud' by transferring data directly from one device to another. This simpler transfer procedure enables more secure data transfer, an important factor when working with sensitive data.[3] Bluetooth and Wi-Fi are similar in their use of radio waves for data transfer over short distances, but they differ in their design, capabilities, and purpose. Bluetooth is simpler than Wi-Fi, and it requires less power, but this comes at the expense of reduced range and data transfer speed, making it ideal for consumer electronics, mobile sensors and small electrical devices where these trade-offs are acceptable.[4]

A critical assessment of the technologies considered should be carried out to understand their implication in a healthcare context. This means considering factors such as a reduction of efficiency when switching to a new technology, the cost of implementing a new system and whether changes will upset the overall work ecosystem.

## DIGITAL TECHNOLOGY IN A HEALTHCARE CONTEXT

Electronic health records are the patient and population health information that is collected and stored in a digital format, as opposed to the more traditional, physical paper forms and reports used in the past. This has been recognised as one of the integral parts of modernised healthcare service and has been implemented in a variety of ways across the world.[5,6] Weighing up the impact of EHRs is a useful proxy for understanding the broader impact of digitisation on the healthcare sector.

The installation of EHR systems has been supported by cloud computing storage facilities and widely available internet connectivity, which provides the infrastructure for digital EHRs to be quickly and securely accessed and shared among staff and hospitals.[7] Following the widespread implementation of EHR systems over the past decade, it is possible to assess how much progress has been made with the problems they were intended to solve, as well as discussing some of the hindrances that have been encountered.[8]

There is considerable evidence to support that practices using EHRs have had quicker patient identification times, improved treatment decision support, fewer complications, reduced costs and lower mortality rate.[9–11] Furthermore, EHRs provide invaluable data for epidemiological studies and played an integral part in public health decision making during the COVID-19 pandemic. Many countries deployed COVID-19 monitoring applications for people to voluntarily download on their smartphones,[12] allowing users to update information regarding symptoms and test results, while using Bluetooth signals to continually track encounters with others.[13] This offers real-time data about spread of the disease as well as the ability to alert people to self-isolate if their phone detects they have been precariously close to someone who had COVID-19 at the time.[14]

Although EHRs and their knock-on effects have been shown to be beneficial in many respects, there has been some criticism and doubt regarding the digitisation of medical information. For example, although digitisation should theoretically increase working efficiency due to a streamlined access to information, there are other important factors that can prove challenging, such as the transition process from paper to digital, the digital education of staff, the quality of the EHR software and compatibility among the EHRs of different hospitals. Studies have shown instances where the efficiency gains of using EHRs are offset by a reduction in productivity while the technology is being implemented as well as by physicians being dissatisfied with the ease of use of these systems.[15–17]

Assuming that a high-quality EHR system has been implemented in a conscientious way, there are still other hurdles to consider. If EHR systems are reliant on cloud computing alone, when faced with a server failure (which can be caused by natural disasters or simply a technological failure) a hospital could be left temporarily or, even worse, permanently without access to its records, and this, of course, has the potential to be life threatening.[18] A common approach to minimising the chance of such a catastrophic failure is by introducing server redundancy, where copies of the same data are stored on multiple servers in different locations.

However, with more servers and infrastructure comes more opportunity for security flaws, and this brings to light another concern with EHRs regarding security.[19] Given the sensitive nature of the data, it provides an attractive target for malicious intent. As such, the companies providing the servers continually put tremendous effort into protecting their servers from hackers by staying ahead of the latest techniques and exploits.[20,21] Nonetheless, regardless of how secure the servers are, a concern that was much less of an issue prior to digitisation is still present: privacy.

Even if the data are protected, it is still questionable whether it is ethical for governments to have open access to such sensitive data. There are concerns that digital health ethics has not kept up with the rate of development of technology, and it tends to be regulated *reactively* (often following a serious incident) rather than *proactively*.[22] It is clear that weighing up the impact of EHRs is not trivial. Most of these concerns can be, and have been, diligently thought through and addressed over the past few years, and whilst EHRs are not perfect, they have the scope to solve the issues of lost records, duplication of effort, mistaken identity, and idiosyncratic clinical decisions.[8]

This discussion on EHRs can be extended to digital healthcare as a whole; digitisation and its implications offer powerful opportunities, provided that there is a careful implementation. Distinct efforts to minimise issues must be made, and the management of such systems should be meticulous, constantly responding to the ever-changing needs of patients and healthcare professionals.

## OUTLOOK FOR DIGITAL HEALTHCARE TECHNOLOGIES

The healthcare sector continues to accommodate a rapidly growing number of digital health innovations that improve the quality of life, diagnostic and treatment options, as well as the efficiency and cost effectiveness of the healthcare system.[23] The spread of digital health technologies means there is a huge amount of data generated on a daily basis.[24] The term assigned to datasets that are too large and complex to work with manually or using traditional statistical software, is 'big data'.[25,26] Although tricky to work with, these datasets can provide insights that improve healthcare in multiple respects, including helping societal health promotion and disease prevention initiatives, diagnosis and treatment of patients, and healthcare system efficiency.[27]

One of the most prevalent tools used to extract value from big data is machine learning (ML). ML is a branch of artificial intelligence focused on building algorithms that find patterns in massive amounts of data.[28] The insights provided can prove invaluable in aiding physicians with the diagnosis,[29,30] treatment,[31,32] and optimisation of patient management.[33,34]

Digital technologies can also aid healthcare workers during their training. Virtual reality (VR) is a technology that allows the user to explore and manipulate computer-generated real or artificial three-dimensional environments in real time. Recent studies support the notion of VR becoming a routine part of the training process of health professionals such as surgeons, similarly to how pilots use flight simulators.[35-37]

The future is evidently very exciting for digital healthcare. The technologies mentioned throughout this chapter and beyond give the opportunity for science-fiction healthcare, such as being able to 3D-print new organs,[38] a distinct possibility in the coming years. If the lessons learned from the implementation of EHRs are carried forward, we can be hopeful for vastly different but much improved future healthcare systems.

A good way to demonstrate how the various levels within the digital health landscape we have explored so far tie together, we will explore *Flexio* and its physiotherapy platform as a case study.

Home exercise programmes (HEPs) are one of the primary forms of treatment within the musculoskeletal physiotherapy domain but are notorious for suffering from particularly low patient adherence. Studies suggest that amongst physiotherapy patients, levels of non-adherence to HEPs could be as high as 70%.[39] There are a multitude of factors that have been found to affect adherence levels, with notable examples including low level of physical activity prior to the HEP starting, previous periods of non-adherence within the programme and low self-efficacy.[40] There are various approaches one could use to tackle these issues, and our case study, a UK-based start-up called Flexio, is an example of a company working to provide a digital solution. With their digital platform, Flexio aims to facilitate the tracking of a patient's recovery journey, both for the patient themselves and for their physiotherapist.

As it stands, Flexio provides a telehealth service with two different interaction options: one for the physiotherapists and another for their patients. To the physios, it is a website where their patients and their respective treatments can be supervised and adjusted as appropriate. For the patients, Flexio takes the form of a mobile app where an overview of their HEP and the exercises included are presented as well as functionality that allows patients to record the physical completion of their exercises, effectively entering information into their physiotherapy specific EHR.

The first step in the overall onboarding process is for the physiotherapist to assign their patient a set of exercises on the Flexio website. These are then accessible to the patient whenever they log into their account on a compatible mobile device. For each exercise there are detailed written instructions in addition to videos of the exercise in practise. Other, more personalised HEP information, such as the number of repetitions that patients are expected to complete, is also included. As a patient is completing an exercise, in-built sensors in the device record the raw movement data, and once the exercise is finished this is sent back to Flexio via Wi-Fi. All the information within the app is kept up to date thanks to an active connection with the Flexio servers that constantly passes the latest information to the app.

It is within these servers that the power of cloud computing is leveraged, and an intelligent automated analysis is performed that calculates various physiotherapy metrics such as the number of repetitions and the range of motion. Once calculated, this is instantly accessible to the physiotherapist, along with the patient's past activity data, allowing them to easily track the patient's progress. A noteworthy point to reiterate is how quick and scalable any customisation is when using such systems. Whether it is the analysis behind the scenes that needs changing or an improved description for a particular exercise is found, optimisations can be made quickly and come into effect in real-time for all users.

However, with the collection of so much novel data, and now the ubiquitous nature of powerful computers, companies such as Flexio aim to bring the most value through their development of machine learning algorithms. Their goal of ultimately helping to provide more personalised, and consequently, higher-quality care as well as increasing adherence to HEPs by facilitating logistical factors has the potential to have more profound effects for healthcare organisations such as the NHS. In Flexio's case, such algorithms could use information detailing past physio decisions and rate of patient progression to provide extra insight about when a patient is ready to progress onto the next step of their rehabilitation programme or provide alerts when a patient is suspected to have bad form for a particular exercise.

This is just one many companies harnessing the ever-growing capabilities of digital technologies to tackle problems in the healthcare sector in innovative ways. It is undeniable that there will be many, often unprecedented, challenges faced as the evolution into digital healthcare continues, and whilst this is something to remain mindful of, this continued innovation inspires an exciting vision for the future of healthcare.

## REFERENCES

1. Ejehiohen Iyawa G, Herselman M, Botha A. Digital health innovation ecosystems: From systematic literature review to conceptual framework. *Procedia Comput. Sci.* 2016;100(2):244–252. doi:10.1016/j.procs.2016.09.149
2. Lupton D. Critical perspectives on digital health technologies. *Sociol Compass.* 2014;8(12):1344–1359. doi:10.1111/soc4.12226
3. Khan M, Kabir M. Comparison among short range wireless networks: Bluetooth, Zigbee, & Wi-Fi. *Advances in Computer Science and Engineering.* 2016;4(2):19–28.
4. Wang XH, Iqbal M. Bluetooth: Opening a blue sky for healthcare. *Mob Inf Syst.* 2006;2(2-3):151–167. doi:10.1155/2006/423567
5. The Department of Health. The Health and Personal Social Services Programmes; 2008. Accessed December 17, 2020. https://assets.publishing.service.gov.uk/government/uploads/system/uploads/attachment_data/file/250880/5103.pdf
6. Schaeffer LD, Schultz AM, Salerno JA. *HHS in the 21st century: Charting a new course for a healthier America.* 2009. doi:10.17226/12513
7. Hossain S. Cloud computing basics - Cloud computing news. Published 2014. Accessed December 24, 2020. https://www.ibm.com/blogs/cloud-computing/2014/02/04/cloud-computing-basics-2/
8. Greenhalgh T, Potts HWW, Wong G, Bark P, Swinglehurst D. Tensions and paradoxes in electronic patient record research: A systematic literature review using the meta-narrative method. *Milbank Q.* 2009;87(4):729–788. doi:10.1111/j.1468-0009.2009.00578.x
9. Amarasingham R, Plantinga L, Diener-West M, Gaskin DJ, Powe NR. Clinical information technologies and inpatient outcomes. *Arch Intern Med.* 2009;169(2):108. doi:10.1001/archinternmed.2008.520
10. Chaudhry B, Wang J, Wu S, et al. Systematic review: Impact of health information technology on quality, efficiency, and costs of medical care. *Ann Intern Med.* 2006;144(10):742. doi:10.7326/0003-4819-144-10-200605160-00125

11. Rothman B, Leonard JC, Vigoda MM. Future of electronic health records: Implications for decision support. *Mt Sinai J Med A J Transl Pers Med.* 2012;79(6):757–768. doi:10.1002/msj.21351

12. Abbas R, Michael K. COVID-19 contact trace app deployments: Learnings from Australia and Singapore. *IEEE Consum Electron Mag.* 2020;9(5):65–70. doi:10.1109/MCE.2020.3002490

13. He Z, Zhang CJP, Huang J, et al. A new era of epidemiology: Digital epidemiology for investigating the COVID-19 outbreak in China. *J Med Internet Res.* 2020;22(9):e21685. doi:10.2196/21685

14. Xu B, Gutierrez B, Mekaru S, et al. Epidemiological data from the COVID-19 outbreak, real-time case information. *Scientific Data.* doi:10.6084/m9.figshare.11974344

15. HIMSS EHR Usability Task Force. Defining and Testing EMR Usability. Published June 2009. Accessed December 16, 2020. https://web.archive. org/web/20120322070808/http://www.himss.org/content/files/HIMSS_ DefiningandTestingEMRUsability.pdf

16. Robeznieks A. 7 big reasons why EHRs consume physicians' days and nights | American Medical Association. Accessed December 16, 2020. https://www.ama-assn.org/practice-management/ digital/7-big-reasons-why-ehrs-consume-physicians-days-and-nights

17. Hoerbst A, Ammenwerth E, Hörbst A. Electronic health records. A systematic review on quality requirements. *Methods Inf Med.* 2010;49. doi:10.3414/ME10-01-0038

18. Verma J. Study of cloud computing and its issues: A review. *Smart Comput Rev.* 2014;4(5). doi:10.6029/smartcr.2014.05.005

19. Rapson J. Radical relaxation of GP records and booking rules | News | Health Service Journal. Published 2020. Accessed December 17, 2020. https://www.hsj.co.uk/primary-care/radical-relaxation-of-gp-records-and-booking-rules/7027486.article?

20. Jain P, Gyanchandani M, Khare N. Privacy and security concerns in healthcare big data: An innovative prescriptive. *J Inf Assur Secur.* 2017;12(1):18–30.

21. Reddy GN, Reddy GJU. Study of Cloud Computing in HealthCare Industry. Published online February 8, 2014. Accessed December 24, 2020. http://arxiv.org/abs/1402.1841

22. Sweeney Y. Tracking the debate on COVID-19 surveillance tools. *Nat Mach Intell.* Published online 2020. doi:10.1038/s42256-020-0194-1

23. Omachonu VK, Einspruch NG. Innovation in healthcare delivery systems: A conceptual framework. *The Innovation Journal: The Public Sector Innovation Journal.* 2010;15(2):1–18.

24. Stewart C. Healthcare data volume globally 2020 forecast. Accessed December 24, 2020. https://www.statista.com/statistics/1037970/ global-healthcare-data-volume/

25. Sagiroglu S, Sinanc D. Big data: A review. In: *Proceedings of the 2013 International Conference on Collaboration Technologies and Systems, CTS 2013.* 2013:42–47. doi:10.1109/CTS.2013.6567202

26. Pramanik PKD, Pal S, Mukhopadhyay M. Healthcare Big Data: A Comprehensive Overview. In: *Healthcare Big Data: A Comprehensive Overview*; 2018:72–100. doi:10.4018/978-1-5225-7071-4.ch004

27. Groves P, Kayyali B, Knott D, Kuiken S Van. *The "Big Data" Revolution in Healthcare.* 2013. Accessed December 24, 2020. https://www.mckinsey.com/insights/health_systems/~/media/7764A72F70184C8EA88D805092D72D58.ashx.

28. IBM Cloud Education. What is Machine Learning? | IBM. Published 2020. Accessed December 24, 2020. https://www.ibm.com/cloud/learn/machine-learning

29. Kadir T, Gleeson F. Lung cancer prediction using machine learning and advanced imaging techniques. *Transl Lung Cancer Res.* 2018;7(3):304–312. doi:10.21037/tlcr.2018.05.15

30. Sadoughi F, Kazemy Z, Hamedan F, Owji L, Rahmanikatigari M, Talebi Azadboni T. Artificial intelligence methods for the diagnosis of breast cancer by image processing: A review. *Breast Cancer Targets Ther.* 2018;10:219–230. doi:10.2147/BCTT.S175311

31. Jiang F, Jiang Y, Zhi H, et al. Artificial intelligence in healthcare: Past, present and future. *Stroke Vasc Neurol.* 2017;2(4):230–243. doi:10.1136/svn-2017-000101

32. Shi Z, Hu B, Schoepf UJ, et al. Artificial intelligence in the management of intracranial aneurysms: Current status and future perspectives. *Am J Neuroradiol.* 2020;41(3):373–379. doi:10.3174/AJNR.A6468

33. Olive | The RPA + AI Workforce Made for Healthcare. Accessed December 24, 2020. https://oliveai.com/

34. Qventus, Inc. | Automate Your Patient Flow. Accessed December 24, 2020. https://qventus.com/

35. Kyaw BM, Saxena N, Posadzki P, et al. Virtual reality for health professions education: Systematic review and meta-analysis by the digital health education collaboration. *J Med Internet Res.* 2019;21(1):e12959. doi:10.2196/12959

36. Rosen JM, Long SA, McGrath DM, Greer SE. Simulation in plastic surgery training and education: The path forward. *Plast Reconstr Surg.* 2009;123(2):729–738. doi:10.1097/PRS.0b013e3181958ec4

37. Kühnapfel U, Çakmak HK, Maaß H. Endoscopic surgery training using virtual reality and deformable tissue simulation. *Comput Graph.* 2000;24(5):671–682. doi:10.1016/S0097-8493(00)00070-4

38. Badwaik R. 3D printed organs: The future of regenerative medicine. *J Clin Diagnostic Res.* Published online 2019. doi:10.7860/jcdr/2019/42546.13256

39. McLean SM, Burton M, Bradley L, Littlewood C. Interventions for enhancing adherence with physiotherapy: A systematic review. *Man Ther.* 2010;15(6):514–521. doi:10.1016/j.math.2010.05.012

40. Jack K, McLean SM, Moffett JK, Gardiner E. Barriers to treatment adherence in physiotherapy outpatient clinics: A systematic review. *Man Ther.* 2010;15(3):220–228. doi:10.1016/j.math.2009.12.004

## CASE STUDY J: FLEXIO, REMOTE PHYSIOTHERAPY

Patients who have suffered a musculoskeletal injury or undergo orthopaedic surgery often require post-operative physiotherapy. These physical exercises aim to encourage movement and improve functional outcome. Early introduction, increasing complexity and regular supervision are considered to provide superior results. Patients are monitored regularly by their physiotherapist in the clinic and their exercises amended accordingly.

Compliance with treatment is an important factor that influences the outcome of that treatment with all treatments. Compliant patients have better outcomes than non-compliant patients. Poor adherence has been recognised across many healthcare disciplines, including physiotherapy. One study found that 14% of physiotherapy patients did not return for follow-up appointments (Vasey, 1990), whilst another suggested non-adherence with treatment as high as 70% (Sluijs et al., 1993). Poor adherence has implications on treatment cost and effectiveness. Poor compliance may be due to patients forgetting how to perform their exercises or losing their instructions and due to language barriers.

### SOLUTION

Flexio is a platform that allows patients to be remotely monitored. It consists of a downloadable iPhone application and linked website. Exercises are prescribed by the physiotherapist via the website and appear on the iPhone screen when the application is initiated. A text description and video clip are also included to remind patients of the exercises they are required to perform.

What is unique to the platform is that if the patient is holding or wearing their smartphone on the appropriate limb as they undertake their exercises, the movement data is recorded and relayed to the physiotherapist on the website.

Benefits of this low-cost solution to improve compliance with treatment plans include empowering patients to manage their treatment and track their progress, allowing early intervention for non-compliant patients, reducing time and travel for patients and protecting medical professionals from litigation. In addition, the platform has the potential for machine learning that could provide an optimised automated programme for patients.

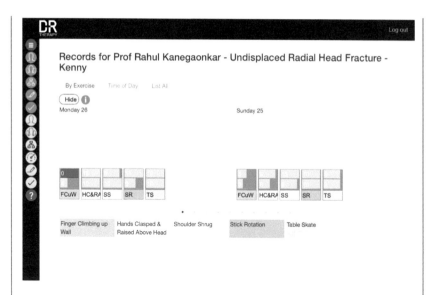

Figure J.1 Movement data is processed to calculate reps, range of motion, time of day and overall compliance via a dashboard.

## Recording for Prof Rahul Kanegaonkar

Undisplaced Radial Head Fracture - Kenny, Phase 4, Stick Rotation, recorded on 17:49 25 Sep 2016

Figure J.2 Movement data is processed to calculate reps, range of motion, time of day and overall compliance via a dashboard.

≡ csp.org.uk ↻

CHARTERED SOCIETY OF PHYSIOTHERAPY 👤 🔍 ≡

**NEWS AND EVENTS**

### Physio trials remote monitoring tool that could improve patient compliance

8 November 2016 - 4:46pm

A doctor has teamed up with a physiotherapist to develop a free app that allows physios to remotely monitor the progress of musculoskeletal patients.

Figure J.3  Feature on the Chartered Society of Physiotherapy.

## BIBLIOGRAPHY

Abhishek Vaish, Saif Ahmed, Anan Shetty. Remote physiotherapy monitoring using the novel D+R Therapy iPhone application. *J Clin Orthop Trauma.* Jan-Mar 2017;8(1):21–24.

Alan Saleh, Fatimah Parkar, Amit Tolat. The use of the D+R Therapy iPhone Application in the management of radial head fracture. *Research and Reviews: Orthopaedics* 2017.

14

# Regenerative medicine

## RICHARD WEBB, ATHINA MYLONA, AND ALWYN D'SOUZA

## INTRODUCTION

Regenerative medicine relies on the utilisation and manipulation of cells, bio-molecules and bio-scaffolds for the *in vitro* generation of transplantable tissues or the acceleration of the body's healing mechanisms to restore normal tissue function. While tissue engineering was originally defined as the cross-section between the use of biocompatible scaffolds, stem cells and bio-active molecules (Langer and Vacanti, 1993) (Figure 14.1), as research has continued over the past 28 years a more complex profile continues to evolve.

As our understanding of the base requirements for tissue engineering continues to grow, mechanical stimulation, oxygen tension, bio-active molecules and scaffolds must interact holistically to develop functional tissue that can be directly applicable to patient treatment (Figure 14.2).

The primary goal of regenerative medicine and tissue engineering is for the development of "off-the-shelf" products to replace damaged or diseased tissue. However, to date, no such engineered functional tissue has been developed to enter the medical marketplace for clinical use.

The most utilised cell therapy remains the bone marrow transplant (Henig and Zuckerman, 2014), followed by autologous cartilage implantation for the treatment of cartilage injury (Zellner et al., 2015). While the latter doesn't cure the problem, it has been shown to delay the requirement for partial or complete joint replacement.

DOI: 10.1201/9781003164609-16

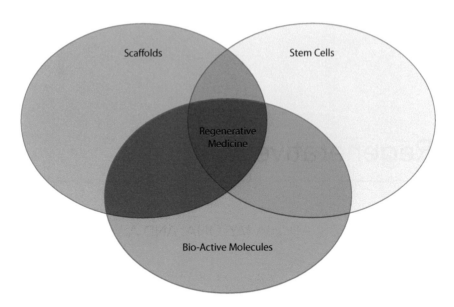

Figure 14.1 Original components of regenerative medicine/tissue engineering. (Adapted from Langer and Vacanti, 1993.)

The growth of three-dimensional tissues from stem cells has been long held as the "holy grail" of regenerative medicine. Bone, cartilage and skin have been extensively investigated as targets for stem-cell–driven tissue regeneration, while muscle, cardiac tissue, liver and lung alveoli regeneration are emerging research fields.

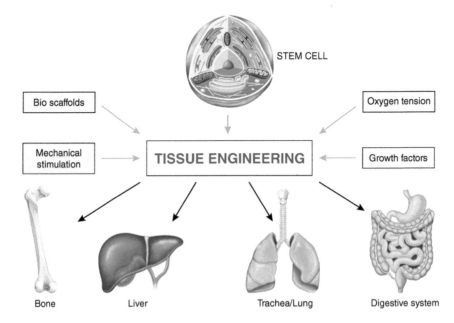

Figure 14.2 Advanced components of tissue engineering/regenerative medicine. (Adapted from Humphries et al., 2022.)

# STEM CELLS

Stem cell maintenance and manipulation is the focal point of any regenerative medicine activity towards engineering new tissues *in vitro*. These are either embryonic or adult stem cells. Embryonic stem cells are found in the inner cell mass of the developing blastocyst and are maintained in *in vitro* adherent cultures for unlimited time (Evans and Kaufman, 1981, Martin, 1981) under specific culture conditions. They are characterised by self-renewal and pluripotency as they can differentiate into any somatic cell lineage. The injection of embryonic stem cells into blastocysts and the generation of chimeric mice have demonstrated that these cells can contribute to every cell lineage, including the germ line *in vivo* (Bradley et al., 1984, Nagy et al., 1990). Often progenitor cells appear as an intermediate derivative during the differentiation process of embryonic stem cells (Sato and Nakano, 2001). Progenitor cells have also the ability to self-renew, albeit for a limited number of cell divisions before committing to a fully differentiated cell type. While embryonic stem cells offer, in theory, many different possibilities in tissue engineering, there are nevertheless serious ethical considerations that render their use as a tool in regenerative medicine impossible.

Stem cells present in adult tissues are largely responsible for tissue regeneration after injury. These can self-renew and differentiate towards at least one but usually more cell lineages, with the balance between self-renewal and differentiation being tightly regulated. Adult stem cells are supported by a specific micro-environment niche, which ensures control of their proliferative and differentiation potentials. The biology of stem cells has been extensively studied in mouse models, with a plethora of adult stem cell populations described in the adult mouse, existing in protective niches, i.e. in the forebrain sub-ventricular zone (SVZ), the hippocampus, the bone marrow, the skin, the bulge of the hair follicle, the crypts of the intestine and the testis (Ohlstein et al., 2004). Human adult stem cells have been identified more recently in the same corresponding tissues.

Of the different adult stem cell categories, one has been the subject of extensive focus in tissue regeneration. These are the mesenchymal stem cells (MSCs), which are multipotent progenitor cells showing highly proliferative and plastic adhesion properties and which can generate fibroblast-like colonies (CFU-Fs) *ex vivo*. MSCs have been successfully isolated from the trabecular compartment at the ends of long bones, bone marrow, adipose tissue and embryonic tissues (e.g. umbilical cord). When mesenchymal stem cells differentiate *in vitro*, they give rise to bone, cartilage or adipose tissue, with the differentiation pathway dependent on cell culture conditions. MSCs are identified through the expression of the cell surface markers CD105, CD90, CD73, CD44. However, this immunophenotype still identifies a heterogeneous cell population, and the determination of cell membrane markers that can describe more homogeneous cell sub-populations with enhanced multipotency is an ongoing effort. One such candidate is the low affinity neurotrophin receptor p75-NTR (also known as CD271), which was described as a marker for a population of true mesenchymal stem cells based on their differentiation capacity (Tormin et al., 2011). For example, p75-NTR positive cells were shown to contribute to osteogenesis after serial transplantations in mice (Ghazanfari et al., 2016). Due to their differentiation capacity MSCs are an ideal tool for the development of treatment protocols targeting conditions where bone or cartilage has been damaged due to either disease progression or injury.

While to date the potential of regenerative medicine has yet to deliver on the predictions and promises of the past, nevertheless the identification of numerous sources of stem or progenitor cells has led to many potential cellular candidates for tissue regeneration. However, so far few have delivered clinically and at best achieved the production of pseudo-tissue. More recently, tissue engineering research has shifted focus towards the components of the stem cell secretome. Deciphering the composition of the secretome and understanding the function of the different molecules that make it up offers new and promising possibilities in the manipulation of adult stem cells either *in vivo* or *in vitro,* with the final goal of speeding up the tissue healing process or developing novel engineered tissue types. The secretome has been shown to be an elaborate combination of signalling proteins, lipids and microRNA. To date, the synergistical composition and how each of the components elicit either immune dampening and/or induce tissue regeneration has yet to be fully elucidated.

Mesenchymal stem cells, when maintained and expanded in cell culture conditions, are known to produce secretomes, which can act towards dampening the immune response and promote tissue repair (Carvalho et al., 2011, Moschidou, 2009, Ning et al., 2013). Table 14.1 shows examples of proteins found within the MSC secretome and associated functions, while Table 14.2 shows examples of miRNA found within the secretome of MSCs.

MSC-secreted proteins are components of the structural matrix, signalling molecules involved in cell communication cascades or immune system modulators (Table 14.2) (Qiu et al., 2019).

## MicroRNA (miRNA) COMPONENT OF MSC SECRETOME

miRNAs are highly conserved sequences that span multiple species and play a vital role in the regulation of gene expression and protein synthesis. They were first discovered by Lee et al. in the early 1990s (Lee et al., 1993) and further expanded upon by Fire et al. in the late 1990s (Fire et al., 1998). Since their original discovery in *C. elegans*, miRNA have been shown to be secreted by human MSCs during cellular expansion and can play a significant regulatory role in both osteogenic and chondrogenic differentiation (Dong et al., 2012, Sun et al., 2019). Examples of miRNAs identified with roles in chondrogenic differentiation and maintenance, or osteogenic differentiation and maintenance are given in Table 14.2.

## SECRETOME ISOLATION

During the isolation and expansion of human MSCs, secreted protein and miRNAs can be isolated at multiple points (Figure 14.3). Early isolation can potentially retain some of the secretome found within the native bone marrow/

Table 14.1 Examples of functional proteins found within the MSC secretome

| Protein | Signalling | Structural | Immunological | Reference |
|---|---|---|---|---|
| TGF-β | YES | NO | YES | Alvarez et al., 2018, Jiang et al., 2016 |
| LG3BP | YES | YES | NO | Adamo et al., 2019a, Adamo et al., 2019b |
| PTX3 | NO | NO | YES | Adamo et al., 2019a |
| S10A6 | YES | YES | NO | Adamo et al., 2019a |
| COX2 | YES | NO | YES | Harting et al., 2018 |
| IL-2 | YES | NO | YES | Chen et al., 2019 |
| IL-10 | YES | NO | YES | Chen et al., 2019 |
| RANTES | YES | NO | YES | Chen et al., 2019 |
| VEGF | YES | NO | NO | Chen et al., 2019, Ahn et al., 2018, Shim et al., 2018, Jiang et al., 2016 |
| BDNF | YES | NO | NO | Chen et al., 2019 |
| NEPRILYSIN | YES | NO | NO | Katsuda et al., 2013 |
| COL VII | NO | YES | NO | McBride et al., 2018 |

adipose/tissue niche, whereas, over time and multiple media changes, the native tissue niche secretome will be diluted to produce, a more-pure MSC secretome. The components of the secretome will depend on whether a 2D or 3D culture is employed, on whether an oxygen rich or depleted environment is used as well as on the composition of the culture media.

Once MSCs are expanded and are undergoing differentiation, the synthesis of the secretome will be impacted again by the cell culture conditions and can change to reflect the disappearance of most progenitor cells and the appearance of more mature differentiated cells.

The utilisation of MSC expansion and differentiation can in the future give rise to multiple therapeutic products based on the secretome protein or miRNA component at either the isolation, expansion, or differentiation stages (Figure 14.3).

Stem- and progenitor-cell–secreted molecules have been used as the basis of biological implants. Acellular implants consist of acellular collagen that is derived from the extracellular matrix. These have been utilised in dental implants (Zafiropoulos and John, 2017, Zafiropoulos et al., 2016, Zafiropoulos et al., 2021), in breast reconstruction utilising acellular dermal matrix (ADM)

Table 14.2 Examples of miRNAs identified to play an active role in osteogenic or chondrogenic differentiation (Gimble et al., 2019)

| miRNA | Osteogenic | Chondrogenic |
|-------|-----------|--------------|
| miR-16 | Yes | No |
| miR-210 | Yes | No |
| miR-17 | Yes | No |
| miR-142-3p | Yes | No |
| miR-21 | Yes | No |
| miR-2861 | Yes | No |
| miR196a | Yes | No |
| miR-218 | Yes | No |
| miR-675 | No | Yes |
| miR-140 | No | Yes |
| miR-320c | No | Yes |
| miR-125b | No | Yes |
| miR-23b | No | Yes |
| miR-22 | No | Yes |
| miR-27a/b, -9 | No | Yes |
| miR-210 | No | Yes |
| miR-199a | No | Yes |
| miR-146 | No | Yes |
| miR-9 | No | Yes |
| miR-98 | No | Yes |

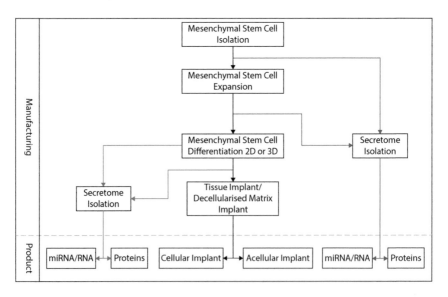

Figure 14.3 Schematic diagram showing the possible manufacturing points for stem cell secretions and cellular/acellular implants. (Adapted from MCh lecture series, Advanced orthopaedic regenerative medicine, Richard Webb 2021.)

(Park et al., 2018) and in bone reconstruction utilising ADM (Cigerim, 2020). The use of de-cellularised matrix products has gained attention since these products have been observed to not generate immune responses when implanted, which is coupled with enhanced cellular attachment and differentiation (Wei et al., 2021). These implants provide a scaffold for stem/progenitor cell proliferation, differentiation and ultimately tissue regeneration. Nevertheless, the question remains whether functional acellular matrix implants can be manufactured *ex-vivo* in the quantity and at the cost level to become the product of choice for tissue regeneration and reconstruction.

Implants and scaffolds can be utilised in a 3D cell culture protocol, where stem/progenitor cells are grown in a differentiation inducing environment. Should differentiation be undertaken in a 3D environment to produce a naïve tissue for implantation, the benefit of the use of a cell free implant compared to a cellular based implant should be taken into consideration.

## REGENERATIVE MEDICINE: CLINICAL TRIALS

Several clinical trials have explored the application of either adult stem cells or progenitor cells in the development of treatment options for tissue damage due to degeneration or lesions. Thus far MSCs have been the primary focus in this effort due to their detailed characterisation using well-defined cell surface markers, the uncomplicated cell culture protocols and their clonal *in vitro* expansion. Bone marrow remains the preferred source of MSCs, with adipose tissue and bone being explored as well.

The utilisation of bone marrow–derived MSCs in a novel bone graft preparation was compared with the gold standard of autogenous iliac crest bone graft in transforaminal lumbar interbody fusion surgery for the treatment of lower spine degeneration or stenosis. The randomised clinical trial showed a promising outcome for the tissue-engineered bone graft, with better spinal fusion rates (Garcia de Frutos et al., 2020).

Facial bone reconstruction can prove to be a complex process where the functional and aesthetic outcomes weigh similarly for patients. Several registered clinical trials have investigated the use of bone marrow–derived MSCs as an improved alternative to autologous bone grafting. In Gjerde et al. (2018), bone marrow MSCs added on a biphasic scaffold were shown to reconstitute the posterior mandibular ridge of the alveolar bone (Gjerde et al., 2018).

However, another clinical trial of equal size concluded that the procedure, although safe for the patients, offered only limited tissue regeneration outcomes for larger defects in the alveolar bone. The authors concluded that larger multicentre trials are necessary to fully evaluate the efficacy of MSC-seeded bone grafts in tissue regeneration (Bajestan et al., 2017).

A larger single-centre clinical trial, the TEOM study, is currently looking at the application of bone marrow MSCs in the reconstitution and regeneration of the maxillomandibular bone following damage from injury or surgery (Shimizu et al., 2019).

Finally, the use of bone marrow MSCs on suitable ceramic and polymer scaffolds was investigated for cranial bone reconstruction. The study, which differs from the previous ones in the use of allogenic and not autologous MSCs, demonstrated the feasibility and safety of the procedure. However, while bone regeneration was considered satisfactory, resorption was later observed. The authors conclude that the choice of scaffold material and 3D design is essential for long-term cranial bone reconstruction (Morrison et al., 2018).

Beyond bone regeneration, tissue-engineering protocols are applicable to improved cardiovascular surgery procedures. Vascular grafts produced with bone marrow mononuclear cells can induce tissue remodelling and improved graft integration following surgery, and these were used to treat patients with univentricular physiology. The feasibility and safety of the procedure were considered satisfactory (Sugiura et al., 2018).

Cardiovascular progenitor cells derived from human embryonic stem cells following differentiation were used to treat patients with ischemic left ventricular dysfunction. The small-scale trial looked primarily at the feasibility and safety of the novel procedure and reported a positive outcome in support for larger similar clinical trials (Menasche et al., 2018).

## REGENERATIVE MEDICINE: CLINICAL PERSPECTIVE

Plastic and reconstructive surgery has progressed at a rapid pace, with microsurgery, advanced imaging including 3D technology and transplantation of organs, including full face transplantation techniques. Despite this, morbidity continues to be a significant restrictive factor, and this applies particularly to the donor site. In addition, it often warrants long-term immunosuppression, and the effects of it pose a significant challenge, with concerns – including mortality – relating to immunosuppression either directly or indirectly. These drawbacks would be either reduced or at best eliminated completely if tissue-engineered cell systems and organs can be applied successfully for reconstruction, with restoration of normal physiology and optimal functional as well as aesthetic results. Therefore, further growth and refinement in regenerative medicine is crucial. The Medical Research Council states that regenerative medicine and tissue engineering "holds the promise of revolutionizing patient care in the twenty-first century".

The successful bio-production of tissues required to repair defects in clinical setting will require interdisciplinary collaboration among cell biologists, material scientists, engineers and associated medical specialties. Plastic and reconstructive surgeons are uniquely placed to be intrinsically involved in the research and development of laboratory-engineered tissues and their subsequent use by facilitating inter-speciality collaboration and research.

Engineered tissue potentially offers many advantages akin to autologous tissue, which include biocompatibility, functionality, appropriately maintained size and shape of tissue, possibility of unlimited expansion and supply, non-immunogenic potential, mechanical stability and escape from donor site morbidity.

The drawbacks at this early stage in research and production include size limited by vascularity, expense, tumorigenic potential and the challenges of producing "physiologically relevant/mature tissue". Further as the science is in it infantile stage the long-term effects are unknown, hence wide-scale clinical application will be a prolonged, laborious process.

From the clinical point of view most advances have been in the area of scaffolds. These include both synthetic materials (Polylactic acid: PLA; Polyglycolic acid: PGA; Polyethylene glycol products: PEG, etc.) and biological substitutes, such as fibrin, elastin and collagen to name a few. Other products, though not entirely laboratory produced, include irradiated skin, irradiated rib and various irradiated fascial and membranous products that are used widely in daily clinical practice with excellent clinical outcome.

There are few areas where tissue-engineered constructs have been used successfully in humans over the years. These included bladder, trachea, urethra, ear and nasal cartilages and vaginal organs. Table 14.3 offers a brief summary.

Overall, advances in tissue engineering rely on the proven synergy between distinct areas such as stem cell biology, bioengineering, and clinical and biomedical research. These offer hope for the development of novel treatment options for patients that go beyond the traditional outlook on tissue damage management. Regenerative medicine is not merely a distant future promise anymore but a reality within our grasp.

Table 14.3 Brief summary of tissue-engineered constructs

| Organ/tissue type | Cell source | Clinical outcome |
| --- | --- | --- |
| Nasal cartilage (Fulco et al., 2014) | Autologous nasal chondrocytes | Structural stability and improved nasal function |
| Ear cartilage (Zhou et al., 2018) | Chondrocytes from microtia cartilage | Functioning and aesthetic auricle |
| Trachea (Macchiarini et al., 2008), (The Lancet, 2018)* | Recipients MSCs | Mechanical properties, normal appearance and functional airway. |
| Bladder (Atala et al., 2006) | Bladder muscle and urothelial epithelial cells | Improved volume and compliance |
| Urethra (Raya-Rivera et al., 2011) | Muscle and epithelial cells | Patent urethra, no strictures |
| Vaginal organs (Raya-Rivera et al., 2014) | Muscle and epithelial cells | Muscle and epithelial structure maintained |

\* Indicates controversial study which resulted in prosecution and imprisonment of lead author (The Lancet, 2018)

# REFERENCES

Adamo, A., Brandi, J., Caligola, S., Delfino, P., Bazzoni, R., Carusone, R., Cecconi, D., Giugno, R., Manfredi, M., Robotti, E., Marengo, E., Bassi, G., Takam Kamga, P., Dal Collo, G., Gatti, A., Mercuri, A., Arigoni, M., Olivero, M., Calogero, R. A. & Krampera, M. 2019a. Extracellular vesicles mediate mesenchymal stromal cell-dependent regulation of B cell PI3K-AKT signaling pathway and actin cytoskeleton. *Front Immunol*, 10, 446.

Adamo, A., Dal Collo, G., Bazzoni, R. & Krampera, M. 2019b. Role of mesenchymal stromal cell-derived extracellular vesicles in tumour microenvironment. *Biochim Biophys Acta Rev Cancer*, 1871, 192–198.

Ahn, S. Y., Park, W. S., Kim, Y. E., Sung, D. K., Sung, S. I., Ahn, J. Y. & Chang, Y. S. 2018. Vascular endothelial growth factor mediates the therapeutic efficacy of mesenchymal stem cell-derived extracellular vesicles against neonatal hyperoxic lung injury. *Exp Mol Med*, 50, 26.

Alvarez, V., Sanchez-Margallo, F. M., Macias-Garcia, B., Gomez-Serrano, M., Jorge, I., Vazquez, J., Blazquez, R. & Casado, J. G. 2018. The immuno-modulatory activity of extracellular vesicles derived from endometrial mesenchymal stem cells on CD4+ T cells is partially mediated by TGFbeta. *J Tissue Eng Regen Med*, 12, 2088–2098.

Atala, A., Bauer, S. B., Soker, S., Yoo, J. J. & Retik, A. B. 2006. Tissue-engineered autologous bladders for patients needing cystoplasty. *Lancet*, 367, 1241–1246.

Bajestan, M. N., Rajan, A., Edwards, S. P., Aronovich, S., Cevidanes, L. H. S., Polymeri, A., Travan, S. & Kaigler, D. 2017. Stem cell therapy for reconstruction of alveolar cleft and trauma defects in adults: A randomized controlled, clinical trial. *Clin Implant Dent Relat Res*, 19, 793–801.

Bradley, A., Evans, M., Kaufman, M. H. & Robertson, E. 1984. Formation of germ-line chimaeras from embryo-derived teratocarcinoma cell lines. *Nature*, 309, 255–256.

Carvalho, M. M., Teixeira, F. G., Reis, R. L., Sousa, N. & Salgado, A. J. 2011. Mesenchymal stem cells in the umbilical cord: Phenotypic characterization, secretome and applications in central nervous system regenerative medicine. *Curr Stem Cell Res Ther*, 6, 221–228.

Chen, S. Y., Lin, M. C., Tsai, J. S., He, P. L., Luo, W. T., Herschman, H. & Li, H. J. 2019. EP4 antagonist-elicited extracellular vesicles from mesenchymal stem cells rescue cognition/learning deficiencies by restoring brain cellular functions. *Stem Cells Transl Med*, 8, 707–723.

Cigerim, L. 2020. Treatment of exposed bone with acellular dermal matrix in a smoker patient after dental implant surgery: A case report. *J Oral Implantol*, 46, 245–249.

Dong, S., Yang, B., Guo, H. & Kang, F. 2012. MicroRNAs regulate osteogenesis and chondrogenesis. *Biochem Biophys Res Commun*, 418, 587–591.

Evans, M. J. & Kaufman, M. H. 1981. Establishment in culture of pluripotential cells from mouse embryos. *Nature*, 292, 154–156.

Fire, A., Xu, S., Montgomery, M. K., Kostas, S. A., Driver, S. E. & Mello, C. C. 1998. Potent and specific genetic interference by double-stranded RNA in Caenorhabditis elegans. *Nature*, 391, 806–811.

Fulco, I., Miot, S., Haug, M. D., Barbero, A., Wixmerten, A., Feliciano, S., Wolf, F., Jundt, G., Marsano, A., Farhadi, J., Heberer, M., Jakob, M., Schaefer, D. J. & Martin, I. 2014. Engineered autologous cartilage tissue for nasal reconstruction after tumour resection: An observational first-in-human trial. *Lancet*, 384, 337–346.

Garcia De Frutos, A., Gonzalez-Tartiere, P., Coll Bonet, R., Ubierna Garces, M. T., Del Arco Churruca, A., Rivas Garcia, A., Matamalas Adrover, A., Salo Bru, G., Velazquez, J. J., Vila-Canet, G., Garcia-Lopez, J., Vives, J., Codinach, M., Rodriguez, L., Bago Granell, J. & Caceres Palou, E. 2020. Randomized clinical trial: Expanded autologous bone marrow mesenchymal cells combined with allogeneic bone tissue, compared with autologous iliac crest graft in lumbar fusion surgery. *Spine J*, 20, 1899–1910.

Ghazanfari, R., Li, H., Zacharaki, D., Lim, H. C. & Scheding, S. 2016. Human non-hematopoietic CD271pos/CD140alow/neg bone marrow stroma cells fulfill stringent stem cell criteria in serial transplantations. *Stem Cells Dev*, 25(21):1652–1658.

Gimble, J. M., Marolt, D., Oreffo, R. O. C., Redl, H. & Wolbank, S. 2019. Cell engineering and regeneration. Reference Series in Biomedical Engineering. Cham: Springer.

Gjerde, C., Mustafa, K., Hellem, S., Rojewski, M., Gjengedal, H., Yassin, M. A., Feng, X., Skaale, S., Berge, T., Rosen, A., Shi, X. Q., Ahmed, A. B., Gjertsen, B. T., Schrezenmeier, H. & Layrolle, P. 2018. Cell therapy induced regeneration of severely atrophied mandibular bone in a clinical trial. *Stem Cell Res Ther*, 9, 213.

Harting, M. T., Srivastava, A. K., Zhaorigetu, S., Bair, H., Prabhakara, K. S., Toledano Furman, N. E., Vykoukal, J. V., Ruppert, K. A., Cox, C. S., JR. & Olson, S. D. 2018. Inflammation-stimulated mesenchymal stromal cell-derived extracellular vesicles attenuate inflammation. *Stem Cells*, 36, 79–90.

Henig, I. & Zuckerman, T. 2014. Hematopoietic stem cell transplantation-50 years of evolution and future perspectives. *Rambam Maimonides Med J*, 5, e0028.

Humphries, S., Joshi, A., Webb, W. R. & Kanegaonkar, R. 2022. Auricular reconstruction: Where are we now? A critical literature review. *Eur Arch Otorhinolaryngol*, 279, 541-556.

Jiang, Z. Z., Liu, Y. M., Niu, X., Yin, J. Y., Hu, B., Guo, S. C., Fan, Y., Wang, Y. & Wang, N. S. 2016. Exosomes secreted by human urine-derived stem cells could prevent kidney complications from type I diabetes in rats. *Stem Cell Res Ther*, 7, 24.

Katsuda, T., Tsuchiya, R., Kosaka, N., Yoshioka, Y., Takagaki, K., Oki, K., Takeshita, F., Sakai, Y., Kuroda, M. & Ochiya, T. 2013. Human adipose tissue-derived mesenchymal stem cells secrete functional neprilysin-bound exosomes. *Sci Rep*, 3, 1197.

Langer, R. & Vacanti, J. P. 1993. Tissue engineering. *Science*, 260, 920–926.

Lee, R. C., Feinbaum, R. L. & Ambros, V. 1993. The *C. elegans* heterochronic gene lin-4 encodes small RNAs with antisense complementarity to lin-14. *Cell*, 75, 843–854.

Macchiarini, P., Jungebluth, P., Go, T., Asnaghi, M. A., Rees, L. E., Cogan, T. A., Dodson, A., Martorell, J., Bellini, S., Parnigotto, P. P., Dickinson, S. C., Hollander, A. P., Mantero, S., Conconi, M. T. & Birchall, M. A. 2008. Clinical transplantation of a tissue-engineered airway. *Lancet*, 372, 2023–2030.

Martin, G. R. 1981. Isolation of a pluripotent cell line from early mouse embryos cultured in medium conditioned by teratocarcinoma stem cells. *Proc Natl Acad Sci U S A*, 78, 7634–7638.

Mcbride, J. D., Rodriguez-Menocal, L., Candanedo, A., Guzman, W., Garcia-Contreras, M. & Badiavas, E. V. 2018. Dual mechanism of type VII collagen transfer by bone marrow mesenchymal stem cell extracellular vesicles to recessive dystrophic epidermolysis bullosa fibroblasts. *Biochimie*, 155, 50–58.

Menasche, P., Vanneaux, V., Hagege, A., Bel, A., Cholley, B., Parouchev, A., Cacciapuoti, I., Al-Daccak, R., Benhamouda, N., Blons, H., Agbulut, O., Tosca, L., Trouvin, J. H., Fabreguettes, J. R., Bellamy, V., Charron, D., Tartour, E., Tachdjian, G., Desnos, M. & Larghero, J. 2018. Transplantation of human embryonic stem cell-derived cardiovascular progenitors for severe ischemic left ventricular dysfunction. *J Am Coll Cardiol*, 71, 429–438.

Molins, L. 2019. Patient follow-up after tissue-engineered airway transplantation. *The Lancet*, 393(10176), 1099.

Morrison, D. A., Kop, A. M., Nilasaroya, A., Sturm, M., Shaw, K. & Honeybul, S. 2018. Cranial reconstruction using allogeneic mesenchymal stromal cells: A phase 1 first-in-human trial. *J Tissue Eng Regen Med*, 12, 341–348.

Moschidou, D. 2009. A New Source of Stem Cells in Amniotic Fluid and Placenta in 1st Trimester of Pregnancy [electronic resource] [Online]. Imperial College London. Available: http://hdl.handle.net/10044/1/5484 [Accessed].

Nagy, A., Gocza, E., Diaz, E. M., Prideaux, V. R., Ivanyi, E., Markkula, M. & Rossant, J. 1990. Embryonic stem cells alone are able to support fetal development in the mouse. *Development*, 110, 815–821.

Ning, G. Z., Tang, L., Wu, Q., Li, Y. L., Li, Y., Zhang, C. & Feng, S. Q. 2013. Human umbilical cord blood stem cells for spinal cord injury: Early transplantation results in better local angiogenesis. *Regen Med*, 8, 271–281.

Ohlstein, B., Kai, T., Decotto, E. & Spradling, A. 2004. The stem cell niche: Theme and variations. *Curr Opin Cell Biol*, 16, 693–699.

Park, T. H., Chung, S. W., Song, S. Y., Lew, D. H., Roh, T. S. & Lee, D. W. 2018. The use of acellular dermal matrix in immediate two-stage prosthetic breast reconstruction provides protection from postmastectomy radiation therapy: A clinicopathologic perspective. *J Mater Sci Mater Med*, 29, 27.

Qiu, G., Zheng, G., Ge, M., Wang, J., Huang, R., Shu, Q. & Xu, J. 2019. Functional proteins of mesenchymal stem cell-derived extracellular vesicles. *Stem Cell Res Ther*, 10, 359.

Raya-Rivera, A., Esquiliano, D. R., Yoo, J. J., Lopez-Bayghen, E., Soker, S. & Atala, A. 2011. Tissue-engineered autologous urethras for patients who need reconstruction: An observational study. *Lancet*, 377, 1175–1182.

Raya-Rivera, A. M., Esquiliano, D., Fierro-Pastrana, R., Lopez-Bayghen, E., Valencia, P., Ordorica-Flores, R., Soker, S., Yoo, J. J. & Atala, A. 2014. Tissue-engineered autologous vaginal organs in patients: A pilot cohort study. *Lancet*, 384, 329–336.

Sato, M. & Nakano, T. 2001. Embryonic stem cell. *Intern Med*, 40, 195–200.

Shim, S. H., Kim, J. O., Jeon, Y. J., An, H. J., Lee, H. A., Kim, J. H., Ahn, E. H., Lee, W. S. & Kim, N. K. 2018. Association between vascular endothelial growth factor promoter polymorphisms and the risk of recurrent implantation failure. *Exp Ther Med*, 15, 2109–2119.

Shimizu, S., Tsuchiya, S., Hirakawa, A., Kato, K., Ando, M., Mizuno, M., Osugi, M., Okabe, K., Katagiri, W. & Hibi, H. 2019. Design of a Randomized Controlled Clinical Study of tissue-engineered osteogenic materials using bone marrow-derived mesenchymal cells for Maxillomandibular bone defects in Japan: The TEOM study protocol. *BMC Oral Health*, 19, 69.

Sugiura, T., Matsumura, G., Miyamoto, S., Miyachi, H., Breuer, C. K. & Shinoka, T. 2018. Tissue-engineered vascular grafts in children with congenital heart disease: Intermediate term follow-up. *Semin Thorac Cardiovasc Surg*, 30, 175–179.

Sun, H., Hu, S., Zhang, Z., Lun, J., Liao, W. & Zhang, Z. 2019. Expression of exosomal microRNAs during chondrogenic differentiation of human bone mesenchymal stem cells. *J Cell Biochem*, 120, 171–181.

The, L. 2018. The final verdict on Paolo Macchiarini: Guilty of misconduct. *Lancet*, 392, 2.

Tormin, A., Li, O., Brune, J. C., Walsh, S., Schutz, B., Ehinger, M., Ditzel, N., Kassem, M. & Scheding, S. 2011. CD146 expression on primary nonhematopoietic bone marrow stem cells is correlated with in situ localization. *Blood*, 117, 5067–5077.

Wei, F., Liu, S., Chen, M., Tian, G., Zha, K., Yang, Z., Jiang, S., Li, M., Sui, X., Chen, Z. & Guo, Q. 2021. Host response to biomaterials for cartilage tissue engineering: key to remodeling. *Front Bioeng Biotechnol*, 9, 664592.

Zafiropoulos, G. G., Al-Asfour, A. A., Abuzayeda, M., Kacarevic, Z. P., Murray, C. A. & Trajkovski, B. 2021. Peri-implant mucosa augmentation with an acellular collagen matrix. *Membranes (Basel)*, 11.

Zafiropoulos, G. G., Deli, G., Hoffmann, O. & John, G. 2016. Changes of the peri-implant soft tissue thickness after grafting with a collagen matrix. *J Indian Soc Periodontol*, 20, 441–445.

Zafiropoulos, G. G. & John, G. 2017. Use of collagen matrix for augmentation of the peri-implant soft tissue at the time of immediate implant placement. *J Contemp Dent Pract*, 18, 386–391.

Zellner, J., Krutsch, W., Pfeifer, C., Koch, M., Nerlich, M. & Angele, P. 2015. Autologous chondrocyte implantation for cartilage repair: Current perspectives. *Orthopedic Research and Reviews*, 7, 149–158.

Zhou, G., Jiang, H., Yin, Z., Liu, Y., Zhang, Q., Zhang, C., Pan, B., Zhou, J., Zhou, X., Sun, H., Li, D., He, A., Zhang, Z., Zhang, W., Liu, W. & Cao, Y. 2018. In vitro regeneration of patient-specific ear-shaped cartilage and its first clinical application for auricular reconstruction. *EBioMedicine*, 28, 287–302.

# 15

# Cardiology

ROBERT BELL

Cardiovascular disease remains the single leading cause of death.[1] Ischaemic heart disease alone is estimated to cost 8.9 million lives worldwide per year.[1] With such high prevalence and early adoption of clinical investigation and evidence-based medicine, cardiologists have benefitted enormously from the data derived from large-scale, high-quality clinical trials that have revolutionised the management of the diseases that have ravished our society. As one example, over the past five decades, death from myocardial infarction has fallen as evidence-based innovations in minimally invasive interventions (including primary percutaneous intervention and optimised medical management) and risk factor identification and optimisation have become common place.[2] Such has been the pace of change that one might be forgiven for wondering whether there is space for further innovation. In the aforementioned example of acute myocardial infarction, death rates remain unacceptably high: there is certainly space to innovate further, to identify the "at-risk" patient earlier (and preferably before a presentation with an acute coronary syndrome) and to continue to optimise the management of those who have been impacted by this crippling and often fatal condition. Moreover, myocardial infarction is just one of a large number of cardiovascular diseases that lead to significant morbidity and disability. Other examples include heart failure, cardiac arrhythmia (such as atrial fibrillation), valve disease, inherited muscle diseases and congenital abnormalities, to name but a few. All are subject to intense research, and examples of innovation are continually emerging.

DOI: 10.1201/9781003164609-17

## PHASES OF INTERVENTION

For diseases that evolve over time, there are three phases of intervention: preventative (before the disease becomes clinically apparent), management of acute presentation(s) and the subsequent management once the disease process has become clinically apparent. All three phases have their own challenges, but all three have the potential to make significant differences in patient outcome on both an individual and population health level (see Table 15.1).

## PRE-CLINICAL/PRIMARY PREVENTION

Pre-clinical prevention, at its core, relies on a clear understanding of the mechanisms of the disease process itself. Many cardiovascular diseases result from the presence of diabetes mellitus and systemic hypertension, which in turn can be a manifestation of lifestyle (exercise, diet, etc.). The benefits of tackling public health cannot be underestimated; the successes in tackling smoking as a cardiovascular risk factor has certainly had significant benefits in diminishing the rates of premature coronary and arterial disease.[2] Hypercholesterolaemia is another recognised risk factor for arterial atheroma formation, for which there are effective treatments and population-based medical interventions. These "modifiable" risk factors that formed the original Framingham risk score[3] are certainly the "low-lying fruit", but there are on-going studies looking at the human genome, seeking evidence of genetic traits that may either amplify or attenuate cardiovascular risk.[4] With genomic sequencing becoming progressively more affordable, it is foreseeable that particular genetic predispositions could be identified and facilitate a more personalised approach to preventative medicine, both as primary prevention and as secondary risk-reduction once the disease has become manifest.

Elucidating the mechanisms of the pathophysiology of cardiac disease has also moved forward. We now have sophisticated pre-clinical models of disease that range from in-silico modelling, through in-vitro cellular to animal models. These have been matched by changes in clinical data collection, through electronic health

Table 15.1 Phases of intervention

| 1. Pre-clinical presentation/ primary prevention | 2. Acute management of clinical presentation | 3. Post-presentation management and secondary prevention |
|---|---|---|
| *Example:* Identification of modifiable risk factors and initiation of appropriate therapy. | *Example:* Development of new, more effective intervention; optimisation of existing interventional approach. | *Example:* Interventions that minimise injury or optimise recovery following acute presentation; reduction of risk for future events. |

records and clinical investigations that include novel biomarker identification and modern imaging techniques that include radiological, nuclear medicine and magnetic resonance imaging that enable fundamental questions to be addressed directly in humans. Integration of the knowledge gained through research into the mechanisms of disease with the increasingly well-phenotyped clinical presentations should facilitate a more nuanced approach to primary prevention. If the "high-risk" individual can be identified with more accuracy, there is the possibility for intervention at an early stage, avoiding the higher costs associated with hospitalisations and specialist intervention as well as the socioeconomic impact of the consequent morbidity and mortality which can then be avoided.

Innovations for the future of disease prevention or mitigation will, therefore, include optimal implementation of the interventions that we already know work. The evidence base is already well-known, but there are multiple barriers to their implementation. Artificial intelligence algorithms have the potential to probe clinical data and flag particular lifestyle and drug therapy advice, although there are barriers to uptake: what if medical insurance companies were to use such algorithms to calculate insurance premiums? Putting aside such concerns for a moment, genetic testing could identify potential metabolic or genetic weaknesses long before biomarkers would become positive, and it could open the gate for personalised medicine and lifestyle advice. For those at high risk of developing a cardiovascular condition, wearable technologies (tracking heart rhythm, blood pressure, etc.) and even implantable technologies such as biometric "chips" (Figure 15.1) that could measure serum biomarkers, electrolyte concentrations and tissue water content could be useful to warn the individual that an event

Figure 15.1 An example of a small silicone chip. Actual devices will likely be encapsulated and be covered with biometric and chemical sensors that will facilitate diagnosis and management of chronic conditions. An example of such technology that has been in use for some time is the implantable loop recorder, that can record heart rhythms for many months or years, downloading and transmitting data via a base station to the physician's clinic where the data can be interpreted and acted upon.

may be about to occur, or even alert emergency services that a life were in danger. Such innovations are not the subject of science fiction but are techniques and technologies that are being worked on today and have the potential of becoming science fact in the near future. How other consumer electronics might start to impact upon medical management is only starting to emerge, as current, comparatively crude devices such as fitness trackers and smart watches are already identifying abnormal heart rhythms with increasingly proven clinical utility (for example, in the diagnosis of paroxysmal atrial fibrillation using a smart watch).[5]

## ACUTE DISEASE PRESENTATION

Without doubt, the greatest trend over the past two decades has been the move to minimally invasive interventions and optimisation of medical therapy – and there is no doubt that this trend will continue. While there is clearly still a vital role for surgical interventions – and indeed there remain clear outcome advantages for surgery over other techniques and strategies – there are populations and specific patient groups where minimally invasive intervention is preferable and is generally the patient's preferred choice. Catheter-based coronary interventions are the prototypical procedure for this, and more recently, aortic valve replacement via transaortic valve intervention/replacement (TAVI/TAVR) has been employed as an alternative to surgical aortic valve replacement, particularly in those thought to be at too risk for surgery (Figure 15.2).[6] There is increasing interest in minimally invasive mitral and tricuspid repair and even replacement, although the

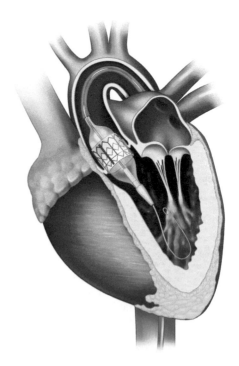

Figure 15.2 A cartoon demonstrating the balloon deployment of a TAVI within the native aortic valve. The principle of this technique are not dissimilar from coronary stents in that the valve is typically deployed on a stent structure that is expanded in place by a balloon (shown inflated here), deploying the valve and its supporting structure within the native valve. When the balloon is deflated, aortic flow is restored with the replacement tissue valve now taking over from the original valve, which is now effectively pushed aside circumferentially and functionally redundant.

large mitral valve size means that catheter-based mitral valve replacement currently remains only for selected patients where the prosthesis will not lead to an undersized valve and thus a relative "stenosis" compared to a more conventional valve replacement. Innovations in deployable valve design and techniques may, however, lead to a broadening of what can be done using these devices.

In respect to patient selection, as with genetic screening for prevention of disease, imaging biomarkers, such as the quantity and distribution of calcification within a valve and its annulus, may lead to more specific choices of valve. Similarly, with three-dimensional imaging techniques and modelling of movement, optimisation of device deployment within, for example an existing valve, will lead to improved outcomes in terms of reducing post-deployment paravalvular leak, and strut strain analysis will ensure that the prosthetic structure is durable in the position into which it is deployed.[7] These analyses may reveal a particular valve design as being more optimal than others – another example of personalised medicine where interventions can be tailored to optimise the final outcome and longevity of an intervention.

Any intervention will, of course, carry a risk, however small. Choosing the right patient at the right time is currently the greatest challenge. Current modalities including echocardiography, radiology and magnetic resonance imaging, all contribute to determining the structural and functional parameters that will be important in making these decisions. Combine this with functional testing at the time of imaging, and further dynamic data can be obtained to inform decision making. Away from the clinic, there may be additional options for problems to be identified while the vulnerable patient is in the community – again, utilising wearable technology (heart rhythm, heart rate, blood pressure response) and perhaps even the monitoring of biomarkers (for example, looking at cardiac strain and/or injury) may alert the clinician to problems even before a scheduled clinic appointment, and facilitate informed decision making in terms of the timing of an intervention or, in some cases, perhaps avoiding unnecessary interventions altogether.

The character of some interventions may also change over time. One current innovation in the field of cardiac pacing is a good example of this. Current pacemaker devices sense atrial and ventricular electrical activity using leads placed within the heart chambers (the right atrium and right ventricle for the commonly used dual-chamber pacemaker). These leads also electrically activate the myocardium that they are placed in contact with so as to "pace" the heart to ensure a minimum heart rate or a minimum pacing delay between atrial and ventricular activation. Thus, the traditional pacing lead has been the enabler of the often life-saving pacemaker intervention. However, pacing leads can be problematic. They can be the source of complications at the time of implantation (lead displacement), and the process of lead implantation, depending on the approach used, can lead to pneumothorax, vascular damage or infection of the pacemaker wound and pocket. In the longer term, the electrical leads can fail (fracture of the electrical cables) or even, on rare occasions, become infected, requiring often extremely challenging extraction. Devices are available now on the market that avoid the need for these wires, and while there are certainly going to be limitations to this technology (it can pace only a single chamber – currently the right

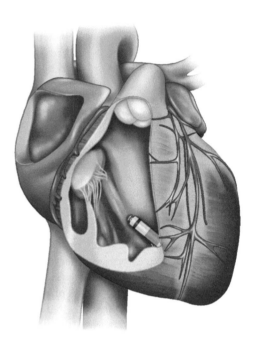

Figure 15.3 A leadless pace-maker placed at the apex of the right ventricle. The approach is via a catheter approach commonly used in cardiology and in this case passed via the venous system. The current principal limitation versus more conventional pacing devices is that the device currently can pace only a single cardiac cham-ber and does not offer a defibril-lator option. But if this approach is commercially successful for the device manufacturers, one may expect further developments to emerge.

ventricle), the technology will clearly have benefits to selected patients where single chamber pacing is acceptable (Figure 15.3).[8]

In addition to innovation in device design, future devices will likely benefit from the broader development of battery technology that we are observing in other fields of non-medical product design. With increasing energy density stor-age, it is conceivable that the devices of the future will be both be smaller and have a longer life time. Current devices have an approximate life span of ten years and have to be replaced: this procedure is routine but does carry with it a risk of procedural complications, including infection; a device that has a longer dura-tion of function may, in future, be "fit and forget" – at least in terms of battery life. Moreover, given that the chassis of the pacemaker will be fitted under the skin, the potential to load other sensors that may help optimise the management of cardiac conditions, such as heart failure, will almost certainly not be overlooked as these devices continue to be developed in the coming years.

## POST-EVENT MANAGEMENT AND SECONDARY PREVENTION

As previously mentioned, while the mortality of acute myocardial infarction has declined decade by decade, there has been a reciprocal increase in the inci-dence and prevalence of heart failure. Current heart failure therapy, at least for those with reduced left ventricular systolic function, has improved significantly over recent years with developments of medical therapy, but the prognosis of advanced heart failure remains dire and worse than many cancers.[9] For patients with heart failure with preserved left ventricular function the challenge is even greater, with no clear, efficacious medical interventions. However, advances in fundamental medicine and concomitant improvements in imaging modalities, such as cardiac magnetic resonance and nuclear medicine imaging, have started to identify sub-groups within the heart failure population that may be amenable to medical intervention.[10] A good example of this is amyloidosis: treating the underlying cause (e.g. myeloma or TTR amyloidosis) is having an impact upon the progress of the disease and offering encouraging directions for future management.[11] Thus, innovations in the understanding of underlying disease, innovations in imaging and biomarkers to identify the disease in individuals, and subsequent development of small-molecules to inhibit the progression and lead to regression of the disease offer a great deal of hope. However, much work is needed to understand the diastolic heart failure of the older population, who are more frequently female, diabetic and/or hypertensive, so that management may progress beyond purely symptomatic control.

As discussed in previous sections, one can easily foresee how artificial intelligence (AI) techniques may lead to optimised medical regimes in individual patients, even to ensure that current knowledge is effectively applied to all. Small-molecule therapies will continue to be developed, and the community is keen to see existing drugs being repurposed to optimise challenging patients. However, there will always be patients with organ damage that is too extensive to be effectively managed with drugs and devices alone. Heart transplant therapy is now well established, and the outcomes from such interventions are now generally very good following patient selection and donor genetic matching along with matching of other more physical constraints. However, such selection inevitably reduces the ability of an available heart to be effectively matched to a donor, and many donor hearts may have other injuries that will render them unsuitable for transplantation. This, combined with a general scarcity of donor organs, has resulted in incredibly challenging waiting times and to the deaths of those waiting for a suitable donor to materialise – despite the employment of mechanical ventricular assist devices and optimised and carefully monitored medical management of heart failure therapy. This is an ethically charged area, and recent developments with genetically modified pig hearts may provide one solution to a significant problem. Another is tissue engineering and three-dimensional printing of the human heart. This sounds to be in the realm of science fiction, particularly as some solutions would seem to require access to the microgravity environment of low-Earth orbit to achieve,[12] but innovations are likely to emerge from many directions. If it were to be possible to "manufacture" a heart – or indeed any other human organ – from the recipient's own stem cell lines, then this could represent an extraordinary step to regenerate or even replace a damaged heart.

## SUMMARY

We are entering an exciting period when advances in technologies both inside and outside of medicine are increasingly able to leverage novel innovations that have the potential to at least start to tackle current intractable problems such as heart failure and optimise and improve existing interventions, from cardiac valve replacement to medical devices such as pacemakers. Indeed, the potential to do more with what we already have is immense. Integrating advances from other fields, from data through wearable devices and technologically integrated clothing to novel developments in monitoring biomarkers, imaging and the ability to personalise interventions and therapies about what is known about the individual will be certain to have significant impact upon medical practice within the speciality of cardiology.

## REFERENCES

1. DALYs GBD, Collaborators H. Global, regional, and national disability-adjusted life-years (DALYs) for 315 diseases and injuries and healthy life expectancy (HALE), 1990-2015: a systematic analysis for the Global Burden of Disease Study 2015. *Lancet* 2016;388(10053):1603–58. doi: 10.1016/S0140-6736(16)31460-X [published Online First: 2016/10/14]

2. Mensah GA, Wei GS, Sorlie PD, et al. Decline in cardiovascular mortality: possible causes and implications. *Circ Res* 2017;120(2):366–80. doi: 10.1161/CIRCRESAHA.116.309115 [published Online First: 2017/01/21]

3. Wilson PW, D'Agostino RB, Levy D, et al. Prediction of coronary heart disease using risk factor categories. *Circulation* 1998;97(18):1837–47. doi: 10.1161/01.cir.97.18.1837 [published Online First: 1998/05/29]

4. Swerdlow DI, Hingorani AD, Humphries SE. Genetic risk factors and Mendelian randomization in cardiovascular disease. *Curr Cardiol Rep* 2015;17(5):33. doi: 10.1007/s11886-015-0584-x [published Online First: 2015/04/22]

5. Caceres BA, Hickey KT, Bakken SB, et al. Mobile electrocardiogram monitoring and health-related quality of life in patients with atrial fibrillation: findings from the iPhone Helping Evaluate Atrial Fibrillation Rhythm Through Technology (iHEART) Study. *J Cardiovasc Nurs* 2020;35(4):327–36. doi: 10.1097/JCN.0000000000000646 [published Online First: 2020/02/06]

6. Nguyen TC, Terwelp MD, Thourani VH, et al. Clinical trends in surgical, minimally invasive and transcatheter aortic valve replacementdagger. *Eur J Cardiothorac Surg* 2017;51(6):1086–92. doi: 10.1093/ejcts/ezx008 [published Online First: 2017/03/23]

7. Bosi GM, Capelli C, Cheang MH, et al. A validated computational framework to predict outcomes in TAVI. *Sci Rep* 2020;10(1):9906. doi: 10.1038/s41598-020-66899-6 [published Online First: 2020/06/20]

8. Boveda S, Lenarczyk R, Haugaa KH, et al. Use of leadless pacemakers in Europe: Results of the European Heart Rhythm Association survey. *Europace* 2018;20(3):555–9. doi: 10.1093/europace/eux381 [published Online First: 2018/01/24]

9. Mamas MA, Sperrin M, Watson MC, et al. Do patients have worse outcomes in heart failure than in cancer? A primary care-based cohort study with 10-year follow-up in Scotland. *Eur J Heart Fail* 2017;19(9):1095–104. doi: 10.1002/ejhf.822 [published Online First: 2017/05/05]

10. Shah SJ, Borlaug BA, Kitzman DW, et al. Research priorities for heart failure with preserved ejection fraction: National Heart, Lung, and Blood Institute Working Group Summary. *Circulation* 2020;141(12):1001–26. doi: 10.1161/CIRCULATIONAHA.119.041886 [published Online First: 2020/03/24]

11. Garcia-Pavia P, Rapezzi C, Adler Y, et al. Diagnosis and treatment of cardiac amyloidosis: A position statement of the ESC Working Group on Myocardial and Pericardial Diseases. *Eur Heart J* 2021;42(16):1554–68. doi: 10.1093/eurheartj/ehab072 [published Online First: 2021/04/08]

12. Cubo-Mateo N, Podhajsky S, Knickmann D, et al. Can 3D bioprinting be a key for exploratory missions and human settlements on the Moon and Mars? *Biofabrication* 2020;12(4):043001. doi: 10.1088/1758-5090/abb53a [published Online First: 2020/09/26]

# 16

# Genetics and genomics horizon scanning

## JULIAN BARWELL AND TOM CALDERBANK

A review of the role of genetics in clinical practice and how the dawn of genomics could impact clinical care in the 21$^{st}$ century.

## GENETICS IN MEDICINE UP TO 2015

Genetics has been shown to underpin biology through three mechanisms: firstly, the process of reproduction through semi-conservative replication; secondly, the 'central dogma' where the DNA molecule codes for the production of proteins through intermediary RNA molecules that help to build and maintain cellular organisation and function; thirdly, a biological mechanism for evolution through the selective reproductive success of organisms with advantageous genetic variation. The advantageous genetic variation has now been supported by gene mapping comparisons between species with closely related phenotypes.

DOI: 10.1201/9781003164609-18

Clinical genetics is the study of Mendelian (single-gene caused) disorders. One in 17 individuals have a rare inherited disorder, and approximately 3–10 in 100 cancers are caused by a faulty inherited gene.[1,2] Although conditions such as myotonic dystrophy, neurofibromatosis type 1, gross chromosomal abnormalities and cystic fibrosis are rare in our standard practice, we often fail to recognise the steps we have taken in everyday practice to identify and manage some of these, such as Guthrie cards, familial hypercholesterolaemia and rhesus disease of the newborn (which do not actually use genetic tests to detect). The study of genetics has given us many useful insights into the origin of life, human variation and the impact of biological evolution and how these interplay with our new modern psychosocial environmental construct that may underpin common problems such as chronic anxiety and obesity.

There is no doubt that genetics has improved the understanding of inheritance, reproduction, protein expression, identification of individuals, evolution, carcinogenesis, antimicrobial resistance and the aetiology of single-gene-related (Mendelian) disease-causing traits. Significant progress has been made in predicting the lifetime risk of disease in individuals with a significant familial medical history and offering reproductive health advice (where pathogenic variants are detected). However, the significance of identifying hundreds of subtle gene variations through whole-genome sequencing in well individuals without a clear family history is not as well characterised. Complex interactions between other inherited and environmental factors are also poorly understood (see Table 16.1).

Patients are increasingly concerned about the significance of variants detected either through commercial testing or through incidental findings when the test was carried out for another reason (see Table 16.2). The health and economic benefits of detecting families with pathogenic variants is offset by concerns regarding over-diagnosis and medicalising well individuals. These issues and understanding of common complex diseases will be resolved only with the collection and integration of large datasets matched to longitudinal outcomes.

## THE DAWN OF GENOMIC MEDICINE

New technological genomic advances are strategically important and well supported politically in the United Kingdom. These advances include clinical genetics but also the study of complex multifactorial traits; the use of targeted testing to distinguish between disease-causing and microbiome microorganisms; tumour analysis by characterising oncogenes; pharmacogenetics to predict drug metabolism; the release of cell free DNA from the placenta (or from a tumour); as well as the integration of clinical, molecular, social, consumer choices and wearable biometric data to create mathematical algorithms to make better predictions of disease.

These uses open up opportunities to make better predictions for future well-being and health, as outlined in the 'Beyond the Fog' Royal Free Charity commissioned report.[3] This level of thinking, already adopted by large commercial software companies, will require significant political lobbying, but a combination of dynamic clinical academic leadership and clarity of vision will aid in shifting the paradigm. We are very much at the beginning of this transformative health and social care journey, and barriers include insufficient bioinformatics capacity to deliver and present the data; education; and the concerns patients have with respect to how they perceive the integration of doctors, primary care and computer-driven technology.

Bioethical issues about confidentiality, discrimination and the misuse of data are also substantial challenges. Making healthcare in the 21st century safe, reliable and inexpensive will require clinical oversight and critical analysis of health and economic implications. Analysis will include assessing the impact of linked diagnostics and therapeutics (see Table 16.2). The mantras required include 'Move to a world beyond the microscope by treating disease for what it is and not what it looks likes' and 'Screen based on risk rather than age alone'. This so-called 'smarter' rationing of resources and integrated risk-modelling will need political debate with multiple stakeholders. Some current healthcare will need to be removed, creating winners and losers as the concept of routine or standard care is removed. Many providers are starting to work in this space, including commercial genomic companies, mobile phone companies, Facebook and Alexa. Food and Drug Administration (FDA) and European Medicines Agency (EMA) approved drugs have to include pharmacogenetics data within their application. This means the 'worried well' (unaffected individuals) will start to present with commercially derived risk data to their general practitioners, and those with chronic co-morbidities will begin asking about the implications of polypharmacy. Understandably, many people have concerns about how this data will be stored and used in the future either for financial gain or discrimination.

## THE GENOMIC CHALLENGE AND HOW TO HELP DRIVE THROUGH TECHNOLOGIES ALONGSIDE OUR CURRENT COMMITMENTS

Does genetic data have a role in proactively identifying and managing inherited disease, and how will we respond to rising health and social care demands and costs in an under-resourced healthcare system? The answers may include genomic and information technology (IT) solutions (note Table 16.1). The government's approach to the identification of risk appears to be through newly established and centrally commissioned genomic medicine services and consolidated laboratories (fewer laboratories doing larger-scale testing) overseeing the mainstreaming of genetic and genomic testing. This is mainly concentrated in secondary care with standardisation of multiple aspects of care: testing criteria, gene panels available, the consent process and the classification of detected variants. The aim is that these will be supported by clinical genetics and the cascading of genetic information and computer-modelled risk through genetic counsellors. This approach attempts to reduce the risk of population-detected over-diagnosis of conditions that would not potentially result in disease if undetected or treated, at least until more sophisticated and robust risk algorithms are implemented. To make this universally applicable, careful consideration will be required in how genomic data and matched phenotypic data should be captured and presented with relevant disease information.

Consideration is also required for management, escalation plans and data integration into health records. Patient-controlled electronic records, such as Patient Knows Best, offer a number of potential solutions.[5] A further challenge for primary healthcare professionals is the cost of genetic diagnostics and therapeutics. It is possible that future diagnoses for prescription medications, including antimicrobials, will be informed by molecular-based technologies, based either on the pathological process or predicted response of the individual to the therapy itself and its metabolism-smarter prescribing (see Table 16.2). To this aim, from 1st April 2020, the strategy for the National Health Service (NHS) was to deliver a nationwide standardised test directory for rare diseases and cancers, derived from the 100,000 genome project.[4] The plan is for a universal consent form with an "opt in" for future research opportunities. The patient will be also given the opportunity to receive additional incidental and potential treatments when the whole genome is sequenced.

Table 16.1 How to tackle genomic challenges in our practice

| Common genomic challenges | How these can be addressed |
| --- | --- |
| Irrelevant to common disease and my practice | Describe benefit beyond rare disease and cancer, including reduced prescribing of ineffective or potentially harmful medication or tracking of infections |
| Difficult to explain what could be found | Patient and public debate on tackling disparities and approach to consent |
| Too much infrastructure to deliver | Acceleration of diagnostic odyssey and precision of care balanced with consolidation of laboratories and IT/clinical infrastructure and cost |
| Complicated to understand results and too much uncertainty about significance | Standardisation of variant interpretation and mainstreaming of diagnostic testing so clinical genetics can assist with complex disease and results |
| Risk of over-diagnosis and limited predictive power | Opportunity to integrate genetic, genomic, clinical and social data sets to health and mental well-being outcomes to make better predictions and use AI algorithms |
| Concern over downstream screening and personalised medicine costs | Target treatments and screening to those that need it |

Table 16.2 Examples of the use of genetic and genomic technologies

| Application | Technique | Example |
|---|---|---|
| Confirmatory test | Targeted gene or panel of gene tests to confirm molecular basis of condition | Trinucleotide expansion in HD gene in a patient with dementia and chorea |
| Predictive test | Family cascading of Mendelian trait/ multi-layered data for complex disease | BRCA test in daughter of a lady with breast and ovarian cancer/ population based cardiac risk assessment |
| Planning treatment | Somatic test of a tumour/near-patient SNP for pharmacogenetics/ microbial genomics | PARP inhibitors for ovarian cancer/ detection of COVID-19 by PCR |
| Non-invasive genetic testing | Plasma-based cell free-DNA | Down syndrome screening in pregnancy/ liquid biopsies in cancer |
| Molecular manipulation | Pre-implantation genetic diagnosis/CRISPR/use of oligonucleotides | Embryo selection/CART for leukaemia and also solid tumours/HD anti-sense therapy |

## SCREENING AND MODELLING

Economic modelling will be required because not all disease-causing variants result in disease, and we will also need a political and ethical debate about how data is collected and used as well as the subsequent impact on increasingly personalised health information given to us in a depersonalised fashion and health rationing (see Table 16.1). We will need to review the use and impact of polygenic single nucleotide polymorphism (SNP) risk scores on population screening, with a resulting move towards screening based on risk, not age. In particular, how the general public will respond to being offered either less preventative healthcare (if the risk is felt to be low) or increased opportunity for intervention if the risks are thought to be higher will need to be considered in the years ahead.

## OUTREACH AND ENGAGEMENT

Patients struggling with active disease or psychological problems often fail to be referred for genetic treatment or diagnosis. Clinical genetics currently relies on referrals from primary and secondary care; it is often the highly educated worried well who prospectively seek out genetic services to clarify their risk. The failure of patients with active disease to use advancing genetic medicine for diagnosis or treatment can impact on future health or reproductive choices, thereby worsening the problem. At a population level, it is worth reflecting on the power of celebrity and patient-centred stories for explaining to the wider population the current innovative progress in genomic testing and precision medicine for screening and therapeutic purposes.

Approaching equity of access issues for seldom-heard-from groups with more specific problems and health needs can be tackled directly through reaching out and working directly with the community on their terms, such as in the University of Leicester 'Play dominoes, talk prostate cancer' campaign for Men of African Descent, or by involving social media partnerships or marketed community visits.[6] These are best supported by simplified electronic referral systems and aids for doctors, linked to postgraduate training programmes that may include face-to-face sessions, webinars, peer-supported and facilitator-led online courses or channels. These methods are relatively cheap to develop and easy to monitor, use and assess feedback.

In terms of the patient's lived experience, which is vital in the data rich internet-age, patient-led stakeholder groups have a unique insight into understanding the logistic and emotional impact of the disease on themselves and their relatives. These should be used to provide insight into designing and delivering clinical services as well as providing oversight governance into service developments. Through working with academic networks and political lobbying in partnership with organised, informed, enthusiastic and energised support groups, it is possible to assist and influence the implementation of new technologies into every day clinical practice (see Table 16.3).

## GENOMIC-BASED THERAPIES

Functional genomics, driven by the data produced by genome sequencing, focuses on the function and interplay of the vast number of genes present in humans and animals. This has revealed numerous ideas *in vitro* that could have significant therapeutic potential in clinical medicine. Unfortunately, they are not currently a mainstay of clinical practice for a number of reasons, for example, the difficulty in translating from *in vivo* to *in vitro* experiments, ethical issues associated with alteration of the genome and other external factors such as research funding and political backing. Nevertheless, the field of genomic medicine is expanding rapidly with the development of techniques such as anti-sense oligonucleotides, prime editing and functional assays (see Table 16.2).

Oligonucleotides are short, single-stranded DNA or RNA molecules, 18 to 30 base pairs in length, engineered to bind to (via complementary base pairing) a specific mRNA molecule.[7] They can exert effects at different stages of the gene expression cycle, for example, by changing the splicing process of pre-mRNA or by preventing ribosomal translation by steric blocking.[7] These processes all alter the transcription or translation of specific genes, either by altering the amino acid profile of proteins, or by reducing/silencing gene expression completely. ASOs could offer a highly specific treatment option, particularly in the case of Mendelian disorders, where a pathological phenotype can be traced to a single gene.

ASOs, like all therapeutics in medicine, are not without drawbacks. For example, ASOs have been generated to reduce the amount of mutant HTT protein produced in patients with the Huntington's disease phenotype. However, the potential effects of reduced HTT protein are unknown; this could impact the side-effect profile of such medications, and therefore, the risks and benefits of a certain treatment. The pharmacology of ASOs is also fairly complex, requiring specific delivery systems to optimise the bioavailability of the drug, for example intrathecal administration for neurological disorders. Despite these challenges, since the first clinical trial using ASOs in CMV retinitis, there have been trials of treatment for various malignancies, inflammatory disorders such as Crohn's disease and neurological disorders such as Huntington's and Spinal Muscular Atrophy.[7]

Whilst ASOs focus their efforts on genes post-transcription, other techniques, such as CRISPR-Cas9 and the more recent Prime editing, exert their effects on genes pre-transcription. CRISPR-Cas systems are an integral part of the immune process of bacteria and archaea, working by recognition and elimination of foreign DNA. Modified versions of these proteins have been developed for use in humans, their mechanism of action involving creating double-stranded DNA breaks, which are then repaired by either non-homologous end joining (NHEJ) or homology direct repair (HDR), both of which can be manipulated for a desired effect.[8] Unfortunately, allowing the cell itself to repair broken DNA strands occasionally results in unpredictable effects (most often from random insertion/deletion of DNA during the repair process of NHEJ).[8] CRISPR-Cas9 is currently being investigated for therapeutic options for a number of diseases, particularly haematological conditions such as leukaemia and sickle cell disease. CRISPR-Cas systems are still under investigation for use as therapeutic agents, particularly in haematological conditions such as leukaemia, lymphoma and sickle cell disease.[9,10]

Prime editing, on the other hand, has become an attractive alternative. As a modified Cas protein attached to a reverse transcriptase, it is able to insert 'corrected' DNA up to 12 base pairs, without causing the double-stranded break that leads to unpredictable repair.[11] *In vitro*, this has been able to correct mutations for sickle cell disease and Tay Sachs disease. Given the potential benefits of prime editing over CRISPR, it may be unsurprising if in the future it was to overtake CRISPR. Prime editing, could provide a way of intercepting the vast majority of known pathogenic mutations, therefore providing a potential genetic therapy for conditions in every aspect of human medicine.

The Coronavirus (COVID-19) pandemic has brought genomic-based therapies further into the public eye. Messenger-RNA (mRNA) vaccines have emerged as an integral pillar for the prevention and reduction of severity of COVID-19. In contrast with more traditional vaccines, mRNA vaccines do not involve introduction of inactivated or weakened pathogens. Instead, the specific mRNA pattern is used to produce part of the 'spike protein' of the virus. This protein will then be recognised as 'foreign' by the host immune system, activating an immune response and leading to the production of COVID-19–specific antibodies, conferring an element of resistance to the virus. Whilst this mRNA technology has been used in the laboratory for a number of years, it is likely that following its use in the COVID-19 pandemic, it may become a mainstay for future vaccines.

Table 16.3 A vision for human genetics

Clinical genetics involved in framing testing and subsequent clinical management advice within a context of mental health problems and complex family dynamics
Challenge: A new commissioning model

Mainstreaming of genetic testing for simplex disease (a single, already-diagnosed condition such as a cardiomyopathy, with either no relevant or a consistent family history with the identified affected family member) with support from education/training and sample flow logistics working parties
Challenge: Education and clinical band-width

Clinical genetics tackling diagnostic challenges through review of personal and family history, syndromic pattern recognition and unclear variant calls.

Clinical Genetics involved in multisystem disease management coordination and supporting reproductive health decision making
Challenge: Commissioning model and variant interpretation

Institutions (including NHS, university and commercial groups) to support research, innovation and implementation of genomic testing and therapeutic technologies: microbial, oncogenic, pharmacogenetics and non-invasive genetic testing, often through near-patient testing technologies
Challenge: Change science, acute and social care financial strain and cost of precision medicine therapeutics

A governance structure to ensure equity of access to testing, appropriate interpretation of results and subsequent implications on clinical management
Challenge: Commissioning model

A bioinformatic revolution around capacity to interpret genomic variants supported by multidisciplinary meetings, and integration of different data sets to improve health predictions using artificial intelligence
Challenge: Commissioning a change in work force and education

A socio-political think tank regarding the storage and use of genomic and other data for predicting healthcare outcomes for personalised screening and disease management.
Challenge: Recognition of the need for this before a political backlash of a Big-Brother style healthcare system is aimed at genomic medicine and progress is stalled or reversed

# GENOMIC CONCLUSIONS

Progress is being made with Mendelian disease with respect to access to testing and the probability of diagnosing disease. There remains a challenge for data interpretation for which improved phenotypic databases and functional assays will help. The UK and the NHS are world leading in this area, and it is part of a government-applied health science strategy (see Table 16.3). Embedding a culture of advances in genomic medicine is important throughout the healthcare system. However, taking patients through issues of consent, the testing process and the interpretation of results requires focused clinician training when the tests are available.

The extent of variation found in the coding sequences of normal unaffected individuals makes non-focused whole-genome sequencing difficult to use to predict future health. The key to making better predictions about future health will be through integrated data sets linked to health outcomes and machine-based learning algorithms.

Although there are good examples of gene therapy being used in conditions such as ADASCID, the implementation on gene (or gene expression) manipulation routinely is still some way off, but current *in vitro* approaches do suggest that prime editing could have a role in targeting a large proportion of mutational mechanisms.

With the rise of the internet and machine-based learning, it is likely that our relationship with knowledge and using our personal anecdotal experience of conditional probability will be challenged in the years ahead. We have the opportunity to critically assess and shape the changing landscape and then prepare ourselves and the doctors of tomorrow for the exciting opportunities that lie ahead.

# REFERENCES

1. European Commission. ec.europa.eu. [accessed 3/8/20]. Available at: https://ec.europa.eu/info/research-and-innovation/research-area/health-research-and-innovation/rare-diseases_en
2. Cancer Research UK. Cancerresearchuk.org. [accessed 3/8/20]. Available at: https://www.cancerresearchuk.org/about-cancer/causes-of-cancer/inherited-cancer-genes-and-increased-cancer-risk/family-history-and-inherited-cancer-genes#How%20common%20are%20cancers%20caused%20by%20inherited%20faulty%20genes?
3. Beyond the Fog. Vision4Health. [accessed 3/8/20]. Available at: https://medium.com/healthbeyondthefog
4. The 100,000 Genomes Project. Genomics England. [accessed 3/8/20]. Available at: https://www.genomicsengland.co.uk/about-genomics-england/the-100000-genomes-project/
5. Patients Know Best. [accessed 3/8/20]. Available at: https://patientsknowbest.com
6. UMatter. University of Leicester [accessed 3/8/20]. Available at: https://www.umatterleicester.co.uk/play-domino/
7. Scoles D R, Minikel E V, Pulst S M. Antisense oligonucleotides: A primer. Neurology Genetics. 2019;5(2):e323

8. Ann Ran F, Hsu P D, Wright J, Agarwala V, Scott D A, Zhang F. Genome engineering using the CRISPR-Cas9 system. Nature Protocols. 2013;8:2281–2308.
9. Jensen T I, Axelgaard E, Bak R O. Therapeutic gene editing in haematological disorders with CRISPR/Cas9. British Journal of Haematology. 2019;185:821–835.
10. Montano A, Forero-Castro M, Hernandez-Rivas J-M, Garcia-Tunon I, Benito R. BMC Biotechnology. 2018;18:45.
11. Anzalone A V, Randolph P B, Davis J R, Sousa A A, Koblan L W, Levy J M, Chen P J, Wilson C, Newby G A, Raguram A, Liu D R. Search-and-replace genome editing without double-strand breaks or donor DNA. Nature. 2019;576(7785);149–157.

## CASE STUDY K: PINPOINT

### CURRENT SITUATION

The COVID-19 pandemic has created a backlog of patients in need of investigation whilst diagnostic capacity continues to be reduced (by as much as 50% in some centres). Delayed investigation of cancer symptoms can lead to later-stage diagnosis, stage shift and an increase in lives lost. NHS trusts lack the time, money, facilities and specialist staff to procure, house and run new diagnostic equipment. Hence, the COVID-19 backlog is a challenge to clear.

### THE PinPoint TEST

- A machine-learning algorithm that rapidly triages symptomatic patients who might have cancer
- Developed with NHS and academic partners and performed in NHS labs
- A low-cost blood test which 'red flags' symptomatic patients with the highest chance of cancer
- CE-marked for 98% of the NHS two-week wait (2WW)
- Connects to any NHS lab, and has overcome the key systems integration and Information governance issues
- Currently executing an SBRI project involving four AHSNs and five Cancer Alliances in England

### THE PROBLEM WITH THE CURRENT STANDARD OF CARE

- At its inception in 2010, the 2WW pathway received 1 million referrals. This has grown to over 2.5 million referrals at a rate in excess of 10% year on year, at a cost of ~ £1.5 billion.

- 93% of referrals thankfully do not have cancer, but there is currently no reliable alternative to triage and prioritise patients with the greatest need.

## HOW IT WORKS

- The PinPoint Test aggregates data from a range of blood test results through machine learning/AI to provide a calibrated probability a symptomatic patient has cancer.
- The PinPoint Test is CE marked, uses standard NHS infrastructure and has overcome the numerous systems integration and IG challenges.

## COLLABORATORS

The PinPoint team has collaborated with several eminent clinicians, including Professor Sean Duffy, a former national clinical director for cancer, and Professor Richard Neal, a professor of primary care oncology. Professor Peter Selby CBE is the honorary chair of the Scientific Advisory Board.

**NHS England Press Release (January 2022):**

https://www.england.nhs.uk/2022/02/nhs-backs-pioneering-new-cancer-innovations-set-to-transform-cancer-diagnoses-in-england/

# 17

# Artificial intelligence and machine learning

RAJ JENA

## INTRODUCTION

Concurrent advances in computing power and the exponential increase in the volume of digital heath data have led to significant interest in the use of artificial intelligence and machine learning (AI/ML) in the healthcare sector over the past seven years (Figure 17.1). A recent bibliometric analysis of AI/ML-related research papers shows that publication output used to grow at a rate of 17% per year from 1994 to 2014. However, since 2014 the growth rate has increased to just over 45% per annum [1]. The terms artificial intelligence and machine learning are often used interchangeably but have distinct meanings. Artificial intelligence is the broader term and refers to a range of innovations from domains such as robotics, computer vision, speech and natural language processing, and machine learning. Machine learning has been concisely defined as a means to build computers that improve automatically through experience [2]. From a biologist's perspective, it is fascinating that modern AI/ML algorithms have converged on information processing structures that mimic the anatomy of neural information processing in animals.

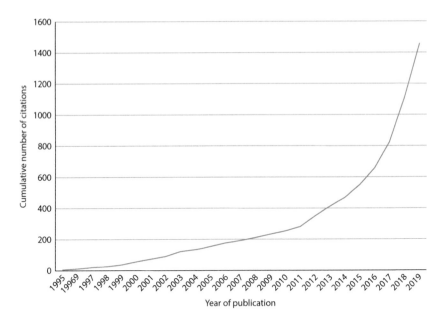

Figure 17.1 Cumulative number of research papers on AI/ML in healthcare since 1995, based on data from Guo et al [1].

## THE ANATOMY OF A MACHINE-LEARNING MODEL

It is important to understand the difference between an AI/ML *algorithm* and an AI/ML *model*. An AI/ML algorithm refers to the underlying structure of a neural network used to process data and the way in which that neural network is programmed into a computer. Examples of an AI/ML algorithm would be a deep convolutional neural network. An AI/ML *model* relates to the way in which the algorithm is configured to solve a specific data processing task. From an innovation perspective, healthcare innovations are enabled by the development of new machine learning algorithms, whilst the design, development, and clinical evaluation of an AI/ML model is a unique healthcare innovation in its own right.

The development of useful AI/ML models in healthcare typically follows a set pattern (Figure 17.2). Let us consider as a timely example a model that is designed to detect radiographic changes associated with Covid-19 pneumonitis on chest radiographs. The first step is to assemble a set of data and annotations that will be used to train the model. This process is known as dataset curation and would involve collecting radiographs from a large number of patients with and without Covid pneumonitis. Annotation refers to the process of human expert observers applying labels to the clinical data, often described as the 'ground truth' annotations. In this example, expert radiologists would score each radiograph for the presence and severity of pneumonitis, ideally using a clinically validated scoring system.

| Dataset curation | Model design | Model training | Model evaluation |
|---|---|---|---|
| • Export source data from clinical systems<br>• De-identify source data<br>• Create 'ground truth' labels from expert clinical observers<br>• Remove poor-quality datasets<br>• Package data ready for import into AI/ML framework | • Selection of a task appropriate AI algorithm<br>• Tune the model for best performance on the incoming data<br>• Design a numerical 'cost function' to measure how well the model output matches the 'ground truth' labels from the clinician<br>• The cost function is usually expressed as an 'error.' Lower error equates to a better fit to the expert labels. | • Data is broken up into small batches<br>• The computer tries changing the strength of connection between the different nodes in the model<br>• After each change, performance is assessed by calculating the 'cost function'<br>• The computer processes all available data through the model, and retains the model that with the lowest 'cost function' | • Hold-out. A small proportion of the original dataset that was not used for training is used to evaluate the model<br><br>• External cross validation. The model is assessed using data from another source, e.g. another hospital. |

*Iterate steps until clinical useful performance is observed*

Figure 17.2 The process of AI/ML model development. Regardless of the nature of the task, these four steps will need to be taken and carefully evaluated to create an AI/Ml model with clinical utility.

The next step is to choose an appropriate AI/ML algorithm and a set of assumptions about the nature of the data that will permit data processing, which is known as model creation. Model training is an iterative process in which an algorithm defines a set of evolving rules that link features in the input data to the appropriate ground truth annotations by stepping through each item in the dataset. In this process, the computer seeks to maximise a numerical score that describes the goodness of fit between the computer's prediction and the ground truth annotation. Once the model has been trained, it is typically tested on a different set of data that was not used for training the model (a hold-out dataset) to assess task-related performance. One weakness of machine learning models is their propensity for over-fitting to the training data. If a model is allowed to train for a very long period of time on a specific set of data, it can model the data too well. In our example, the model might be given images from one hospital that uses a particular brand of X-ray imager and a particular set of X-ray exposure settings in its emergency department. If the model were applied to radiographs from another hospital, using different scanning hardware and different exposure settings, model over-fitting would result in poor performance in the second hospital. Therefore, it is good practice to validate a machine learning model on another dataset that has been curated from another institution, and a different patient population. This final step is known as external cross-validation, and when reading about the performance of any new and promising AI/ML model in healthcare, great care should be taken in the interpretation of results in the absence of robust external cross-validation [3].

## PROBLEMS THAT CAN BE SOLVED WITH AI/ML

When horizon scanning for innovation opportunities around AI/ML in healthcare, it is worth considering that the current genre of AI/ML algorithms lend themselves to specific problem types. Highly structured data present the least challenge to machine learning research. Examples of highly structured data are tables of clinical observations from an electronic healthcare record, cross-sectional imaging data from CT scanners and gene-sequencing data. In each case, the data has a highly standardised inherent structure that makes it easier to encode for a machine learning model. Normal range values may allow rapid annotation of ordinate data from clinical records, and the standardisation of grey scale intensity values (Hounsfield units) across all CT scanners facilitates processing of image data. All three examples also benefit from a clear data model – only a certain range of values is to be expected in each dataset. A standard data model also facilitates de-identification of data when clinical data must be transferred to an academic or commercial partner for development of the machine learning model.

Through the increased availability of low-cost high-performance parallel computing devices, modern machine learning algorithms use large neural networks to process data, Key examples of such networks are deep convolutional neural networks and generative adversarial networks [4]. It is not uncommon for a model to have millions of trainable parameters. There are four broad problem types that can be solved with such machine learning:

1. **Data classification:** The model is given an input dataset and must correctly attribute it to a specific class. This could be a diagnostic class, such as diagnosis of stroke on a diffusion-weighted MRI scan, or a categorisation task, such as the grading of Covid pneumonitis on a chest radiograph as mentioned above.
2. **Data enumeration and segmentation:** This is a task typically appropriate to image data. The model is tasked with correctly identifying all instances of a specific finding in an image and marking the boundary of this finding.
3. **Correlation tasks and prediction tasks:** This is a type of task that crosses the fields of applied statistics, data science and machine learning. A clinical dataset is curated that contains information from multiple sources about a patient, and the aim is to build a model that correlates factors from multiple datasets to a specific clinical outcome or endpoint. An example of this approach is integrative cancer medicine for breast cancer treatment. In such a model, information about the pathology findings, imaging findings, genetic analysis and baseline clinical data may be used to correlate clinical features to clinical outcome. The multiple sources create a high-dimensional dataset, and in place of traditional techniques such as multiple linear regression analysis, an AI/ML model is tasked with learning the correlations between key findings in this high-dimension data and the clinical outcome. It is self-evident that an AI/ML model that has been trained and appropriately validated can also be used for prediction tasks.

An additional special case of correlation and prediction model relates to time-series data. Where most integrative medicine models will use data from a patient gathered at a single point in time (usually the diagnosis of a specific condition), AI/ML models may also be developed that look for correlations in data that occur over time. Again, in such models, a trained and validated time-series correlation model can also be used for time-series prediction. There are specific families of AI/ML algorithms that are useful for time-series data analysis.

4. **Data-synthesis tasks:** These tasks are made possible through the development of a recent form of machine learning algorithm known as generative adversarial networks (GANs) and once again applies best to image data. In recent times, the power of one of these algorithms, known as DeepFake, has been used to create fake photo and video footage of political leaders [5]. Here the model is trained to learn the relationship between paired input data. An example from the healthcare domain would be a CT scan and an MRI scan from the same patient taken at the same time. After training the model on the paired data, it is possible to provide the algorithm with an MRI scan for a patient as an input, and the algorithm syntheses an equivalent CT scan.

From the perspective of a machine learning researcher and a healthcare innovator, it is important to note a key transition that occurs in these four problem types. In tasks 1 and 2, which are the most mature in healthcare, the AI/ML algorithm is largely tasked with matching performance of a human expert observer. In task 3, as we move to increasingly high-dimensional datasets, the capability of the human mind to observe relationships in datasets that exceed 3 dimensions becomes limited. Here an AI/ML algorithm has the potential to exceed human performance in a given task. Finally in task 4, the AI/ML algorithm vastly exceeds the ability of the human observer to create consistent synthetic data.

## CASE STUDIES OF INNOVATIVE AI/ML FROM THESE FOUR PROBLEM TYPES

### Data classification

Over the past ten years, data classification AI/ML models have yielded significant results in the area of computer aided diagnosis (CAD), overtaking most other forms of feature engineering and image analysis algorithms. One application that has received significant research interest is the detection of lung nodules on lung CT scans, a common radiological problem where the problems of radiology workload and fatigue amongst observers raise concerns about small (<10mm) but significant lung nodules being missed during radiology readings. Such applications would be a necessary tool for any large-scale lung cancer screening project that utilised CT scanning. Robust clinical guidance now exists for the classification of such lung nodules, making it easier for algorithms to be deployed in different hospitals around the world [6]. In addition, the clinical community has curated large repositories of labelled chest CT images, shared with the research community under open-access terms [7]. The first lung-nodule detection models based on AI/ML were published in 2015 [8], and by 2016 leading AI/ML algorithms were yielding accuracy rates of 87.14% and a false positive rate of just 7% [9]. At the time of writing, several SME and larger healthcare technology companies now offer FDA 510k cleared solutions for AI/ML based lung-nodule detection. Optellum is an example of a machine learning company, based in Oxford UK, who produced one of the first AI/ML-based CAD solutions to obtain device registration [10]. From an innovation perspective, a key success metric for companies working in the diagnostic imaging space is their ability to partner successfully with several large healthcare organisations around the world.

## Data segmentation

Here we focus on image segmentation in two distinct applications. In the area of cardiology, cardiac CT scanning is being used as a non-invasive alternative to coronary angiography for the management of coronary artery disease. Heartflow is a company that provides an AI/ML-based solution for automatic segmentation of the coronary arteries, which is combined with a computational fluid dynamic model to produce a quantitative report on coronary artery blood flow [11]. The initial model adopted by Heartflow was an innovative solution. The company provided a service agreement to clients, such that cases which could not be processed by the AI/ML-based autosegmentation would be processed by a human expert. In addition, the company provided a lower cost per patient for their analysis if the de-identified patient data could be retained for further refinement of their models.

In radiation oncology, segmentation of tumour and healthy tissues is a key rate-limiting step in preparation of a precision radiotherapy treatment. This segmentation step takes approximately 40 minutes for patients with prostate cancer, whilst the increased complexity of the anatomy in the head and neck region means that this segmentation task typically takes 120 minutes. Our own work at the InnerEye team at Microsoft Research has led to an AI/ML-based solution for automatic segmentation of CT scans to assist clinicians treating patients with prostate and head and neck cancer [12]. To optimise performance, our model uses an ensemble of three machine learning models to process the images and agree on a consensus output, which is presented to the radiation oncologist. Clinical evaluation of the model demonstrates that oncologists can achieve a 13-fold acceleration in treatment preparation using this technology and that variation between expert observers and the model is less that the variation observed between expert observers. From an innovation perspective, the solution uses cloud-based machine learning resources, and the entire solution has been released to the community as open-source code.

## Correlation tasks

A wide range of precision medicine programmes utilise combinations of clinical, pathological, genomic and imaging data to build correlative models of human disease. The most ambitious programmes remain in the research setting. However, smaller-focused applications exist that have already demonstrated clinical utility. An example is the use of methylation classifiers to aid the diagnosis of brain tumours. The WHO 2021 classification recognises over 160 types of brain tumour, and in some cases there is significant diagnostic uncertainty regarding the underlying diagnosis of a specific brain tumour. In methylation array analysis, high-throughput gene sequencing is used to evaluate the gene methylation signal for multiple genes in a tumour sample [13]. *In vivo*, DNA methylation leads to silencing of specific genes, but for diagnostic purposes it can provide a unique signature that identifies the tumour, as it has been observed that tumours of the same underlying subtype share similar DNA methylation profiles. Given the volume of data available, no human pathologist would be able to analyse and interpret the methylation data, but the AI/ML model developed for this purpose has been validated in clinical use, and continues to refine its prediction as new cases are added to the model.

## Data synthesis

In the area of cancer imaging, technologies can often be used in combination to overcome the weaknesses of each individual technique. An example is the PET-CT scanner for cancer staging. The low spatial resolution of PET imaging is enhanced by concurrent acquisition of a CT scan. The CT data is used to enhance the spatial accuracy of the PET image, and the PET data enhances the sensitivity of CT by identifying small but metabolically active lesions. This concept has now been extended to PET-MRI scanners, which avoid the exposure to ionising X-ray radiation associated with CT scanning. This makes the device more applicable as a cancer screening tool in the general population, but the spatial resolution of the PET image is compromised. Generative adversarial network algorithms (GAN) have been utilised to train a model to produce a synthetic CT scan from paired CT and MRI images [14]. The authors used 119 pairs of whole-body CT and MRI scans to train the model, with the goal of making the synthetic CT scans accurate enough to help with PET reconstruction rather than diagnostic use. The author's analysis showed that the mean residual error in PET image reconstruction between synthetic CT and real CT was less than 1%. From an innovation perspective, data synthesis AI/ML is an early but rapidly developing area and at the time of writing, both Siemens and Philips have started to evaluate GANs for commercial synthetic CT workflows [15]

## CONCLUSION

It is clear from these case histories that innovative AI/ML is already starting to make inroads into clinical practice. Sharing of machine learning algorithms and widespread availability of high-performance computing helps AI/ML innovators enter the commercial space at low cost. However, access to appropriate clinical data remains a significant challenge in the clinical domain due to the unique information governance challenges. When evaluation innovations in this domain, equal thought should be given to the quality of the software engineering and computer science that went into the development of the model, and the ability of the clinical team to curate data and validate the model outputs. The responsibility for developing well designed and useful healthcare AI/ML should lie equally between the software engineer and the clinician.

## REFERENCES

1. Guo Y, Hao Z, Zhao S, Gong J, Yang F. Artificial Intelligence in Health Care: Bibliometric Analysis. J Med Internet Res 2020;22(7):e18228. https://doi.org/10.2196/18228.
2. Jordan MI, Mitchell TM. Machine Learning: Trends, Perspectives, and Prospects. Science. 2015 Jul 17;349(6245):255–260. doi: 10.1126/science. aaa8415.
3. Ho SY, Phua K, Wong L, Bin Goh WW. Extensions of the External Validation for Checking Learned Model Interpretability and Generalizability. Patterns (N Y). 2020 Nov 13;1(8):100129. doi: 10.1016/j. patter.2020.100129.
4. LeCun Y, Haffner P, Bottou L, Bengio Y. Object Recognition with Gradient-Based Learning. In: *Shape, Contour and Grouping in Computer Vision*. Lecture Notes in Computer Science, 1999, vol 1681. Springer, Berlin, Heidelberg. https://doi.org/10.1007/3-540-46805-6_19.
5. Christoph Bregler, Michele Covell, Malcolm Slaney. Video Rewrite: driving visual speech with audio. In Proceedings of the 24th annual conference on computer graphics and interactive techniques (SIGGRAPH '97). ACM Press/Addison-Wesley Publishing Co., USA, 1997, pp. 353–360. https://doi.org/10.1145/258734.258880.
6. Brandman, Scott, Ko, Jane P. Pulmonary Nodule Detection, Characterization, and Management With Multidetector Computed Tomography. Journal of Thoracic Imaging. May 2011;26(2):90–105. doi: 10.1097/RTI.0b013e31821639a9.
7. Armato SG 3rd, McLennan G, Bidaut L, McNitt-Gray MF, Meyer CR, Reeves AP, Zhao B, Aberle DR, Henschke CI, Hoffman EA, Kazerooni EA, MacMahon H, Van Beeke EJ, Yankelevitz D, Biancardi AM, Bland PH, Brown MS, Engelmann RM, Laderach GE, Max D, Pais RC, Qing DP, Roberts RY, Smith AR, Starkey A, Batrah P, Caligiuri P, Farooqi A, Gladish GW, Jude CM, Munden RF, Petkovska I, Quint LE, Schwartz LH, Sundaram B, Dodd LE, Fenimore C, Gur D, Petrick N, Freymann J, Kirby J, Hughes B, Casteele AV, Gupte S, Sallamm M, Heath MD, Kuhn MH, Dharaiya E, Burns R, Fryd DS, Salganicoff M, Anand V, Shreter U, Vastagh S, Croft BY. The Lung Image Database Consortium (LIDC) and Image Database Resource Initiative (IDRI): A Completed Reference Database of Lung Nodules on CT Scans. Medical Physics. 2011 Feb;38(2):915–931. doi: 10.1118/1.3528204.
8. Ciompi F, de Hoop B, van Riel SJ, Chung K, Scholten ET, Oudkerk M, de Jong PA, Prokop M, van Ginneken B. Automatic Classification of Pulmonary Peri-Fissural Nodules in Computed Tomography using an

Ensemble of 2D Views and a Convolutional Neural Network Out-of-the-box. Medical Image Analysis. 2015 Dec;26(1):195–202. doi: 10.1016/j.media.2015.08.001.

9. Wei Shen, Mu Zhou, Feng Yang, Dongdong Yu, Di Dong, Caiyun Yang, Yali Zang, Jie Tian, Multi-crop Convolutional Neural Networks for Lung Nodule Malignancy Suspiciousness Classification. Pattern Recognition. 2017;61:663–673. https://doi.org/10.1016/j.patcog.2016.05.029.

10. Massion PP, Antic S, Ather S, Arteta C, Brabec J, Chen H, Declerck J, Dufek D, Hickes W, Kadir T, Kunst J, Landman BA, Munden RF, Novotny P, Peschl H, Pickup LC, Santos C, Smith GT, Talwar A, Gleeson F. Assessing the Accuracy of a Deep Learning Method to Risk Stratify Indeterminate Pulmonary Nodules. American Journal of Respiratory and Critical Care Medicine. 2020 Jul 15;202(2):241–249. doi: 10.1164/rccm.201903-0505OC.

11. Driessen RS, Danad I, Stuijfzand WJ, Raijmakers PG, Schumacher SP, van Diemen PA, Leipsic JA, Knuuti J, Underwood SR, van de Ven PM, van Rossum AC, Taylor CA, Knaapen P. Comparison of Coronary Computed Tomography Angiography, Fractional Flow Reserve, and Perfusion Imaging for Ischemia Diagnosis. Journal of American College of Cardiology. 2019 Jan 22;73(2):161–173. doi: 10.1016/j.jacc.2018.10.056.

12. Oktay O, Nanavati J, Schwaighofer A, Carter D, Bristow M, Tanno R, Jena R, Barnett G, Noble D, Rimmer Y, Glocker B, O'Hara K, Bishop C, Alvarez-Valle J, Nori A. Evaluation of Deep Learning to Augment Image-Guided Radiotherapy for Head and Neck and Prostate Cancers. JAMA Network Open. 2020 Nov 2;3(11):e2027426. doi: 10.1001/jamanetworkopen.2020.27426.

13. Jaunmuktane Z, Capper D, Jones DTW, Schrimpf D, Sill M, Dutt M, Suraweera N, Pfister SM, von Deimling A, Brandner S. Methylation Array Profiling of Adult Brain Tumours: Diagnostic Outcomes in a Large, Single Centre. Acta Neuropathologia Communications. 2019 Feb 20;7(1):24. doi: 10.1186/s40478-019-0668-8.

14. Dong X, Wang T, Lei Y, Higgins K, Liu T, Curran WJ, Mao H, Nye JA, Yang X. Synthetic CT Generation from Non-attenuation Corrected PET Images for Whole-body PET Imaging. Physics in Medicine and Biology. 2019 Nov 4;64(21):215016. doi: 10.1088/1361-6560/ab4eb7.

15. https://www.siemens-healthineers.com/magnetic-resonance-imaging/clinical-specialities/synthetic-ct [accessed 19/12/21]

18

# The evolution of robotic surgery

## *Current status and future concepts*

SASHI S. KOMMU

## INTRODUCTION

The word "Robot" was first coined by the Czech writer Karel Capek and used to describe an artificial automata in the 1920 play *R.U.R. (Rossumovi Univerzální Roboti – Rossum's Universal Robots)* [1]. The first robot appeared in film in the 1927 German expressionist science-fiction drama *Metropolis,* directed by Fritz Lang.

The use of the robot as an assistive tool to aid conventional surgical procedures has successfully led to ways of overcoming the limitations of established minimally invasive surgical procedures (Figure 18.1). This has led to its widespread use in most surgical specialties. Herein, we explore the current status and future concepts as it applies to robot-assisted surgery as it continues to evolve.

DOI: 10.1201/9781003164609-20

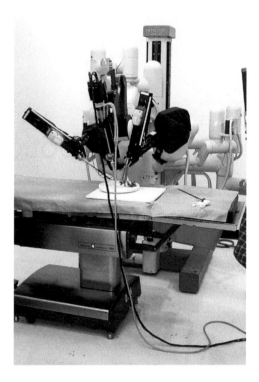

Figure 18.1 Laparoscopic surgery robot. (Nimur at the English-language Wikipedia, CC BY-SA 3.0 http://creativecommons.org/licenses/by-sa/3.0/, via Wikimedia Commons.)

## INITIAL CONCEPTS AND DEVELOPMENT

In 1985, a robot-assisted surgical procedure was performed with the aid of the PUMA 560 robotic surgical arm. The robot was used to perform a stereotactic neurosurgical biopsy of brain tissue under computed tomography (CT) guidance [2]. Robot-assisted surgery has been subsequently used for laparoscopic cholecystectomy [3], prostatic surgery [4] and orthopaedic joint-replacement surgery [5].

In 1998, the ZEUS Robotic Surgical System (ZRSS) was introduced with a view to performing telerobotic surgery [6] and has been successfully used to perform fallopian tube surgery [7], coronary artery bypass grafting [8] and cholecystectomy.

The Stanford Research Institute International, with grant support from National Aeronautics and Space Administration (NASA) and the Defense Advanced Research Projects Agency (DARPA) developed a telesurgical robotic system in 2003. This was the foundation of the initial da Vinci robot. This minimally invasive advanced tool gained widespread interest, and in 2000 the da Vinci robot became the first robotic surgical system to gain FDA approval for general laparscopic surgery in the United States. The da Vinci system was successfully applied to perform the first robotically assisted cardiac bypass surgery

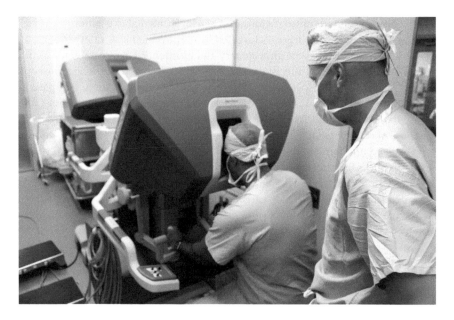

Figure 18.2 The Da Vinci platform. ("Brooke Army Medical Center performs first robot-aided pediatric surgery" by Army Medicine is marked with CC BY 2.0.)

procedure in 1998 [9] and the first robotic-assisted kidney transplant surgery in 2009 [10]. The first robot-assisted laparoscopic radical prostatectomy was performed by Dr Jochen Binder in 2000 [11].

Currently, the da Vinci robot remains the surgical robot of choice and utility in most centres (Figure 18.2). However, a plethora of new surgical robotic platforms have been developed ushering in a welcome competitive environment.

## EndoAssist camera-holding robot

Conventional laparoscopic surgery involves a surgeon working in tandem with an assistant who usually "drives" the camera to permit an optimal field of view for the surgeon. Some surgeons are proponents of the concept that the operating surgeon should ideally have full control of all instrumentation, including the camera. This concept has led to the exploration of surgeon-driven non-human (robotic) cameras and holding/driving robotic tools. Advantages cited include the reduction of assistant fatigue, elimination of fine motor tremor and delivery of a steady target images for the surgeon to function optimally.

The EndoAssist Camera-holding robot was developed to enable a camera interface which would be under the full control of the operating surgeon. The specific control of the camera was designed such that the head movements of the surgeon would translate into the exact movement of the camera, thus permitting the view received by the surgeon to be the optimal intended view without the dependence upon a second human interface driving the camera. The platform was designed with a head-mounted infrared emitter. A sensor located above a monitor is programmed to detect the surgeon's targeted head movements. A safety foot clutch was incorporated to prevent unnecessary and unintentional movement. Kommu et al. in 2007 evaluated the EndoAssist camera-holding robot in laparoscopic urological surgery prospectively [12]. This included nephrectomy (simple and radical), pyeloplasty, radical prostatectomy and radical cystoprostatectomy. This study found that EndoAssist was a safe, effective and responsive device for the purpose of robotic camera drive.

The Food and Drug Administration (FDA) approved a robotic surgical system made by the American Company Intuitive Surgical™ in 2000. The platform was called the da Vinci Surgical System. It is comprised of a surgeon interface (console) and a patient interface (bedside cart). Initially it was launched with three robotic arms, but subsequently a fourth interactive robotic arm was incorporated. The robot was designed to deliver translation of movement guided by the surgeon at the console to the working tools. The platform works as a master–slave device and is not autonomous. The robotic arms were designed to permit the use of specific purpose-built tools at the target tissue, including graspers, scissors and monopolar and bipolar diathermy. More recently, advanced tools such as stapling devices and advanced coupled diathermy and tissue cutting devices have been added. Since its approval in 2000, especially so over the past decade, the platform has received near exponential uptake in the performance of selected urological, gynaecological, colorectal, upper gastrointestinal, head and neck, transoral, ENT and cardiothoracic procedures.

## ADVANTAGES OF ROBOTIC SURGERY

The advantages of robotic surgery can be largely divided into patient benefits and surgeon benefits. There has been some debate about the true advantages of robotic surgery. However, proponents and sceptics have recognised that the robot provides the surgeon with an increased level of dexterity, *the seven degrees of freedom*, and permits the performance of target tasks in small and "difficult to access" areas of the human body with precision (Table 18.1). In contrast to conventional open surgery, minimally invasive access offers smaller incisions, reduced pain, reduced in-hospital/post-operative stay and quicker times to recovery. Cited surgeon benefits include comfortable ergonomic surgeon position, natural intuitive

Table 18.1 The seven degrees of freedom (N.B. the tip of each instrument allows 90 degrees of articulation)

| | |
|---|---|
| Translational | Up and down |
| | Left and right |
| | Forward and backward |
| Rotational | Roll |
| | Yaw |
| | Pitch |
| One grip | Cutting, grasping etc. |

Table 18.2 Advantages of robotic surgery over pure laparoscopic surgery

| Robotic surgery | Laparoscopic surgery |
| --- | --- |
| 3D vision | 2D vision |
| Motion scaling | Not possible |
| Wrist articulation | Limited range of movement |
| Fluid movement | Rigid movement |
| Tremor filter | Tremor magnified |
| Remote sensing technology | Abdominal wall is fulcrum |
| Ergonomically intuitive | Poor ergonomics |
| x 25 magnificaction | x 10 magnification |
| Haptic feedback | Limited tactile feedback |
| Telesurgery possible | Not possible |

movements, better vision with the 3-D HD vision, better hand-to-eye alignment and ability to enable, in tandem, both instrument and endoscope movement (Table 18.2).

Other advantages of robotic surgery include advanced supplementary/applicable tools, including, in particular with the da Vinci robot, Tilepro for superimposing images for image aided surgery, other real-time, image-guided surgery, advanced vision components and software. Furthermore, it offers tools such as the FDA-cleared dye indocyanine green (ICG) for image-guided surgery with the aim of precise vessel identification, deciphering the extent of solid organ perfusion, assessing the status of renal and liver parenchyma and assessing soft tissue perfusion.

The accepted lack of precise haptic feedback is being explored by several groups at present. The coupling of tools to permit optimal tactile feedback during robotic surgery is seen by many as essential. Others question the real advantage of haptic feedback as numerous current procedures across many specialties are being conducted safely and with non-inferior results to open or laparoscopic surgery without haptic feedback.

One of the resounding "disadvantages" of the da Vinci Surgical System cited by many is the high economic burden. This includes many centres that find the consumable costs unsustainable when placed into their health economic models. Others, particularly high-volume centres, argue that the overall costs including length of hospital stay balances costs and, in some instances, actually generates profitable incomes [13, 14].

## ROBOTIC SURGERY BY SPECIALTY

Since its introduction into current surgical practice, robotic surgery has catapulted in its uptake exponentially over the last two decades. Virtually every major surgical specialty has validated and safely conducted selected cases. These specialties include urology, gynaecology, general surgery, head and neck, cardiothoracic surgery and orthopaedics.

## UROLOGY

Urology, as a specialty, has been at the forefront in the uptake and successful application of technology and innovation in general. Introduction of the da Vinci robot ushered with it a plethora of applications for urological extirpative and reconstructive surgery. These include robot-assisted radical prostatectomy, robot-assisted radical nephrectomy/nephroureterectomy, robot-assisted radical cystectomy and ileal conduit formation, robot-assisted partial nephrectomy and robot-assisted lymph node dissection. Reconstruction procedures include robotic ureteric reimplant and diverticulectomy.

*Robot-assisted radical prostatectomy:* This approach has rapidly evolved, and its widespread use and positive results have led many units to offer this procedure as the preferred option. Techniques continue to evolve, and a plethora of studies report favourable perioperative and long-term outcomes when compared with open and laparoscopic procedures. Yaxley et al. compared outcomes of robotic surgery with that of an open approach and found, in that randomised controlled trial, results in favour of the robotic approach with respect to blood loss, adverse events, shorter length of stay and reduced pain [21]. The alignment of the prostate within the cave of Retzius makes the robotic approach a good option in trained hands. The configuration of the robotic arms remains standard and permits optimal extirpation, reconstruction and lymph node dissection when necessary. Smaller scars favour a robotic approach, which leads to a shorter hospital stay postoperatively. More recently other robotic platforms, such as the Versius Surgical Robotic System (CMR Surgical™), have been successfully used to perform robot-assisted radical prostatectomy and it is anticipated that other surgical systems may expand into this field.

*Robot-assisted radical nephrectomy/nephroureterectomy:* The first robotic nephrectomy was described in 2000. However, the role of robotic nephrectomy has been challenged due to the purported higher costs and no definite proven advantage over the conventional laparoscopic approach.

Those who advocate a robotic approach to nephrectomy have argued that one potential advantage involves the use of the fourth robotic arm to aid in "lifting" the kidney upwards, allowing for superior dissection, especially around the hilum. Some have also included a robotic clip applicator in their support of the robotic approach with what they argue is better precision and safety. Sceptics of the robotic approach to simple and radical nephrectomy are more supportive of nephroureterectomy for urothelial tumours involving the kidney. A robotic approach allows for ergonomic access to the distal ureter, with ligation and suturing in the pelvis. Currently there are no large-scale studies in favour of the global advantage of the robotic versus the laparoscopic approach. The overriding deterrent to the robotic approach for nephrectomy remains cost in most centres.

*Robot-assisted partial nephrectomy:* Since its introduction, robot-assisted partial nephrectomy has become the preferred form of nephron sparing surgery in many high-volume centres of excellence. Recent advances in the technique and technical modifications have allowed favourable oncological, functional and perioperative outcomes. The robotic platform allows ergonomic handling of sutures with closure of the renal bed coupled with hilar isolation and control. Few argue that the robotic platform delivers optimal results as for as partial nephrectomy is concerned [16].

*Robot-assisted radical cystectomy:* Surgical extirpation and reconstruction remains the established gold standard in the management of muscle-invasive bladder cancer. The robotic platform allows a radical cystectomy, pelvic lymph node dissection and urinary diversion to be performed in a safe and efficient manner in trained and experienced hands. Currently, the robotic approach is the approach of choice in many centres. Critics of the robotic approach, with its inherent cost implications, cite the RAZOR Trial, a randomised controlled trial looking primarily at the oncological outcomes of the open versus robotic approach [17]. This multicentre trial found no inferiority of the robotic approach compared with the open approach in two-year progression-free survival rates. Perioperative outcomes, including blood loss, transfusion rates, lengths of stay and operating time, were all extensively investigated. Cata et al. found that blood transfusion rates correlated with overall and cancer-specific survival [18] and also correlated with recurrence free survival, respectively, in patients undergoing robotic cystectomy. The need for further large scale multi-centred studies remains.

## GYNAECOLOGICAL SURGERY

Robotic surgery is currently largely reserved for gynaecological malignancy. The alignment of the robotic arms allows ergonomic access to the pelvis and its inherent organs. Gynaeoncological procedures are no exception. Anterior and posterior exenteration, robot-assisted radical hysterectomy, total mesometrial resection, ovarian cancer surgery and pelvic and para-aortic lymphadenectomy remain the most commonly performed procedures. Several studies have shown that the oncological outcome of minimally invasive surgical approach is at least equivalent to that of open surgery [19].

## GENERAL SURGERY

In established high-volume centres, the laparoscopic approach to general surgical cases is established as a viable and often preferred option. Those who support the laparoscopic approach are confronted with the challenges and cost implications of establishing a routine robotic service. General surgical procedures are diverse. Whilst some find the robotic approach to cholecystectomy difficult to justify, others would champion pelvic and "difficult to access" target organs/regions, as is the case with extirpation of the mesorectum and mesocolon using the robotic platforms as safe and efficacious. Oesophgectomy, antireflux surgery, gastric bypass procedures, splenectomy and pancreatic surgery have all been safely and successfully completed via a robotic approach. Advances in hepatic surgery, including selective metastatectomy, continue to evolve. Like most surgical procedures where robotic surgery is a viable option, cost implication debates continue.

## HEAD, NECK, AND EAR, NOSE AND THROAT SURGERY

Robotic approaches have ushered in paradigms in the approach and access to several areas of head and neck surgery. The intricate anatomy, coupled with small challenging zones renders robot-assisted approaches desirable. Oropharyngeal tumours in the early stages (T1-2) have successfully been treated by transoral robot-assisted surgery (TORS) [21]. Park et al. compared TORS to open trans-cervical surgery in patients with tumours involving the hypopharynx and found shorter postoperative recovery times, hospital stays and postoperative functional outcomes, including swallowing, in favour of TORS.

TORS has been successfully deployed to perform pharyngeal and paraphyn-geal tumour excision. Reconstruction of tissue defects after lateral oropharyn-geal resection has also proved a safe and achievable option using TORS.

A robotic approach to thyroidectomy has been shown to decrease sensory side effects and overall discomfort including swallowing and to improve cosmetic results.

A transoral robotic approach to the base of skull can be performed in tandem with endoscopic approaches to expose the posterior skull base, nasopharynx, and the infratemporal fossa [23]. Oncological outcomes of TORS are favourable, although there remains a paucity of long-term data.

The role of computer-assisted flexible endoscope systems continue to be explored. The Flex System may prove to be an alternative to transoral laser micro-surgery. This platform can be exploited where there are issues with cervical spine alignment or restricted space due to limitations of mouth opening or restricted neck extension.

## CARDIOTHORACIC SURGERY

The robotic approach to cardiothoracic surgery has evolved at an equal pace with other subspecialties over the past two decades. Robotic approaches have been successfully applied to mitral valve surgery, atrial fibrillation surgery, coronary revascularisation, left ventricular lead placement and congenital surgery [25]. Boon et al. [26] reported their experience of transthoracic robotic esophagectomy (TRE). Further studies continue to be conducted to validate its potential on a more widespread basis. At present, no prospective data com-paring robotic esophagectomy with standard laparoscopic or open procedures exists. There remains a paucity of long-term survival studies especially in cancer patients.

## FUTURE PERSPECTIVES

Robot-assisted surgery has evolved rapidly over the past two decades. Numerous robotic platforms continue to be introduced, and attempts to validate safety and efficacy while at the same time maintaining cost benefit remain a challenge. Improved haptic feedback, improved optics and increasing accessibility make these platforms exciting tools in our surgical armoury.

# BIBLIOGRAPHY

1. Morrell ALG, Morrell-Junior AC, Morrell AG, Mendes JMF, Tustumi F, DE-Oliveira-E-Silva LG, Morrell A. The history of robotic surgery and its evolution: When illusion becomes reality. Rev Col Bras Cir. 2021 Jan 13;48.

2. Kwoh YS, Hou J, Jonckheere EA, Hayati S, Kwoh YS, et al. A robot with improved absolute positioning accuracy for CT guided stereotactic brain surgery. IEEE Trans Biomed Eng. 1988 Feb;35(2):153–160.

3. Litynski, Grzegorz S. Erich Mühe and the rejection of laparoscopic cholecystectomy (1985): A surgeon ahead of his time. J. Soc. Laparoendosc. Surg. 1998;2(4):341–346.

4. Harris SJ, Arambula-Cosio F, Mei Q, Hibberd RD, Davies BL, Wickham JE, Nathan MS, Kundu B. Harris SJ, et al. The Probot—an active robot for prostate resection. Proc Inst Mech Eng H. 1997;211(4):317–325.

5. Paul HA, Bargar WL, Mittlestadt B, Musits B, Taylor RH, Kazanzides P, Zuhars J, Williamson B, Hanson W. Development of a surgical robot for cementless total hip arthroplasty. Clin Orthop Relat Res. 1992 December;285:57–66.

6. Baek SJ, Kim SH. Robotics in general surgery: An evidence-based review. Asian J Endosc Surg. 2014 May;7(2):117–123.

7. Margossian H, Garcia-Ruiz A, Falcone T, Goldberg JM, Attaran M, Miller JH, Gagner M, Margossian H, et al. Robotically assisted laparoscopic tubal anastomosis in a porcine model: A pilot study. J Laparoendosc Adv Surg Tech A. 1998 Apr;8(2):69–73.

8. Boyd WD, Rayman R, Desai ND, Menkis AH, Dobkowski W, Ganapathy S, Kiaii B, Jablonsky G, McKenzie FN, Novick RJ. Closed-chest coronary artery bypass grafting on the beating heart with the use of a computer-enhanced surgical robotic system. J Thorac Cardiovasc Surg. 2000 Oct;120(4):807–809.

9. Loulmet D, Carpentier A, d'Attellis N, Berrebi A, Cardon C, Ponzio O, Aupècle B, Relland JY. Endoscopic coronary artery bypass grafting with the aid of robotic assisted instruments. J Thorac Cardiovasc Surg. 1999 Jul;118(1):4–10.

10. Shroff S, Navin S. World's first robot-assisted kidney transplant performed. Indian Transplant Newsletter 2008 Oct–2009 Jun;8(27).

11. Binder J, Kramer W. Robotically-assisted laparoscopic radical prostatectomy. BJU Int 2001;87:408–410.

12. Kommu SS, Rimington P, Anderson C, Rané A. Initial experience with the EndoAssist camera-holding robot in laparoscopic urological surgery. J Robot Surg 2007;1(2):133–137.

13. Kommu SS, Murphy D, Patel SP. Robot assisted pyeloplasty vs. laparoscopic pyeloplasty – a preliminary cost comparison in the United Kingdom setting. J Endourol 2006;20S1:MP19–04.

14. Dobbs RW, Magnan BP, Abhyankar N, Hemal AK, Challacombe B, Hu J, Dasgupta P, Porpiglia F, Crivellaro S. Cost effectiveness and robot-assisted urologic surgery: Does it make dollars and sense? Minerva Urol Nefrol. 2017 Aug;69(4):313–323.

15. Yaxley JW, Coughlin GD, Chambers SK, et al. Robot-assisted laparoscopic prostatectomy versus open radical retropubic prostatectomy: early outcomes from a randomised controlled phase 3 study. Lancet 2016;388:1057–1066.
16. Mohammed Kamil Quraishi, Edward Ramez Latif, Milan Thomas, Ben Eddy, Elio Mazzone, Alexandre Mottrie. Robot-Assisted Partial Nephrectomy: Evolving Techniques in "Kidney Cancer". *In Edited by* Sashi S. Kommu & Inderbir S. Gill; InTech. Dec 2019. ISBN: 978-953-51-5910-0.
17. Parekh DJ, Reis IM, Castle EP, et al. Robot-assisted radical cystectomy versus open radical cystectomy in patients with bladder cancer (RAZOR): An open-label, randomised, phase 3, non-inferiority trial. Lancet 2018;391:252536. 10.1016/S0140-6736(18)30996-6
18. Cata JP, Lasala J, Pratt G, et al. Association between perioperative blood transfusions and clinical outcomes in patients undergoing bladder cancer surgery: A systematic review and meta-analysis study. J Blood Transfus 2016;2016:98.
19. Boggess JF. Robotic surgery in gynecologic oncology: Evolution of a new surgical paradigm. J Robot Surg 2007;1(1):31–37.
20. Gómez Ruiz M, Lainez Escribano M, Cagigas Fernández C, Cristobal Poch L, Santarrufina Martínez S. Robotic surgery for colorectal cancer. Ann Gastroenterol Surg 2020 Dec 10;4(6):646–651.
21. Weinstein GS, O'Malley BW Jr., Magnuson JS, Carroll WR, Olsen KD, Daio L, Moore EJ, Holsinger FC. Transoral robotic surgery: A multicenter study to assess feasibility, safety, and surgical margins. Laryngoscope 2012;122:1701–1707.
22. Lee J, Chung WY. Robotic surgery for thyroid disease. Eur Thyroid J. 2013;2(2):93–101.
23. Carrau RL, Prevedello DM, de Lara D, et al. Combined transoral robotic surgery and endoscopic endonasal approach for the resection of extensive malignancies of the skull base. Head Neck. 2013;35(11):E351–E358.
24. Reade CC, Johnson JO, Bolotin G, et al. Combining robotic mitral valve repair and microwave atrial fibrillation ablation: Techniques and initial results. Ann Thorac Surg. 2005;79(2):480–484.
25. Suematsu Y, del Nido PJ. Robotic pediatric cardiac surgery: Present and future perspectives. Am J Surg. 2004;188(4A Suppl):98S–103S.
26. Boone J, Schipper ME, Moojen WA, Borel Rinkes IH, Cromheecke GJ, van Hillegersberg R. Robot-assisted thoracoscopic oesophagectomy for cancer. Br J Surg. 2009;96:878–886.

# 19

# Innovation in public health

## *Tools and methods*

J. YIMMY CHOW AND JONATHAN FOK

The ancient art and science of public health has used the same methods and tools of detection and control, that of crude contact tracing and quarantine, as a core part of public health outbreak management from the plague through to several influenza pandemics. However, over the span of 20 years between the emergence of SARS-CoV-1 in 2003 and SARS-CoV-2 in 2019, and particularly over the COVID-19 pandemic, the large-scale global spread and pace of change has forced the scientific community and epidemiologists in public health to innovate and develop modern tools and methods to control the spread of emerging infectious diseases.

In this chapter, we explore these innovations through four aspects: surveillance, data analytics, detection and communication.

## SURVEILLANCE

The COVID-19 pandemic significantly changed how public health specialists conduct surveillance for notifiable diseases. From how data is accessed at an individual level to how surveillance is carried out nationally and internationally,

DOI: 10.1201/9781003164609-21

traditional public health methods of surveillance have had to advance and innovate to keep up with the evolving COVID-19 pandemic.

Public health contact tracing has historically been reliant on individual case follow-up and subjective case recall. Although this is still partially the case, there have been new advances that have changed how individual data is collected and how data is utilised for surveillance purposes. Many traditional surveillance mechanisms are still in place, such as identifying the number of test positive cases in the community or utilising community syndromic surveillance; however, current advances in technology have allowed surveillance to expand further by adding extra layers previously not available. An example of this is internet-based surveillance tracking,[1] which has allowed surveillance to capture how people use, search and interact with online data and resources. A local community that has a significant increase in online searches of symptoms such as 'loss of taste and smell', might be an early signal for targeted public health interventions, rather than waiting for people to present to healthcare settings, where data may not be fully available until two to three days later.

Current technological advances have also meant less reliance on traditional subjective case recall for contact tracing. Individuals have greater access to smart phones and other technologies, such as wearables, that can not only help track and recall individual movements but can also help an individual better understand their source of illness and their own transmission pathways. Greater access to these forms of data and willingness to share this personal data have allowed public health specialists to identify potential outbreaks and utilise public health interventions at a much earlier stage of prevention.

Harnessing existing and new technologies has been vital to the success of UK contact tracing, particularly through the co-development of the NHS COVID-19 app.[2] This app used existing Bluetooth technology to facilitate identifying positive cases in the community, facilitate tracking individual locations, identifying an individual's close contacts during their infectious period, and furthermore identifying settings of concern, through the use of a QR code system. At the scale with which the pandemic was growing, manual individual case follow-up was neither practical nor sustainable. Although the efficacy of these apps has yet to be fully proven, they have provided epidemiologists, data analysts, clinicians and policy-makers access to wide-scale data in real time. This has also provided public health specialists more time to focus on the management of complex outbreaks.

At a population level, the pandemic has compelled public health specialists to look at existing public health tools that may have been under-utilised and embrace change in different settings. Environmental studies, such as waste-water sampling and ventilation studies, have historically always been available in public health management of outbreaks; however, with the pandemic, these have played a much more crucial role in enriching understanding of disease vectors and disease transmission. When it comes to horizon scanning and surveillance at our UK ports of travel, the pandemic has allowed innovation at pace and the embracing of technology which previously would not have been implemented at scale. From infrared temperature scanning to help detect symptomatic individuals to advances in biometric data systems and online data capturing tools to help with passenger flows and passenger locator forms, ports of travel around the UK have had to adopt new strategies to improve disease surveillance.

## DATA ANALYTICS

The traditional collection of epidemiological data and surveillance, as described above, has been the cornerstone of public health. During the COVID-19 pandemic, to aid the planning of interventions and to provide a rapid response, data for epidemiological modelling and predictions played a more fundamental role. Innovations within this field include a more complex and sophisticated method of collecting and analysing a wide range of data from multiple sources. Data to input into models include prevalence studies, real-time transmission studies, hospital attendance rates, even transport mobility data and international comparators. This robust analysis gave more-accurate models and estimation of the various impacts of public health interventions, such as the use of lockdowns, on the reproduction number (R) and growth rate during the outbreak and aided decision-making to reduce health, economic and societal impact.[3]

Along with the plethora of modern-day information via the internet and other sources, the COVID-19 pandemic has changed the way public health specialists think of communication. To be able to communicate effectively, especially risk communication, there is a continual need to understand public sentiment, their attitudes to and how they will respond to non-pharmaceutical interventions such as 'social distancing', lockdowns, mass testing and mask wearing. Through this need there has been greater innovation in research methodology, evidence gathering and interpretation within the behavioural sciences[4] to help shape the public messages and communication throughout the different phases of the pandemic.[5] These tools include public surveys and tracker opinion polls, traditionally used in the consumer and political world.

The sharing and communication of epidemiological and statistical data to both the scientific community and the public is vital in the control of a fast-paced pandemic. The appropriate level, quality and transparency in the data allow people to follow the rationale of any mass testing, restrictions or control measures imposed on a community, follow infection rates, and see progress in interventions such as vaccination rates.[6] Throughout this modern pandemic, there have been great strides made in the display of data to make it accessible to all. Epidemiologists, website designers and journalists have provided innovative ways to share data, including interactive maps, metrics documentation and downloadable data for consumption and further analysis to aid the public health response at different levels, ranging from international, national and regional to local.

In addition, explaining and communicating complex, fast-changing control measures to the whole population has been aided by innovative infographics,[7] blogs and tweets via published and social media.

## DETECTION

Traditionally, infectious diseases were detected by clinicians, within healthcare facilities, in symptomatic patients. If a notifiable infectious disease[8] is diagnosed, then the attending clinician will inform the public health authorities for wider source investigations, contact tracing and prophylaxis or vaccination to be carried out for exposed persons. These measures are designed to control the source, whether it is via food poisoning, animal reservoirs, airborne transmission or transmitted directly from humans to other humans via secretions and bodily fluids, to prevent further illness and transmission in the wider population. Although these time-tested methodologies work well for most outbreaks in a contained cohort of individuals, in a situation such as a pandemic, where there is high incidence and prevalence widespread in an immune naïve community, this method of detection for surveillance and public health response is of limited value to prevent serious morbidity and mortality. In addition, for diseases that can be transmitted whilst the patient is not experiencing symptoms, such as COVID-19, the need to detect infection early and faster is vital to reduce chains of transmission. This is particularly important for vulnerable populations such as the elderly and the clinically vulnerable.

During the first two years of the COVID-19 pandemic, a sophisticated test, trace and isolate programme was set up in the UK. A vital part of the 'test' element was conducted through new technology. Alongside the standard lab-based polymerase chain reaction (PCR) tests, which traditionally required samples to be taken in a healthcare facility with results available in a few days, lateral flow tests (LFTs), which are rapid point-of-care test kits, were developed in record time. These COVID-19 antigen tests are simple to use and accurate, and sampling can be for both symptomatic and asymptomatic individuals. The accessibility of these tests at a population level allows testing at a scale not seen before, generating faster surveillance data and enabling quicker isolation of cases, reducing chains of transmission in the community and controlling outbreaks in vulnerable settings such as homeless hostels, prisons and care homes.

Infectious organisms, including bacteria and viruses, will have different strains and change over time to gain an evolutionary advantage. The use of whole genomic sequencing (WGS) to analyse infectious organisms has mushroomed over the past 20 years. Harnessing and using modern techniques to ramp up the speed with which WGS can be conducted enables detailed investigations into genomic clusters and outbreaks while also providing useful information for surveillance purposes through horizon scanning nationally and internationally. During the COVID-19 pandemic, the large circulating pool of SARS-CoV-2 viruses led to unprecedented growth of new variants.[9] Each new variant under investigation will have a series of mutations that would affect the viruses' ability to grow and transmit and will vary in the severity of the disease that it can cause. In addition, the effectiveness of existing vaccines against each variant will also vary. The ability to be able to detect and analyse each new emerging variant in real time has been a beneficial tool to the response of the pandemic.

## COMMUNICATIONS

Public health messaging and communication with members of the public has always been at the forefront of effective public health management. This can be simplified into how data is received and processed by an individual, and how clinicians communicate and convey public health messages.

Modern-day information, especially during the COVID-19 pandemic, comes at a frantic pace, and people often have difficulty processing the sheer quantity and speed of new information. In addition, members of the public must contend with identifying whether information has come from a valid, verified source and if the information is accurate. With the ease of access to media platforms, nearly anyone is able to post information, and this is often released without scientific rigour and evidence. Managing public health interventions and messaging during an outbreak can in itself already be complex. However, the extra variables of growing anti-vaccine sentiments and anti-vaccine misinformation; a lack of control over what, how and where media is released; and intelligent computer algorithms that can target and reinforce potentially negative healthcare behaviours add many further extra hurdles that need to be considered when communicating with the general public. With all the additional communication challenges, there is also further risk around general information fatigue and information overload.

Despite these challenges, the COVID-19 pandemic has advanced how public health messaging and interventions are carried out, especially in an ever-changing digital and communications landscape. Public health messaging now is not a one-size-fits-all approach, and public health and communication teams have had to adapt their communication strategies. For example, the use of traditional print and advertising media may work well for an older population, but these approaches are unlikely to have much reach or impact on the working-age or student population, who may gravitate more towards websites, online resources and social media platforms. Not only have teams had to change how they deliver public health messaging, they have also had to adapt to the potential restrictions on each respective platform and adapt the tone they use to deliver their message to their intended target audience. As more communications migrate to online and social media platforms, new roles that may not have existed during the 2003 SARS pandemic have come to light. Data analytics and data scientist were jobs that likely did not exist in 2003 but have now allowed further insights into how people use and interact with online resources. This, in turn, will allow more targeted public health communications. As local populations become more diverse and continue to access information through different media platforms, public health and healthcare specialists will need to continue to build on and adapt their strategies to be able to best target and communicate with their intended audiences.

## SUMMARY

In this chapter, we have tried to give the reader a flavour of how recent challenging public health incidents have galvanised the need to modernise existing public health tools. The all-consuming nature of the COVID-19 pandemic, in a modern era, has required concerted efforts from different disciplines from technological, commercial, academic and scientific worlds to invent new methods and refine existing tools to prevent and reduce morbidity and deaths from infectious diseases. The valuable tools described above will be the legacy of this modern pandemic which will be deployed for control of other new and emerging infectious diseases for years to come.

## NOTES

1. https://ukhsa.blog.gov.uk/2020/04/23/coronavirus-covid-19-using-data-to-track-the-virus/
2. https://www.wired.co.uk/article/nhs-covid-19-tracking-app-contact-tracing
3. SPI-M-O: Consensus Statement on COVID-19, 19 January 2022 - GOV.UK (www.gov.uk)
4. SPI-B: The role of behavioural science in the coronavirus outbreak, 14 March 2020 - GOV.UK (www.gov.uk)
5. SPI-B: Publications to date by SPI-B participants and relevant polling work of possible interest to participants, 6 March 2020 - GOV.UK (www.gov.uk)
6. England Summary | Coronavirus (COVID-19) in the UK (data.gov.uk)
7. COVID-19 variants (who.int)
8. Notifiable diseases and causative organisms: how to report - GOV.UK (www.gov.uk)
9. COVID-19 variants identified in the UK - GOV.UK (www.gov.uk)

# 20

# Wearable and implantable medical devices

## A fantastic voyage

WESLEY McLOUGHLIN AND IAN McLOUGHLIN

## INTRODUCTION

The 1966 novelisation of *Fantastic Voyage* by Isaac Asimov imagined a future medical team in a submarine miniaturised to molecular size. Few healthcare professionals considered that to be a foretaste of the future, but how many imagined technology at near-cellular size, sensing remote parts of the inner anatomy? Or miniaturised implantable devices delivering treatment at exactly the right timings, degree and locations? Or artificial intelligences (AI) inferring new treatments based on large patient databases? Yet these are today's reality.

This chapter considers wearable and implantable medical devices (WIMD) – technology that makes such cutting-edge medical examples possible. Our voyage of discovery will begin with current reality and then head towards the horizon. We will identify principles, constraints and enabling factors. While we cannot possibly predict every future WIMD, we can chart how such devices are

DOI: 10.1201/9781003164609-22

increasingly altering medical practice. We can also sample some endpoints likely in the 5 and 10 year range.

As with the tech industry in general, nascent WIMDs are continually improving. Incremental advances enable reduced size and cost – positively impacting where, when and how often such devices are used. Technology improvement in turn leads to faster, more efficient action and improved quality, together unlocking new applications in a virtuous cycle. We will explore these aspects: the impact on current medical procedures, how technological advances affect it and enhanced practices which then become possible.

Alongside natural refinement of technology, periodic disruptive ideas emerge to unlock novel paradigms. We will look at the potential for these, firstly by exploring factors that either encourage or restrict such progress and secondly by analysing emerging WIMD areas and their potential to disrupt.

Let us end this section with a story. A patient, Bob, is feeling unwell and so heads off to see his general practitioner (since Bob is a little old fashioned, preferring a human to an app). The GP, after an inconclusive examination, sends Bob home with instructions to return if there is no improvement in two weeks. However, she first passes Bob a bracelet-like device, asking him to wear it continually for a week before he returns. This disposable device measures Bob's blood pressure, oxygen saturation, respiration rate, red and white blood cell counts, blood pH, glucose and electrolyte levels, body temperature, ECG (and HRV), movement patterns, sleep cycle, environmental air quality and more. Measurement rates vary as needed between 100 per second and once per minute, communicated instantly via 5G to his medical record database. Dedicated AI monitors the records, alerting Bob and his GP to anything adventitious.

If Bob returns to the GP after a week, she could see a summary, a detailed analysis comparing the data to Bob's own baseline as well as to other similar patients, and access the raw data if so desired. Perhaps also recommend for further specialist investigation or potential diagnoses. While Bob's story is set in the future, all of those measurements can be obtained with current WIMD – albeit not in a single clinical device or one that a health authority could afford to make disposable.

So if that is what today's technology can do, what of the future?

## WEARABLES AND CONTEMPORARY MEDICAL PROCEDURE

Medical devices represent a broad subset of the medical technology industry. In the EU, the European Medical Agency defines them as '...products or equipment intended generally for medical use' (1). Wearable medical devices are utilised by both consumers, using pseudo-medical devices such as smart watches and fitness trackers, and by medical personnel via devices such as pulse oximeters and pacemakers (2, 3). The market value of wearables doubled over five years, reaching USD$50 billion in 2019. Sustained growth is forecast for another decade (4).

Wearable technology has progressed significantly since inception. Consider the humble wrist watch, first created in 1812, progressing through the eponymous

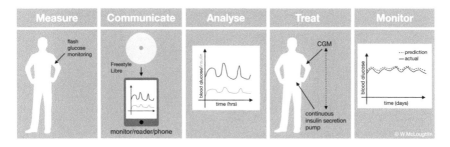

Figure 20.1 Medical device functionality classes. This can be viewed as a process (measure, communicate, analyse, treat and monitor) achieved by multiple devices and stages, or seen as increasingly being integrated into single devices. In the two-device examples shown, a type 1 diabetes mellitus (T1DM) patient uses a wearable glucose measurement sensor and an insulin secretion pump to provide insulin release.

Casio calculator watches of the '80s, to devices which are now essentially smartphones-on-a-wrist (5). Some incorporate pseudo-health functions such as oxygen saturation and heart rate measurement, from which they can infer 'stress levels' (6) and even recommend lifestyle changes to users. The infrared heart sensors in mobile phones (7, 8) could even potentially communicate with surgically implanted pacemakers (9).

Broadly, wearable and implantable medical devices (WIMD) can impact five aspects of functionality, representing a simple progression: measuring, communicating results, analysing, potentially treating and then monitoring outcomes. Current functionality uses different devices at different times, but the trend is towards integration. For example, Figure 20.1 shows separate implantable devices sensing glucose and administering insulin (10) for T1DM management. Yet everything can be combined into a single dialysis machine which equilibrates compound levels in a closed loop system (11).

## SMALLER, FASTER, BETTER TECHNOLOGY

As noted, general technology trends are towards smaller, faster and better devices, typically with reduced cost. Unsurprisingly, WIMDs follow the same tendencies. For example, consider the pacemaker, illustrated in Figure 20.2. This began as an external device and then became internal. It was incrementally reduced in size and cost and also benefitted from improved lifetime service rating (12). Newer devices can now communicate externally (13) and perform increasingly complex interventions and may soon be symbiotically self-powered (14).

Improvements to current technology can be as simple as changing their construction materials, for example, smart textiles (15, 16) – which can self-heal (17), be bio-resolvable (18) or self-assemble (19). Research advances have increased resistance (20) to microbial adherence or, conversely, improved integration and adhesion to bone (21). Such research provides important enabling technology for physical placement of future WIMDs.

**An innovation evolution – the development of pacemakers**

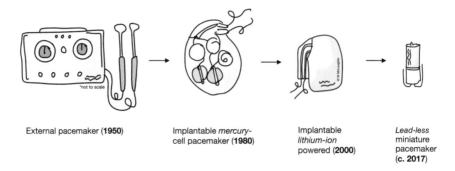

External pacemaker (**1950**)   Implantable *mercury-cell* pacemaker (**1980**)   Implantable *lithium-ion* powered (**2000**)   *Lead-less* miniature pacemaker (**c. 2017**)

Figure 20.2 The evolution of pacemakers since inception. A brief overview of the major changes and developments that have occurred in the design and technology used in pacemakers from the 1950s to the current technology in use now.

Other advances reduce power consumption, while battery technology simultaneously improves. These aspects alone allow more to be done for longer on battery power, significantly improve usability and enable applications that were hitherto impossible.[i] Very recent research into biochemical or symbiotic power sources harness biochemical gradients within the body (22), and of course wireless-powered technology (23) is increasingly common.

Wireless technology also enables communication functionality in many WIMDs. One example is the FreeStyle Libre as used by type 1 diabetic patients. This is a disposable implantable device that measures blood glucose every minute. Stored 15-minute records can be communicated to an external NFC (near field communication) reader (25). Most modern smartphones have NFC, hence reducing the need for specialist equipment and significantly increasing patient convenience.

## ENHANCING MEDICAL PRACTICE WITH WEARABLES

With decreasing budgets for healthcare providers, and a constant shortage of staff, from nurses to radiographers and doctors, technology presents an alternative, complementary method to reduce costs and maintain services. WIMDs are already established as standard practice in many specialties – e.g. pacemakers and pulse oximeters (26). The benefit is unarguable in many cases. For example, wearable cardiac defibrillators now can defibrillate successfully 75% of the time. A meta-analysis found that this contributed to an average survival rate exceeding 94% across 12 studies (27).

The convenience of WIMDs is enabling a shift from static and discrete data collection towards more frequent measurement. Returning to our example of blood glucose monitoring, patients would previously measure blood glucose via

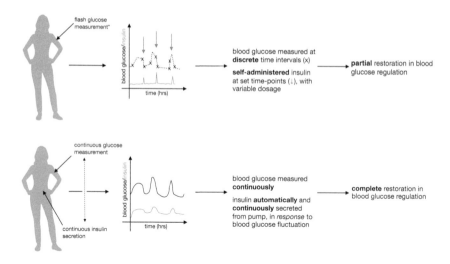

Figure 20.3 Current (top) and future (bottom) medical device treatments for T1DM patients. Current practice involves combining an implantable continuous glucose-monitoring sensor, providing readings over 15 minutes, and self-administered insulin. Future practice will increasingly involve integrated closed loop systems measuring blood glucose much more frequently (or continuously) and automatically administering micro-doses of insulin accordingly. (*FreeStyle [© Abbott Laboratories Limited, Berkshire, UK] measures blood glucose every minute and stores 15-minute readings. ©W McLoughlin.)

a finger-prick process about four or five times a day (28). The FreeStyle Libre, mentioned above, samples that many readings per hour. The increased data time-points allow for more accurate and potentially more robust analysis. But still, even such frequent discrete sampling may not detect every swing in blood glucose level, and therefore, only partially restores its regulation. This is illustrated in Figure 20.3, where the discrete sampling timepoints in the upper diagram prompt self-administered insulin injections. The open loop nature of this system is vulnerable to hypoglycaemic episodes (29) as diabetics can have decreased awareness to low glucose, potentially leading to life-threatening outcomes (30). Self-testing and administration can, of course, be problematic with the young and some of the elderly (31).

Closing the loop means automatically administering insulin – providing significant improvement by removing reliance on a patient's compliance during both testing and administration. Sampling can also be more frequent, better able to track rapid natural variations in blood glucose level and faster to respond to hypoglycaemic episodes. A recent example is the BetaBionics' iLet pump, which continuously measures and adjusts blood glucose levels through seamless and continuous provision of insulin, acting similarly to a normal pancreas (32). Such systems, illustrated in the bottom half of Figure 20.3, are also potentially able to track their own effectiveness and modify operation accordingly.

Consider allying such devices with AI to predict blood glucose changes before they happen. Utilising information from calendars, fitness and calorie tracking apps as well as past history, a pump could, for example, proactively respond to a large carbohydrate-rich Christmas dinner, which might require more insulin than normal, before it is even digested.

In summary, WIMDs are increasingly able to combine several factors together which can improve medical practice:

- Small size, long life, low cost, ease of use
- Frequent/continuous sampling
- Convenient communications capabilities
- Closed loop action (therapy) in response to measurement stimuli
- Capable processing and AI advances

## BARRIERS AND ENABLERS OF PROGRESS

As with any development, WIMD innovation is constrained by obstacles and hindrances while being driven by enabling factors. Obvious barriers to innovation include technology limitations, development affordability and commercial viability of an end product (both limiting development funding). Lack of commercial viability leads to many innovations being held back by popular public appetite. Atari founder Nolan Bushell's pre-GPS car navigation and Sir Clive Sinclair's C5 e-bike come to mind: ground-breaking innovations but too far ahead of their time for widespread uptake. More pertinent for WIMDs is the question of ethicality: testing the limits of current regulations or social acceptability, especially when regulations are slow to keep up with technology. The onus for predicting future ethical and moral boundaries lies primarily with innovators and is a serious responsibility (33). Recent data-centric technology approaches to medicine are a case in point – constrained more by general data protection laws than by medical ethics. It is likely that there will be greater legislative regulation in the future.

A number of enabling factors combine to overcome such barriers. Foremost is economics – consumer demand and funding, sometimes from investors but often in the form of government grants. Differing perspectives apply to (i) healthcare consumers and everyday patients, who generally yearn for greater information and control in the diagnosis and maintenance of their health, to (ii) healthcare workers, who often are overworked or in short supply (34) and strive to ease demands of work with faster methods of analysis, treatment and disease management and to (iii) funding bodies and healthcare providers such as the NHS, NIH and public health authorities, focusing on cost efficiency, increased benefit and enhanced outcomes. Sometimes the goals of different parties align, enabling significant gains. An example is 23AndMe (35) where participants can volunteer to contribute genetic information to a national database (36). Users are advised on predisposition and ancestry, but researchers/governments also benefit by using the database to inform public health decisions, or conduct genetics research.

# HORIZON SCANNING: NEW DEVICES ENABLE FUTURE MEDICAL PRACTICE

We have discussed current WIMD trends, seen how healthcare practice can improve and considered barriers and enablers of progress. Next, we consider novel WIMDs in breakthrough areas, leading to disruptive healthcare innovation: 'new devices, new sensors, new therapies'.

In today's tech-enabled world of thriving innovation, medical research frequently heralds potential novel treatments or possible new WIMDs. However, while R&D can be rapid, the realisation of concepts into products is far slower. To gauge how close an invention is to realisation, NASA developed a classification in the '70s called the Technology Readiness Level (TRL) (37) on a scale from 1–9, shown in Figure 20.4. As we discuss WIMDs at the cutting edge and beyond, we will estimate the TRL to assess how far 'over the horizon' they currently are.

As mentioned, technology refinement and incremental advancement naturally provide higher resolution information, better spatial sensitivity and seamless action, often in a closed loop. This, in turn, enables development of sustainable round-the-clock care. One example is 24/7 care of the ageing population (38), which is beyond the capabilities of current healthcare systems at scale yet becomes achievable with WIMDs – either with automated closed-loop monitoring and therapy or with sensors and therapies supplementing human oversight (39, 40).

Another incremental advance is the miniaturisation of previously bulky hospital machines into wearable, and later perhaps implantable, sensors, for example, pathology lab devices analysing electrochemical traces, pH, gas composition, ion levels and toxins. Some are currently done via disposable tests such as urine dipsticks or applied to samples collected from blood, CSF, lymph and so on. But in future, implanted sensors could provide consistent and continuous measurement of those quantities at source [TRL2].

*Biomimetic* technology is that modelled on biological functions, yet future WIMDs are not confined by this; they could potentially replicate any existing (or envisaged) large-scale monitoring/therapy, including surgery, endocrinology, physiology, neurology [TRL1].

Figure 20.4 NASA's technology readiness level scale, applied by the authors to WIMD development.

Future WIMDs may perform molecular-level sensing, a form of cytometry, analysing and counting cell behaviours (41) [TRL2]. Many disease pathologies begin with irregularities in cell behaviour which, if detected early, would lead to better prognoses. On an even smaller scale we envisage genetic treatment and diagnostics [TRL1]. Chromosomal damage can be measured or even countered through stimulating natural repair mechanisms in the way lobsters and other crustaceans technically 'live forever', by extending their telomeres (42), sensing telomere damage and effecting repair internally; this could potentially slow down ageing in humans [TRL1 or less].

Continuous anatomical measurement [TRL1], monitoring growth and morphology of bones, organs and tissue over time [TRL1], could become accessible. This would allow us to watch for ectopic growth and pathology (tumours and other lesions) without radiation exposure (X-Rays) [TRL1]. Alternatives like MRI are costly – high-maintenance machines requiring skilled operators (43). Furthermore, interpretation of scans requires a lot of training. AI is already being utilised to reduce this workload – even pigeons (natural, not artificial, intelligence) can reportedly be trained to recognise tumours on scans (44) [TRL2].

EEGs (electroencephalograms) (45) are already portable, either head mounted or even worn in-ear [TRL3], perhaps eventually implantable [TRL2]. This could allow warning of incipient epileptic seizures, for example [TRL3]. Indicators can also be visual (46). Epileptic brains feature abnormal levels of neuronal activity (47), producing reverse wave patterns. Could seizures potentially be prevented, or their symptoms reduced, by 'cancelling out' ectopic activity by a suitably equipped WIMD [TRL1]?

Moving to the GI (gastro-intestinal) tract, pro-biotic and active bacterial function could be replicated artificially to promote gut health or encourage weight loss (48, 49) [TRL1]. As bacteria ingest a range of compounds in the GI tract (50), and the GI-neuro axis is an established concept (51), such intervention could provide benefits ranging from improved mental health to reduced infection risk [TRL2].

In summary, the principle here is that any biological function could potentially be replicated artificially by future WIMDs. Meanwhile large-scale equipment, external treatment or regimes can likewise be miniaturised or assisted by future WIMDs (Figure 20.5).

## DATA-DRIVEN MEDICINE

Increased connectivity and concomitant access to vast amounts of pertinent data has defined this century so far. Unsurprisingly, healthcare represents an important and rapidly evolving front that integrated healthcare systems such as the NHS are uniquely placed to harness.

Large amounts of aggregated data can provide insights for new techniques and methods [TRL3/4]. As much as 'evidence-based medicine' was the past century's idiom (52), 'data-driven medicine' will become a shibboleth for this one. Such insights come not only from human analysis of data but also from AIs [TRL4].

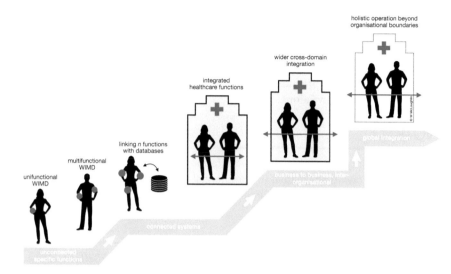

Figure 20.5 Overview of the evolution of WIMDs. Outlining the general trend of progression for WIMDs (and other technologies) in healthcare organisations and their likely future.

Data aggregation will accelerate. For example, any smartphone and a smart home device generate data indicating what users are doing, where, when and with whom (53). This includes lifestyle indicators such as exercise, weight and eating habits. Financial information reveals more, as does travel, communications and search history. Smart home devices can capture coughs [TRL3], detect the hoarseness of a sore throat, and potentially sense diseases from breathing patterns (54) [TRL3]. There is obvious medical potential in these data sources. However, this heralds additional legal and ethical problems – along with a future mired in endless terms & conditions, end-user license agreements, and permissions boxes. Hopefully the health benefits will outweigh the inconvenience and privacy risk that this entails.

## CONCLUSION

We no longer require a team of specialists and their submarine, miniaturised to molecular size, to be injected into the body in order to search out a problem and treat it [TRL0]. In addition to large and expensive imaging and diagnostic devices, we have a growing selection of tiny sensors that can be worn or implanted to provide a vast array of high-quality medical data [TRL2/3]. Meanwhile, wearable or implantable therapeutic devices are increasingly available to deliver therapies where, when and in the way they are needed [TRL1/2]. Furthermore, monitoring sensors are able to assess the effectiveness of therapy long after the submarine would have departed, and do so continuously. Connecting everything and aggregating data allows for better outcomes, while improving quality and timeliness of data continues to yield medical benefits.

As we have seen, WIMD technology is undoubtedly improving. But is society ready? Future WIMDs will cost less than alternatives, and they have much greater diagnostic capabilities. Combined with increased life expectancy, easier diagnosis correlates to more medical intervention. Health will improve but will also increase financial pressure on healthcare systems – and this problem is one technology cannot solve alone.

## NOTE

i. Body hacking and biological augmentation with 'cyborg-like implants' represent a growing alternative to commercial WIMDs. It is mostly unregulated (24) but provides a unique source of creative solutions and ideas.

## REFERENCES

1. European Medicines Agency. Medical Devices [Internet]. 2020 [cited 2020 May 20]. Available from: https://www.ema.europa.eu/en/human-regulatory/overview/medical-devices

2. Godfrey A, Hetherington V, Shum H, Bonato P, Lovell NH, Stuart S. From A to Z: Wearable technology explained. Maturitas [Internet]. 2018;113(April):40–7. Available from: https://doi.org/10.1016/j.maturitas.2018.04.012

3. Yetisen AK, Martinez-Hurtado JL, Ünal B, Khademhosseini A, Butt H. Wearables in medicine. Adv Mater. 2018;30(33).

4. James H. Wearable Technology Forecasts 2019-2029. Cambridge; 2019.

5. Reeder B, David A. Health at hand: A systematic review of smart watch uses for health and wellness. J Biomed Inform [Internet]. 2016;63:269–76. Available from: http://dx.doi.org/10.1016/j.jbi.2016.09.001

6. Schubert C, Lambertz M, Nelesen RA, Bardwell W, Choi JB, Dimsdale JE. Effects of stress on heart rate complexity-A comparison between short-term and chronic stress. Biol Psychol. 2009;80(3):325–32.

7. Jarchi D, Salvi D, Velardo C, Mahdi A, Tarassenko L, Clifton DA. Estimation of HRV and SpO2 from wrist-worn commercial sensors for clinical settings. 2018 IEEE 15th Int Conf Wearable Implant Body Sens Networks, BSN 2018. 2018;2018-Jan(March):144–7.

8. Jarchi D, Salvi D, Tarassenko L, Clifton DA. Validation of instantaneous respiratory rate using reflectance ppg from different body positions. Sensors (Switzerland). 2018;18(11).

9. Rajappan K. Permanent pacemaker implantation technique: Part I. Heart. 2009;95(3):259–64.

10. Russell SJ, El-Khatib FH, Sinha M, Magyar KL, McKeon K, Goergen LG, et al. Outpatient glycemic control with a bionic pancreas in type 1 diabetes. N Engl J Med. 2014;371(4):313–25.

11. El-khatib FH, Russell SJ, Nathan DM, Sutherlin RG, Damiano ER. A bihormonal closed-loop artificial pancreas for type 1 diabetes. Sci Transl Med. 2010;2(27).

12. Aquilina O. A brief history of cardiac pacing. Images Paediatr Cardiol. 2006;8(2):17–81.
13. Shimonov N, Vulfin V, Sayfan-Altman S, Ianconescu R. Design of an implanted antenna inside the human body for a pacemaker application. In: 2016 IEEE International Conference on the Science of Electrical Engineering (ICSEE). 2016. pp. 1–3.
14. Ouyang H, Liu Z, Li N, Shi B, Zou Y, Xie F, et al. Symbiotic cardiac pacemaker. Nat Commun. 2019;10(1):1–10.
15. Rogers JA, Ghaffari R, Kim D-H. Stretchable Bioelectronics for Medical Devices and Systems. Springer I. Basel, Switzerland; 2016.
16. Poon CCY, Liu Q, Gao H, Lin W-H, Zhang Y-T. Wearable Intelligent Systems for E-Health. J Comput Sci Eng. 2011;5(3):246–56.
17. Liu Y, Wang H, Zhao W, Zhang M, Qin H, Xie Y. Flexible, stretchable sensors for wearable health monitoring: Sensing mechanisms, materials, fabrication strategies and features. Sensors (Switzerland). 2018;18(2).
18. Wang L, Lou Z, Jiang K, Shen G. Bio-Multifunctional Smart Wearable Sensors for Medical Devices. Adv Intell Syst. 2019;1(5):1900040.
19. Cholkar K, Acharya G, Trinh HM, Singh G. Therapeutic Applications of Polymeric Materials. In: Emerging Nanotechnologies for Diagnostics, Drug Delivery and Medical Devices [Internet]. Elsevier; 2017. pp. 1–19. Available from: http://dx.doi.org/10.1016/B978-0-323-42978-8.00001-2
20. Nanda SS, Yi DK, Kim K. Study of antibacterial mechanism of graphene oxide using Raman spectroscopy. Sci Rep [Internet]. 2016;6(March):1–12. Available from: http://dx.doi.org/10.1038/srep28443
21. Guo CY, Matinlinna JP, Tang ATH. Effects of surface charges on dental implants: Past, present, and future. Int J Biomater. 2012;2012.
22. Alcaraz JP, Menassol G, Penven G, Thélu J, El Ichi S, Zebda A, et al. Challenges for the implantation of symbiotic nanostructured medical devices. Appl Sci. 2020;10(8).
23. Xue R, Cheng K, Je M. High-efficiency wireless power transfer for biomedical implants by optimal. IEEE Trans Circuits Syst. 2013;60(4):867–74.
24. Duarte BN. Entangled agencies: New individual practices of human-technology hybridism through body hacking. Nanoethics. 2014;8(3):275–85.
25. Blum A. Freestyle libre glucose monitoring system. Clin Diabetes. 2018;36(2):203–4.
26. Teng XF, Poon CCY, Zhang YT, Bonato P. Wearable medical systems for p-health. IEEE Rev Biomed Eng. 2008;1(February):62–74.
27. Piccini JP, Allen LA, Kudenchuk PJ, Page RL, Patel MR, Turakhia MP. Wearable cardioverter-defibrillator therapy for the prevention of sudden cardiac death: a science advisory from the American Heart Association. Circulation. 2016;133(17):1715–27.
28. Olansky L, Kennedy L. Finger-stick glucose monitoring: Issues of accuracy and specificity. Diabetes Care. 2010;33(4):948–9.

29. Brown SL, Bright RA, Tavris DR. Medical device epidemiology and surveillance. Medical Device Epidemiology and Surveillance. 2007. 219–236 p.

30. Martín-Timón I, Cañizo-Gómez FJ del. Mechanisms of hypoglycemia unawareness and implications in diabetic patients. World J Diabetes. 2015;6(7):912–26.

31. Leroith D, Biessels GJ, Braithwaite SS, Casanueva FF, Draznin B, Halter JB, et al. Treatment of diabetes in older adults: An Endocrine Society* Clinical Practice Guideline. Journal of Clinical Endocrinology and Metabolism. 2019;104:1520-74.

32. Russell SJ, Hillard MA, Balliro C, Magyar KL, Selagamsetty R, Sinha M, et al. Day and night glycaemic control with a bionic pancreas versus conventional insulin pump therapy in preadolescent children with type 1 diabetes: A randomised crossover trial. Lancet Diabetes Endocrinol [Internet]. 2016;4(3):233–43. Available from: http://dx.doi.org/10.1016/S2213-8587(15)00489-1

33. Eaton ML, Kennedy DL. The Modern History of Human Research Ethics. In: Eaton, Margaret L, Kennedy D, editors. Innovation in Medical Technology. Baltimore: Johns Hopkins University Press Eaton; 2007. pp. 37–46.

34. Portoghese I, Galletta M, Coppola RC, Finco G, Campagna M. Burnout and workload among health care workers: The moderating role of job control. Saf Health Work [Internet]. 2014;5(3):152–7. Available from: http://dx.doi.org/10.1016/j.shaw.2014.05.004

35. Stoeklé HC, Mamzer-Bruneel MF, Vogt G, Hervé C. 23andMe: A new two-sided data-banking market model. BMC Med Ethics [Internet]. 2016;17(1):1–11. Available from: http://dx.doi.org/10.1186/s12910-016-0101-9

36. Slevin P, Caulfield B. Patient-generated health data: looking toward future health care. In: Wearable Technology in Medicine and Health Care [Internet]. Elsevier Inc.; 2018. pp. 261–73. Available from: http://dx.doi.org/10.1016/B978-0-12-811810-8.00013-0

37. Mai T. Technology Readiness Level | NASA [Internet]. 2017 [cited 2020 Jun 2]. Available from: https://www.nasa.gov/directorates/heo/scan/engineering/technology/txt_accordion1.html

38. de Meijer C, Wouterse B, Polder J, Koopmanschap M. The effect of population aging on health expenditure growth: A critical review. Eur J Ageing. 2013;10(4):353–61.

39. Pang I, Okubo Y, Sturnieks D, Lord SR, Brodie MA. Detection of near falls using wearable devices: A systematic review. J Geriatr Phys Ther. 2019;42(1):48–56.

40. Ramachandran A, Karuppiah A. A survey on recent advances in wearable fall detection systems. Biomed Res Int. 2020;2020.

41. Alvarez DF, Helm K, DeGregori J, Roederer M, Majka S. Publishing flow cytometry data. Am J Physiol - Lung Cell Mol Physiol. 2010;298(2).

42. Klapper W, Kühne K, Singh KK, Heidorn K, Parwaresch R, Krupp G. Longevity of lobsters is linked to ubiquitous telomerase expression. FEBS Lett. 1998;439(1–2):143–6.

43. Sistrom CL, McKay NL. Costs, charges, and revenues for hospital diagnostic imaging procedures: Differences by modality and hospital characteristics. J Am Coll Radiol. 2005;2(6):511–9.

44. Levenson RM, Krupinski EA, Navarro VM, Wasserman EA. Pigeons (Columba livia) as trainable observers of pathology and radiology breast cancer images. PLoS One. 2015;10(11):1–21.

45. Ramaswamy P, Revett K. PIN generation using EEG: A stability study. Int J Cogn Biometrics. 2014;6(2):95–105.

46. Catala A, Cousillas H, Hausberger M, Grandgeorge M. Dog alerting and/or responding to epileptic seizures: A scoping review. PLoS One. 2018;13(12):1–20.

47. Scharfman HE. The neurobiology of epilepsy. Curr Neurol Neurosci Rep. 2007;7(4):348–54.

48. John GK, Wang L, Nanavati J, Twose C, Singh R, Mullin G. Dietary alteration of the gut microbiome and its impact on weight and fat mass: A systematic review and meta-analysis. Genes (Basel). 2018;9(3).

49. Davis CD. The gut microbiome and its role in obesity. Nutr Today. 2016;51(4):167–74.

50. Hao W-L, Lee Y-K. Microflora of the gastrointestinal tract: A review. Methods Mol Biol. 2004;268:491–502.

51. Carabotti M, Scirocco A, Maselli MA, Severi C. The gut-brain axis: Interactions between enteric microbiota, central and enteric nervous systems. Ann Gastroenterol. 2015;28(2):203–9.

52. Nunan D, Sullivan JO, Heneghan C, Pluddemann A, Aronson J, Mahtani K. Ten essential papers for the practice of evidence-based medicine. Evid Based Med. 2017;22(6):202–4.

53. McLoughlin IV. Speech and Audio Processing: A MATLAB®-based Approach. Cambridge University Press; 2016.

54. Pham L, McLoughlin I, Phan H, Tran M, Nguyen T, Palaniappan R. Robust Deep Learning Framework For Predicting Respiratory Anomalies and Diseases. In: 42nd Annual Int Conf IEEE Engineering in Medicine and Biology Society (EMBC), [Internet]. Montreal; 2020. pp. 90–3. Available from: http://arxiv.org/abs/2002.03894

# CASE STUDY L: AN ASSISTIVE DEVICE FOR THOSE WITH HEARING LOSS

Hearing loss is the most common sensory impairment in humans. An estimated 20% of adults suffer from some form of hearing loss (Shannon et al., 1993; Toh and Luxford 2002), with a greater prevalence in the older age group (Colleti et al., 2002). Amongst the paediatric population, the prevalence of permanent childhood hearing impairment of 40 dB HL or greater is approximately 133 per 100,000, with profound congenital loss occurring in 1 in 4000 live births. A hearing impairment may result in significant handicap, disability and social isolation. As a result, every effort is made to provide auditory rehabilitation in those with a significant hearing impairment.

Cochlear implantation may be indicated in those patients with a severe-to-profound hearing loss. Whilst the indications for implantation have gradually evolved to include a greater number of patients, intervention is limited by anatomical, medical, technical, and financial constraints. In those anatomically excluded for cochlear implantation, an auditory brainstem implant may provide direct stimulation centrally at the level of the cochlear nucleus (Grayeli et al., 2003; Nevison et al., 2001). This novel central auditory prosthesis has been shown be of considerable benefit in both post-surgical and trauma patients (Bento, Sanchez and Brito Neto, 1997).

In recent years, voice recognition software technology has become commonplace, with applications extending beyond word processing and telephone operator services. Speech-to-text conversion and appropriate presentation to a user may provide an alternative strategy for improving speech recognition in those with a hearing loss. However, understanding speech, and placing it in context, relies on not only auditory but also non-verbal information including lip reading, facial cues and gestures.

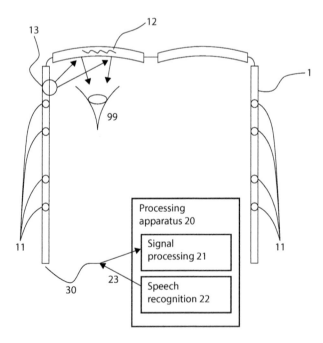

Figure L.1 Glasses with microphone array and integrated display.

Whilst the converted text should be accurately and rapidly displayed the method of presentation should not detract or distract the user from essential non-verbal cues.

We conducted a feasibility study, employing voice recognition software and a spectacle-mounted visual display, to observe any benefit in free field speech recognition in those with a hearing loss. Control subjects were also examined to assess any change in their ability to accurately recognise speech whilst using this system. The results of this study demonstrated a significant cumulative improvement in the understanding of speech when aiding was also included but also identified key issues that require addressing to optimise such a system.

## REFERENCES

Bento RF, Sanchez TG, Brito Neto RV. Critérios de indicação de implante coclear. Arq. Fund. Otorrinolaringol 1997; 1: 66–7.

Colleti V, Carner M, Fiorino F, Sacchetto L, Miorelli V, Orsi A, Cilurzo F, Pancini L. Hearing restoration with auditory brainstem implant in three children with cochlear nerve aplasia. Otology and Neurotology 2002; 23: 682–93.

Grayeli AB, Bouccara D, Kalamarides M, Ambet-Dahan E, Coudert C, Cyna-Gorse F, Sollmann WP, Rey A, Sterkers O. Auditory brainstem implant in bilateral and completely ossified cochleae. Otology and Neurotology 2003; 24: 79–82.

Nevison B, Laszig R, Sollmann WP, Lenarz T, Sterkers O, Ramsden R, Fraysse B; Manrique M, Rask-Anderson H, Garcia-Ibanez E, Colletti V; Wallenberg E. Results from a European Clinical Investigation of the Nucleus Multichannel Auditiry Brainstem Implant. Ear Hearing 2002; 23: 170–83.

Shannon RV, Fayad J, Moore J, Lo WW, Otto S, Nelso RA. Auditory brainstem implant (ABI): Post surgical issues and performance. Otolaryngol-Head and Neck Surgery 1993; 108: 634–42.

Toh EH, Luxford WM. Cochlear and brainstem implantation. Otolaryngologic Clinics of North America 2002; 35: 325–42.

# 21

# Using technology to improve the outcomes of mental health

## RAJ ATTAVAR AND VINOD MUNISWAMY

## INTRODUCTION

Depression is a major form of mental illness. This condition has claimed the lives of numerous individuals who have often suffered silently, sometimes for many years. According to a Centers for Disease Control and Prevention (CDC; Kenneth D. Kochanek, 2019) report based on data from 2017, there were 47,173 cases of death by suicide in the US, which translates to 14.5 suicide deaths per 100,000 population. According to the World Health Organization (WHO) website (Mental Health, 2016), globally close to 800,000 people die by suicide every year, which is one person every 40 seconds.

Depression and stress are the most common cause of work-related sickness and absenteeism. The global cost of mental health has been soaring over the past few decades and continues to rise. Many readers might be surprised to learn that one in four individuals has had, or will have, clinical depression in their lifetime. The socio-economic cost of an illness as pervasive as this is quite staggering, and according to an information sheet from the WHO website (WHO, 2019), the current estimated cost of depression and anxiety to the global economy is $1 trillion. Per a Reuters (Kelland, 2018) report from October 2018, the cost to the global economy is expected to reach $16 trillion by 2030.

Many psychiatrists agree that while genetics cannot be ruled out as a causal factor, the occurrence of depression is thought to be more directly related to stresses

DOI: 10.1201/9781003164609-23

resulting from personal relationships, financial hardships, work-related pressures, struggles related to sexual orientation and gender identity, alcoholism or other forms of substance abuse, lack of sleep/poor quality of sleep, unhealthy diet, in some cases, lack of physical activity and very limited exposure to sunlight. Clearly, depression is linked more closely to the everyday, mundane aspects of life than any physiological factors responsible for many other illnesses associated with the human condition.

The current approach to improving the health outcomes related to depression is still very reactive, and treatment does not begin until there has been a diagnosis of clinical depression. Globally, while there has been significant improvement in the ability of clinicians to diagnose depression, challenges remain with regard to the societal understanding and acceptance of depression as a legitimate form of mental illness.

These prevailing conditions pose a challenge in the diagnosis and curing of depression. Unfortunately, in many parts of the world, due to the societal norms, depression is still a taboo subject, making it difficult for depressed individuals to acknowledge/accept or even openly discuss their condition. This inability to openly discuss their depression with family and friends only serves to further exacerbate the condition, allowing the illness to feed off of itself, becoming even more deep rooted, such that by the time the disease starts to manifest itself in more obvious ways, it is already too late for many individuals who have suffered in silence.

It is not surprising then, that, despite newer pharmaceutical drug-based antidepressants becoming available, the incidence and prevalence of depression continues to rise.

Many experts in this field agree that their desire to more effectively help patients with depression depends on their ability to

- Intervene early
- Intervene often

Unfortunately, given the reactive nature of the current setup, in which a mental health professional cannot offer help until and unless a patient seeks their help, the ability to intervene early does not exist in most cases.

Also, given the current, primarily pharmaceutical drug-based approach, and the considerable cost associated with seeking help from healthcare professionals, let alone mental health professionals, many patients and their families lack the resources to seek intervention often.

It is primarily for this reason that the authors feel that the therapeutic regimen for treating depression should shift from the existing pharmaceutical drug- and psychiatrist-based paradigm to a preemptive approach that is more technology based, as outlined below.

## THE INNOVATION PATHWAY TO DETECTING AND ALLEVIATING DEPRESSION

The 21st century has been chock-full of technological innovations which can be woven into an ecosystem that can be used to detect, treat and monitor the symptoms of clinical depression and, ultimately, cure patients or at the very least, continue to manage their symptoms so that they remain highly productive, happy and content, without succumbing to it – and all of this in a subliminal way, without overtly interfering with an individual's day-to-day existence.

In the authors' vison of the not-too-distant future, where privacy rights have been traded in for big-data-driven personalized solutions focused on mental, physical and fiscal well-being, this technological ecosystem will be a confluence of

- Wearable devices
- Smartphones and other smart devices
- Bluetooth-enabled implantable devices
- Cloud computing
- Artificial intelligence (AI)

Whilst it is true that some of these technologies are not sufficiently mature for the outputs to be considered adequately reliable for the purpose of diagnosis and treatment, what is important to note is that the basic technology already exists and is continuing to mature rapidly to where the authors feel that this will be a highly viable approach within the next five to seven years, if not sooner.

## Wearable devices

Today's world is overflowing with smart devices that can measure everything from a person's heart rate down to their blood alcohol level. Purely from the perspective of depression, the parameters of interest that can or should be measured by wearables would be the following:

- Dietary intake (Brooke M. Bell, 13th March 2020)
- Quality and duration of sleep (Massimiliano de Zambotti, July 2019)
- Exposure to sunlight (Northwestern University, 2018)
- Physical activity (calories, steps counter)
- Blood sugar level (Healthcare Technology Featured Article, 2020)
- Blood alcohol level (Campbell, 2018)

## Smartphones and other smart devices

According to a recent finding published on the Statista website (O'Dea, 2020), the number of smartphone users in 2020 stood at 3.5 billion and was projected to reach 3.8 billion in 2021. Based on this projection, half the world already owns smartphones, and smart device ownership continues to increase.

Complementary to smartphones, the advent of smart devices such as Alexa and Google Assistant has allowed us to connect and interact with our home and surroundings in a more effortless and seamless fashion. These devices help us control almost all aspects of our in-home surroundings, such as security, entertainment, ambience and probably many more such seemingly mundane aspects. Whilst these smart devices are not yet as ubiquitous as smartphones, their adoption continues to grow rapidly to where it is not unimaginable for the majority of homes to have such devices in the next five to seven years, as implied by a study published on Mordor Intelligence's website (Mordor Intelligence, 2019).

Smartphones and other devices have brought the world to our fingertips and help us stay connected with the physical, social, economic, political and even religious aspects of our lives. In today's world, an individual can keep track of a multitude of the aspects related to our daily existence, ranging from the weather to our bank accounts to our health using just our smartphones.

Given that this is the world that we live in, it is not too much of a stretch to imagine an algorithm that can be used to harvest data from those aspects of an individual's existence that would allow the creation of a meaningful juxtaposition of some or all of the factors behind depression and anxiety. The output(s) from such an algorithm could then enable qualified medical professionals, or even an AI-based entity, to provide timely and effective intervention.

## Bluetooth-enabled implantable devices

The adoption of implantable devices to cure or alleviate serious ailments is starting to gain popularity, and the ever-growing advances in the fields of biomedical and biotechnology are bringing to life novel therapies to combat heart disease, diabetes, orthopaedic injuries, macular degeneration, dental disease and even neurological conditions such as epilepsy and migraines.

The potential of neural implants to address depression, which is also categorized as a neurological disease, is very promising. As demonstrated by the recent, highly publicized event held by Elon Musk, it may soon be possible to establish a neural link using implantable technology (Breakthrough Technology for the Brain, 2020). Whilst this research is still in its early stages and has not yet extended to humans, it is no longer science fiction. On the basis of this and other global research efforts, we postulate that some day in the not too distant future brain implants may be able not only to monitor brain activity but also to regulate the flow of hormones and neuropeptides leading to homeostasis and an improved well-being in individuals.

This postulation is also partially based on existing technology that allows researchers to monitor and analyze brainwaves, blood flow to the brain and overall brain activity while completing specific tasks or experiencing specific emotions such as joy, anger, sadness, relief, anxiety and fear, through the use of computed tomography, magnetic resonance imaging (MRI) and functional MRI scans.

The information being compiled using the data from these research efforts is enabling scientists to create an emotional map of the brain, which can then be used to create an algorithm. This algorithm, in conjunction with a Bluetooth-enabled neural implant, could be used to assess and monitor the emotional state of a person and perhaps also provide electrical impulses to alter the mood of an individual. Since the neural implant would be Bluetooth enabled, it would be possible for the data gathered to be linked to an individual's smart device and be viewed by the individual and, with their consent, to a mental health expert for timely and appropriate intervention.

We also envision that, in addition to alerting individuals and their mental health experts to symptoms of depression, in a home or office environment with smart home capabilities the Bluetooth-enabled implant could interface directly with Alexa or Google Assistant (or other smart home setups):

- To adjust some of the triggers that can help uplift an individual's mental state, such as music, lighting or temperature.
- In more overt ways such as send a text suggesting a meditation session, a walk (or any other physical activity), a healthy beverage or snack, or even place a phone call to a close friend or family member. If the implant were to detect an intense emotional state, it could also set up an ad-hoc therapy session administered by either a mental health expert or an AI-driven therapist.

## Cloud computing

We would like to highlight another critical aspect of Bluetooth-enabled implants in our vision of a technology-based ecosystem for improving the health outcomes for patients suffering from depression and anxiety.

With Bluetooth-enabled neural implants, it would also be possible to upload the relevant patient data to the cloud for compilation, analysis and comparison with other similar data sets. Taking this "big data" approach can allow for more effective individualized therapies to be developed.

The big data approach is crucial to the discussion around Bluetooth-enabled implants actively stepping in to intervene covertly and overtly as described above. The big data approach would help to continually improve the fidelity and choice of therapies available to a specific individual, by comparing that individual's current data against previous versions of itself and also against a larger data set from a similar set of individuals. Such an approach would allow the development of a still highly personalized but also highly nuanced intervention session that would be best suited to that individual's state of mind at that specific point in time, by either a mental health expert or an AI-driven mental health therapist.

## Artificial intelligence

As alluded to previously, a big data approach can also be used to create an AI-based solution that can offer a more cost effective, and highly personalized, on-demand therapy session to patients in the comfort of their homes and at a time that is most convenient to them.

Teladoc Health, Inc. is a multi-national telemedicine and virtual healthcare company founded in the US in 2002, and its primary services include telehealth, medical opinions, AI and analytics, telehealth devices and licensable platforms. It is just one specific example of an enterprise harnessing some of the elements of technology described above to treat many ailments, including mental health.

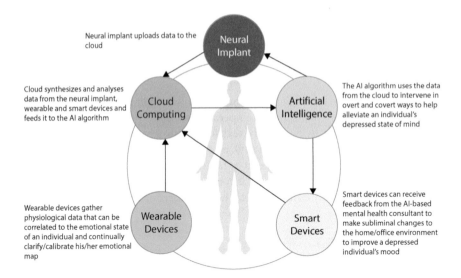

Figure 21.1 Super-consciousness resulting from the melding of human consciousness and artificial intelligence.

Figure 21.1 shows a technology model comprised of the five elements. We use the term "super-consciousness" to describe the heightened sense of awareness of an individual's state of mind resulting from the melding of human consciousness and AI. This super-consciousness is at the core of this technology model and may have applications beyond the scope of those outlined in this chapter.

## COST MODEL

There are several aspects to cost, not all of which are addressed in this chapter. From our perspective, the most important are the costs associated in enabling the five core elements of this technology model.

Due to the already prevalent and still rapidly increasing use of smartphones and other smart devices, most individuals will already have two of the five core elements outlined in the section "The Innovation Pathway to Detecting and Alleviating Depression".

While the cost of implementing the remaining three aspects of this technology model (Neural Implants, Cloud Computing and AI) is likely to be significant, once this technology model is established, it should be largely self-sufficient and require minimal additional investments for maintaining and sustaining it.

The development and implementation of these remaining three elements could be funded by a combination of the government, insurance companies, and private companies whose business model is based on trading in the currency of data to generate profit (e.g. Google, 23andme, etc.,).

As mentioned in Introduction, the current $1 trillion global cost of mental health is expected to be as high as $16 trillion by 2030. For varying reasons, this staggering sum is quite an incentive to all these three entities, and the most significant of these reasons are as follows:

- The government benefits from having a healthy population because of the direct link between health and productivity, which in turn has a direct impact on GDP.
- Health service providers benefit from reducing the very high costs associated with providing mental healthcare.
- The private companies that commercialize data can find new and varying uses for the data collected though this technology model and accrue benefits that directly impact their bottom line.

## ROADBLOCKS AND CHALLENGES

We recognize that there are some significant roadblocks and challenges to realizing our vision of creating a technological ecosystem focused on improving the health outcomes for patients suffering from depression and anxiety. These include the following:

- Neural implants are still not sufficiently mature to perform as outlined in this chapter. However, significant advances continue to be made to where the transition from science fiction to reality should take place in the next five to seven years.
- While the adoption of smartphones and smart devices is sufficiently high, the adoption of a smart home set up is not as high and will probably inhibit some aspects of this ecosystem.
- The ecosystem would require that individuals largely forfeit their right to some aspects of their privacy, such as their finances, social interactions, personal relationships, overall health information, etc. While this data will be randomized and fully protected in other ways, such transparency would be essential to intervening early and when required.
- Some elements of the ecosystem will also require individuals to allow access to their smart devices and smart home set up.

## REFERENCES

Alan S. Campbell, Jayoung Kim, Joseph Wang. (2018 Aug). Wearable Electrochemical Alcohol Biosensors. *Science Direct, Current Opinion in Electrochemistry*, Volume 10, 126–135.

Breakthrough Technology for the Brain. (2020). Retrieved from www.neuralink.com.

Brooke M. Bell, Ridwan Alam, Nabil Alshurafa, Edison Thomaz, Abu S. Mondol, Kayla de la Haye, John A. Stankovic, John Lach & Donna Spruijt_Metz. (13th March 2020). Automatic, wearable-based, in-field eating detection approaches for public health research: a scoping review. *Nature |npj| Digital Medicine*, npj Digit. Med. 3, 38 (2020). https://doi.org/10.1038/s41746-020-0246-2.

Healthcare Technology Featured Article. (2020, January 24). Retrieved from HealthTechZone.com: https://www.healthtechzone.com/topics/healthcare/articles/2020/01/24/444307-two-innovative-wearables-took-diabetes-control-the-next.htm#:~:text=Basically%20the%20Glutrac%20is%20a,uses%20AI%20to%20calculate%20glucose.

Kelland, K. (2018, October 9). *Reuters - Healthcare & Pharma*. Retrieved from www.Reuters.com: https://www.reuters.com/article/us-health-mental-global/mental-health-crisis-could-cost-the-world-16-trillion-by-2030-idUSKCN1MJ2QN

Kenneth D. Kochanek, Sherry L. Murphy, Jiaquan Xu, and Elizabeth Arias. (2019, June 24). *National Vital Statistics Reports*. Retrieved from www.cdc.gov: https://www.cdc.gov/nchs/data/nvsr/nvsr68/nvsr68_09-508.pdf

Massimiliano de Zambotti, Nicola Cellini, Aimee Goldstone, Ian M Colrain, Fiona C Baker. (July 2019). Wearable Sleep Technology in Clinical and Research Settings. *Medicine & Science in Sports & Exercise (American College of Sports Medicine)*, Volume 51, Issue 7, 1538–1557.

Mental Health. (2016). Retrieved from www.who.int: https://www.who.int/mental_health/prevention/suicide/suicideprevent/en/

Mordor Intelligence. (2019). *Smart Homes Market - Growth, Trends, and Forecast (2020 - 2025)*. Retrieved from mordorintelligence.com: https://www.mordorintelligence.com/industry-reports/global-smart-homes-market-industry

Northwestern University. (2018, January 9). *World's Smallest Wearable Device Measures UV Exposure*. Retrieved from sciencedaily.com: https://www.sciencedaily.com/releases/2018/01/180109125342.htm#:~:text=Summary%3A,UV%20light%20from%20the%20sun.

O'Dea, S. (2020, August 20). *Statista> Technology & Telecommunications> Telecommunications*. Retrieved from Statista.com: https://www.statista.com/statistics/330695/number-of-smartphone-users-worldwide/

WHO. (2019, May). *World Health Organization*. Retrieved from WHO website: https://www.who.int/mental_health/in_the_workplace/en/

# 22

# Medical imaging

RICHARD JENKINS AND DIPALEE DURVE

## INTRODUCTION

Radiology is a relatively young medical discipline; nonetheless, medical imaging has always sat at the crossroads of technological innovation and clinical application. This application of academic ingenuity to have real-world impact is in many ways at the core of the speciality of radiology and innovation in the field.

The discovery of X-rays by Wilhelm Conrad Roentgen in 1895 and their extraordinarily rapid introduction into clinical practice revolutionised patient management. Inaugural imaging modalities demonstrated a static image and physical status of a limb or organ, but novel advances in clinical radiology, closely linked with advances in physics, have resulted in the introduction of medical ultrasound, computed tomography (CT), magnetic resonance imaging (MRI) and nuclear medicine imaging. These modalities have not only allowed three-dimensional reconstructions to aid surgical planning and radiotherapy, but recent radiological advances have allowed clinicians to better understand

DOI: 10.1201/9781003164609-24

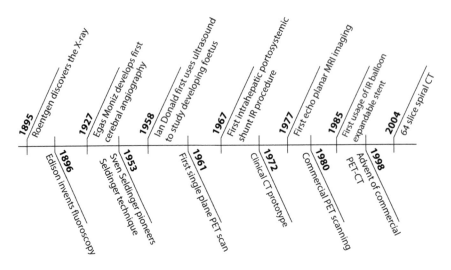

Figure 22.1 Timeline of radiological innovation.

functional change and four-dimensional flow through imaging alone; for example, renal and foetal cardiac function can be assessed through MRI manipulation. This advance has reduced the need for conventional contrast imaging and consequently, the associated risks involved. Interventional radiology (IR), an established branch of radiology, provides an interface between surgical intervention and radiological imaging and has evolved from Egas Moniz's discovery of angiography and the Seldinger technique (Figure 22.1) with promising future developments (discussed later).

The fledgling branch of paediatric radiology has promoted innovative care in a more challenging patient population. Functional magnetic resonance urography or paramagnetic MRI has been developed by Dmitry Khrichenko with post-processing software for use in paediatric imaging. This method is increasingly recognised as an alternative mode of dynamic renal imaging without the need for the radiation dose associated with its predecessor (nuclear medicine), an essential consideration in any choice of imaging when the overall aim is to decrease the long-term effects of cumulative radiation in children (Figure 22.2).

This chapter will discuss innovation in medical imaging. We will consider the future of medical imaging at a granular level, detailing several specific emerging technologies and bringing that technology to an ever-expanding patient base in a clinically meaningful way. As part of this we will put forward a concept of two significant leaps that are needed in imaging innovation: the leap from academic concept to clinical application and the leap from limited patient access to mass adoption. This will be illustrated with specific promising innovative technologies, but the principle can also be seen as a wider approach to innovation in imaging.

MRI–guided focused ultrasound surgery (MRI-FUS) and robotics-assisted interventional radiology both show the potential for widespread clinical adoption in the near future. The revolution of bedside imaging and imaging in the developing world show exciting opportunities by significant widening of access

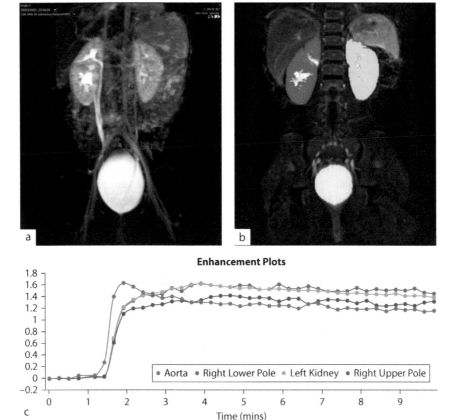

Figure 22.2 MRI Urography provides a functional assessment of renal function. (a) Functional MRI imaging revealing a right duplex kidney from which split function can be extrapolated (b) and (c).

and expanding beyond the borders of a traditional radiology department, particularly when combined with teleradiology.

## NEUROLOGICAL MAGNETIC RESONANCE FOCUSED ULTRASOUND

MRI-FUS is a technology that allows non-invasive thermal ablation of specific neurological targets. It combines MRI localisation, management and monitoring of the target with high-frequency focused ultrasound for tissue destruction.

Focused ultrasound (FUS) is capable of causing a significant temperature rise in a defined voxel of tissue by manipulating the combined effect of multiple ultrasound beams in order to produce thermal coagulative necrosis of a target lesion with minimal effect on adjacent structures. The combination of MRI and FUS allows a blunt instrument to become a precision scalpel whilst allowing real-time monitoring in conscious patients.

## CURRENT USE IN ESSENTIAL TREMOR

Essential tremor is the commonest movement disorder, with an estimated global prevalence of 5%. Clinically, it manifests as involuntary shaking during purposeful movement. Structural neurodegenerative changes in focal areas of the brain have been identified as a cause; multiple areas of the cerebellothalamocortical tract have been implicated, with the ventral intermedius nucleus (Vim) of the thalamus thought to be of particular significance. The Vim has historically been the target of both traditional open surgery and deep-brain stimulation for the treatment of essential tremor. However, both these technologies display clinical drawbacks, such as surgical healing time in the former and patient tolerance in the latter.

MRI-FUS targeting the Vim has shown significant symptomatic improvement with minimal treatment side effects. This approach offers the promise of a safer alternative and a shortened recovery time compared to traditional invasive surgery. It has recently received approval for use in both the USA and UK.

## MAKING THE LEAP FROM ACADEMIC CONCEPT TO CLINICAL APPLICATION

The early success of MRI-FUS in essential tremor serves as an exciting proof of concept, and a large array of possible further targets and clinical conditions have been identified.

Parkinson's disease is a movement disorder producing significant morbidity worldwide. The application of MRI-FUS to targets within the thalamus for the treatment of this condition have suggested improved outcomes. Epilepsy and chronic neuropathic pain have also been the focus of early academic work with promising results. This approach, henceforth, has the potential to replace far more invasive surgical procedures.

MRI-FUS also offers the potential for improved treatment in psychiatric conditions. Trials targeting the anterior limb of the internal capsule in patients with obsessive compulsive disorder and depression have shown symptomatic improvement. This potentially opens the door for a treatment option to a range of historically difficult-to-treat psychiatric conditions.

Finally, temporary disruption of the vascular endothelial lining and increased permeability associated with this therapy may disrupt the blood brain barrier: an extension that may facilitate targeted drug delivery.

## ROBOTIC INTERVENTIONAL RADIOLOGY

The tide is undeniably turning in medical practice away from open surgical treatment to minimally invasive techniques. Interventional radiology (IR) has been at the vanguard of this trend, with an ever-expanding range of conditions now amenable to the work of the interventional radiologist.

Access to endovascular and non-endovascular cavities has revolutionised a number of treatments, such as sclerotherapy of arterio-venous and lymphatic malformations, gastrostomy formation and organ transplant complications. Paralleling this dramatic progress has been significant technological progress. A tissue biopsy can now be targeted in almost any organ system with guidance from ultrasound, CT or MRI, and endovascular treatment now deploys a range of complex devices or targeted treatments in small hard-to-reach vessels for ablation of tumours and the treatment of peripheral vascular disease.

Conversely, increasingly complex interventional radiology procedures have posed two particular problems: increased radiation exposure times for practitioners and ever greater demand on operator dexterity. The integration of robotics presents a promising solution to these problems and opportunities for improved treatment.

The use of robotics in conventional surgery is now widespread. In 2011 more than 100,000 prostatectomies were performed using robotic systems worldwide. It has been shown to have multiple benefits, including precise dissection, 3D vision, tremor filtration and a shorter learning curve. Early robotic prototypes in interventional radiology have now matured into clinically viable devices poised to enter widespread use with the scope for the development of semi-autonomous robotics and remote procedures.

## CURRENT STATE OF PLAY

Image-guided biopsy and ablation are complex procedures requiring high levels of operator skill. These procedures require adequate target visualisation, careful trajectory planning and dextrous navigation. Image guidance can be in the form of ultrasound, computed tomography or magnetic resonance guidance.

Difficult-to-access lesions with at-risk neighbouring structures require a high level of precision. Challenging scenarios such as these can result in prolonged radiation exposure for the operator in CT guided biopsy. Patient- or table-mounted robotic systems offer increased dexterity and precision whilst the operating radiologist is remote to the imaging suite and able to limit their exposure in the radiation field.

Endovascular IR can treat a variety of conditions via minimally invasive catheter and guidewire access to the arterial and venous systems. As with guided biopsy, operator radiation exposure levels can be high and a significant degree of operator dexterity and precision is required. Currently available robotic catheter steering systems offer multiple benefits. For example, systems such as the Hansen Medical Magellan System allow the operator to control catheter position and angulation, offering enhanced steering. This has been shown in animal models to produce shorter cannulation times, precise stent placement, and reduced operator radiation dose exposure. The commercially available CorPath 200 cardiac catheter robot showed 98.6% technical success and 95% operator radiation exposure reduction in multicentre clinical trials.

The current state of robotics-assisted interventional radiology is poised to make the leap seen in robotic laparoscopy from successful clinical trials to large volume clinical use.

# FUTURE PROSPECTS

The pipeline of future robotics-assisted IR techniques is equally exciting to those more established technologies described above. Two areas of particular interest are automated manoeuvres and non-tethered endovascular devices.

The current generation of endovascular robotic devices are operated under direct human control of all parameters. However, with the advent of machine learning there is an opportunity for devices to be capable of certain automated movements. Early research has demonstrated simple automated motions, such as rotation of a retracting guidewire to increase chance of target vessel selection, or guidewire "wiggling" when traversing a lesion. As robotic catheter systems are more widely used, larger training datasets will present opportunities for machine learning to incorporate more complex automated functions.

All current endovascular intervention uses a tethered approach; in other words, all devices remain fixed at the skin surface, with an external component controlled by the operator. Early studies have shown promising results with non-tethered soft ferro-magnetically controlled robots in a non-living vessel phantom. Whilst this is still in its infancy, it offers huge potential in the longer term.

# WIDENING ACCESS TO MEDICAL IMAGING

The story of radiology has been to progress imaging from the lab to the patient. For much of the 20th century this was a journey from academic research to clinical application in the radiology department. The next leap is taking imaging to a much broader patient base both at local institutional sites and ultimately with a more global approach.

On the local level we will explore the revolution of portability that is allowing medical imaging to break out of the radiology department and into a host of other medical settings. On a global level we will explore how medical imaging can be brought to the majority of the world's population who currently have poor access to medical imaging.

# FROM DEPARTMENT TO BEDSIDE ... AND BEYOND

Whilst the role of high quality diagnostic studies performed in the radiology department will remain important, fast and portable bedside imaging has the potential to dramatically improve clinical decision making and patient outcomes.

# ULTRASOUND

Medical ultrasound has a long history, with initial applications as early as the beginning of the 20th century. In recent years, however, it has undergone a seismic shift with the arrival of truly portable, cheap point-of-care ultrasound technology.

Within the hospital setting, ultrasound provides relatively cheap, accessible and most importantly safe imaging as a first line investigation in both healthy and acutely unwell children and adults.

Current portable uses at the bedside provide diagnostic information and treatment of non-mobile patients when transfer of the patient would be considered detrimental to the patient's condition. In global health, this advantage allows a service that can be delivered in remote areas and is economically viable with basic operator training and education, serving the needs of a community, for example, in pregnancy. Remote access to expertise via teleradiology allows images to be shared from one region to another, enabling a spoke-and-hub model of healthcare. Extrapolated to the extreme, this guidance allows medical care in areas as remote as Antarctica and in interplanetary space using non-expert operators. Portable ultrasound equipment design for the global health setting is already underway, with solar powered ultrasound units used successfully in communities as remote as the Himalayas.

## CROSS-SECTIONAL IMAGING ON THE MOVE

Traditional cross-sectional imaging features large fixed scanner units with the need for bespoke room design. Understandably this technology has proved challenging to export from the radiology department. However, in recent years, exciting advances have been made in two areas: lightweight bedside units and truly mobile vehicle-integrated scanners, able to reach far beyond the hospital setting.

### The future is smaller!

The recently released Siemens Somatom On.site portable CT scanner is a truly portable CT scanning unit which can be taken ward to ward by a single trained operator. The device allows CT head imaging to be performed at the bedside, with images available on the patient archiving and communication systems (PACS) to report. This offers to revolutionise cross-sectional neurological imaging in difficult-to-transport patients, such as in the intensive care unit (ITU) setting or the highly infectious patient.

Another example of the use of bedside CT was seen recently in the response to the COVID-19 pandemic. Multiple radiology departments repurposed limited-capability portable CT units for chest imaging, removing the need to transport infectious patients around the hospital. The rapid progression of next-generation portable body CT (such as the Samsung BodyTom) presents an opportunity to greatly expand such uses of CT in the future.

Portable MRI (Swoop developed by biotech company Hyperfine) is being used at the newborn imaging centre at the Evelina London Children's Hospital for neuroimaging in the neonatal intensive care setting (Figure 22.3). Further research and development is hoped to refine the technology so that it can eventually be used globally in countries where health inequity is limited by access to equipment and economic factors.

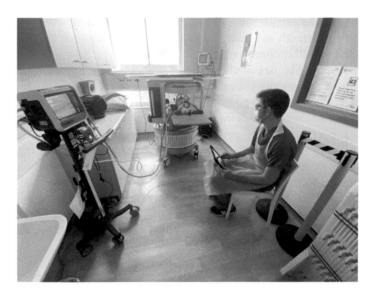

Figure 22.3 Hyperfine Swoop Portable MRI system on site at KHP.

## Further afield

The ability to take imaging to the patient in community and global settings has huge potential benefits. For many patients the suite of imaging available in a hospital is inaccessible in a timely manner. Improving out-of-hospital mobile imaging presents an opportunity for significant impact and consequently, a huge potential benefit in the developing world.

Conventional CT scanners mounted to trailers have offered relocatable CT services for some time. However, these units are designed to operate for extended periods in fixed locations, and relocation requires good transport infrastructure. Providers of healthcare to remote locations have had some success in converting these units to access hard-to-reach communities, but the majority of these populations remain unserved by cross-sectional imaging services.

Mobile stroke units, whereby a compact CT scanner is mounted on a modified emergency vehicle, provide a more mobile solution across a wider range of locations. These have been seen in the developing world for almost 20 years, providing rapid access acute stroke services. Similar technology was recently combined with an air ambulance in Melbourne, Australia. These more mobile units, however, often offer limited-capability CT (typically CT head only).

The next steps in mobile cross-sectional imaging are innovative solutions to reach an ever-increasing range of communities with fully capable cross-sectional imaging. An exciting project on the horizon is the RAD-AID Straightline Medical Airship Program. This aims to provide highly capable diagnostic imaging mounted on a modern hybrid airship that can land on almost any terrain.

## TARGETED GLOBAL HEALTH SOLUTIONS

In conjunction with mobile technologies, innovation in fixed imaging solutions targeted for the developing world can provide a dramatic increase in the access to imaging.

### Low-cost fixed units

The narrative of cross-sectional imaging development has been one dominated by ever-increasing capabilities. However, it has equally been one of extrapolated increasing financial entry costs. To open up cross-sectional imaging to the vast number of patients in poorer economic settings, a parallel development revenue of low-cost alternatives is also required. Until recently very little of this was seen in CT imaging and almost none in MRI imaging.

A recent prototype MRI unit developed at the University of Hong Kong with an estimated cost of $15,000 (a tiny fraction of typical commercial units) is an indicator of the untapped huge prospective market of low-cost technology. The prototype showed robust diagnostic performance in neurological application and would be commercially viable for many low-income countries. It features a fixed magnet requiring only mains power and minimal specific room requirements. Further development in this field presents an opportunity for an explosion in the number of patients able to access modern imaging diagnosis.

## SUMMARY

Medical imaging is a young field which has already revolutionised patient care in its short history. A wealth of opportunities for innovation are seen, and medical imaging remains a growth area in its share of public and private research investment. An even larger opportunity exists, widening access to existing technologies. Many patients in a hospital setting cannot access fixed departmental imaging, and a fraction of the global population have access to modern imaging technology in any setting.

The leap from research to clinical practice and from limited use to wide patient access provides attractive commercial opportunities, and as the investment continues to flow, great strides forward are sure to follow.

## BIBLIOGRAPHY

Bates DDB, Vintonyak A, Mohabir R, et al. Use of a portable computed tomography scanner for chest imaging of COVID-19 patients in the urgent care at a tertiary cancer center. *Emerg Radiol.* 2020;27(6):597–600.

Beaman CB, Kaneko N, Meyers PM, Tateshima S. A review of robotic interventional neuroradiology. *Am J Neuroradiol.* 2021 May;42(5):808–814. doi: 10.3174/ajnr.A6976. Epub 2021 Feb 4.

Ben-David E, Shochat M, Roth I, Nissenbaum I, Sosna J, Goldberg SN. Evaluation of a CT-guided robotic system for precise percutaneous needle insertion. *J Vasc Interv Radiol.* 2018 Oct;29(10):1440–1446.

Bretsztajn L, Gedroyc W. Brain-focussed ultrasound: what's the "FUS" all about? A review of current and emerging neurological applications. *Br J Radiol.* 2018;91(1087):20170481.

Chang KW, Jung HH and Chang JW. (2021). Magnetic resonance-guided focused ultrasound surgery for obsessive-compulsive disorders: potential for use as a novel ablative surgical technique. *Frontiers In Psychiatry.* 12:640832. DOI: 10.3389/FPSYT.2021.640832.

Frija G, Blažić I, Frush DP, Hierath M, Kawooya M, Donoso-Bach L, Brkljačić B. How to improve access to medical imaging in low- and middle-income countries? *EClinicalMedicine.* 2021 Jul 17;38:101034.

Gunduz, S., Albadawi, H. and Oklu, R. (2021), Robotic devices for minimally invasive endovascular interventions: A new dawn for interventional radiology. *Adv Intell Syst.* 3: 2000181

Kassamali RH, Ladak B. The role of robotics in interventional radiology: current status. *Quant Imaging Med Surg.* 2015;5(3):340–343.

Kim Y, Parada GA, Liu S, Zhao X. Ferromagnetic soft continuum robots. *Sci Robot.* 2019 Aug 28;4(33):eaax7329

Kwok JS, Fox K, Bil C, Langenberg F, Balabanski AH, Dos Santos A, Bivard A, Gardiner F, Bladin C, Parsons M, Zhao H, Coote S, Levi C, De Aizpurua H, Campbell B, Davis SM, Donnan GA, Easton D, Pang TY. Bringing CT scanners to the skies: design of a CT scanner for an air mobile stroke unit. *Applied Sciences.* 2022; 12(3):1560.

Liu Y, Leong ATL, Zhao Y, Xiao L, Mak HKF, Tsang ACO, Lau GKK, Leung GKK, Wu EX. A low-cost and shielding-free ultra-low-field brain MRI scanner. *Nat Commun.* 2021 Dec 14;12(1):7238.

Mollura DJ, Azene EM, Starikovsky A, Thelwell A, Iosifescu S, Kimble C, Polin A, Garra BS, DeStigter KK, Short B, Johnson B, Welch C, Walker I, White DM, Javadi MS, Lungren MP, Zaheer A, Goldberg BB, Lewin JS. White Paper Report of the RAD-AID Conference on International Radiology for Developing Countries: identifying challenges, opportunities, and strategies for imaging services in the developing world. *J Am Coll Radiol.* 2010 Jul;7(7):495–500.

Rho JY, Yoon KH, Jeong S, Lee JH, Park C, Kim HW. Usefulness of mobile computed tomography in patients with coronavirus disease 2019 pneumonia: a case series. *Korean J Radiol.* 2020;21(8):1018–1023.

Tacher, V., de Baere, T. Robotic assistance in interventional radiology: dream or reality? *Eur Radiol.* 30, 925–926 (2020).

Turpin J, Unadkat P, Thomas J, et al. Portable magnetic resonance imaging for ICU patients. *Crit Care Explor.* 2020;2(12):e0306. Published 2020 Dec 21.

# 23

# Medical innovation in ophthalmology

ZIYAAD SULTAN AND JOHN BLADEN

## INTRODUCTION

A growing and ageing population has led to an increase in the demand for high-quality care from all medical services, ophthalmology being no exception. In the United Kingdom, there are currently over seven million ophthalmology outpatient appointments each year. Over the next 20 years, the workload of two sub-specialties in particular, medical retina and glaucoma, are estimated to grow by 60% and 40% respectively. This is in part due to demographics but also to medical advances with a greater ability and sensitivity to detect diseases early and a greater choice of medical treatments available. There is, therefore, a need to modify the traditional patient pathway using innovative means such as virtual clinics, patient-led diagnostics, artificial intelligence (AI) analysis of diagnostic data coupled with targeted therapies, gene independent treatments and surgical robotics.

Virtual clinics are now routinely deployed in busy eye departments for either video conferencing or having patients attend for a diagnostics-only appointment, for example a glaucoma patient undergoing visual field testing and optical coherence tomography (OCT) which are later reviewed by a clinician who can then inform the patient whether there needs to be any intervention. Many diagnostic tests that were previously the domain of hospital outpatient departments are now ubiquitously available in high-street opticians and some supermarkets. In

DOI: 10.1201/9781003164609-25

the future, patient-led medical innovation will allow for greater autonomy and engagement by patients: access to portable or home-based medical devices are likely to improve service capacity further in ophthalmology. Diagnostics have been enhanced with the application of AI, to interpret the data and achieve a conclusion that a trained clinician would arrive at, at least with a high degree of certainty. Ophthalmology is data-rich and very much at the forefront of research and innovation in medical AI.

Advances in medical therapeutics have revolutionised management of conditions that were largely untreatable. Monoclonal antibodies therapy is the backbone of treatment of wet age-related macular degeneration, a condition that offered a poor visual prognosis over a decade ago and has recently been managed with laser. In recent years, gene therapy has opened the prospect of treating (slowing disease progression) of otherwise blinding inherited conditions. In the UK, the National Institute of Health and Care Excellent (NICE) has recommended gene therapy to patients with a RPE65 gene mutation. Surgical techniques have become more refined, with microincisions using laser for cataract surgery and robotics employed for vitreoretinal surgery. Rapid advances in these technologies have the potential for direct translation into ophthalmology.

# DIAGNOSTICS

## Imaging

The past 20 years have seen a transformation in the availability of non-invasive tools to assess ocular pathology. Previously, a patient with retinal disease (e.g. age-related macular degeneration) would be examined by a clinician, and invasive adjuvant investigations such a fundus fluorescein angiography (FFA) would be used. However, OCT has revolutionised the assessment of ocular disease (Figure 23.1). The principles of OCT are similar to that of ultrasound scans. OCT

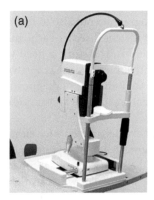
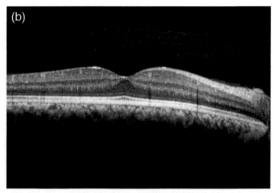

Figure 23.1 **a)** Optical coherence tomography (OCT) machine. **b)** Cross-sectional image of the fovea, showing in detail the layers of the retina.

is based on low-coherence (white light) interferometry; high-frequency light is split into two beams that are directed towards tissue; a proportion of the beams are scattered back towards a sensor, and spatial information is rendered from this. OCT produces high-resolution cross-sectional images of the anterior segment (cornea and iris) and posterior segment (retina and choroid) and has now become an essential tool. Within seconds a cross-sectional image of the retina can identify an abnormality that cannot be seen clinically and before it becomes noticeable to the patient; hence, early intervention can prevent any permanent visual damage. The two main applications for OCT in ophthalmology are medical retina and glaucoma; universally, any patient who now attends a clinic will undergo this investigation. For medical retina patients, that may be every four weeks, which equates to a greater burden on both the patient to attend clinic and the healthcare provider to build capacity.

OCT is now widely available at many high-street opticians, hence the scope to use this tool to meet current and future demands. Further recent advances in OCT technology include hand-held OCT devices that overcome the challenge of examining patients with mobility issues. These hand-held devices may also be able to provide multi-modal functions – such as visual field testing and a wide-field fundus photograph. Because they are portable, it is possible that these devices can be sent to the patient, who can carry out their own test at home, avoiding them coming into the hospital and causing minimal disruption to their daily routine.

## Home testing

Innovation in the flexibility and usability of home testing has the ability to transform patient experience and improve the quality of information that is used to guide management. Patients may not necessarily own the equipment, but it can be shared with patients (much like cardiac telemetry) or in some cases administered by trained staff at home.

Visual-field testing is an objective method of measuring visual function, and it performs a key investigation in monitoring glaucoma (peripheral visual-field defects that are easily ignored by patients until the condition is advanced) or diagnosing neurological conditions (visual-field defects secondary to stroke). Visual-field testing can be cumbersome for the patient and requires concentration for several minutes, with the test sometimes repeated to allow the patient to provide clinically reliable data. Remote home testing would allow the patient time to practise and record reliable data. Through innovation in augmented reality, there are now commercially available head-up virtual reality visual-field tests that can be performed in the convenience of the patient's home. Augmented reality (Figure 23.2) has further applications in measuring visual acuity, and a virtual-reality–based treatment for amblyopia ("lazy eye") in children, was recently approved by the Food and Drug Administration (FDA).[1]

Intraocular pressure readings, much like blood pressure, fluctuate throughout the day; for example pressure tends to be lower in the evening. Typically, measurements are taken by a specialist in a clinic, using either a table-mounted

Figure 23.2 An augmented reality headset. These headsets can be used to perform tests such as visual acuities and visual fields, as well as aid in the treatment of amblyopia. (By Syced – Own work, CC0, https://commons.wikimedia. org/w/index.php?curid=79841904.)

tonometer or a hand-held device. There are now hand-held devices that a patient can use at home, after suitable training, and then share the data with their clinician. This allows multiple daily readings to be taken, which may capture intraocular pressure spikes and guide glaucoma management.

## Artificial intelligence

AI or deep learning (DL) is well suited to ophthalmology, given the data-rich environment – patients may undergo several imagining modalities over several years, and disease progression can often be clearly demonstrated clinically, for example, the gradual reduction in vision or worsening glaucomatous optic nerve damage. AI requires a vast amount of input data, and more specifically, good-quality data, i.e. unbiased and repeatable. Current ophthalmology imaging modalities are able to provide this (see, *Imaging*). This new innovation has the potential to be applied to labour-intensive screening programmes (e.g. diabetic retinopathy screening) or in monitoring patients with an established diagnosis, especially those who are more likely to progress or need change in management. Large studies comparing the accuracy of diabetic retinopathy grading by DL systems versus a licensed ophthalmologist have shown sensitivities and specificities of greater than 90%. This is especially critical if we continue to move to out-of-hospital care formats or virtual clinics. The ethical dilemmas of AI are not unique to ophthalmology, in that any human biases in how data has been collected may be transmitted into the result, and the question of liability arises should the AI system fail to detect a pathology (much like with human error).

# TREATMENT

## Therapeutics

Monoclonal antibodies, with their ability to specifically target a protein/receptor, are used in many diseases, showing promising results in cancer therapy. Anti-VEGF (vascular endothelial growth factor) was serendipitously found to be beneficial in age-related macular degeneration (AMD) when colon cancer patients received Avastin. Subsequently, multiple intravitreal monoclonal antibodies have been developed to target VEGF in the retina for diseases that induce retinal ischaemia. Initially this resulted in monthly injections for patients, putting a massive burden on the health service. Further innovations are in the pipeline to allow once yearly Depo-Provera injections of slow-release anti-VEGF, and a nanoparticle delivery system may allow a topical eye drop delivery of medication for the retina.[2] Nevertheless, these treatments, as so often in medicine, although revolutionary, treat the symptom of the disease rather than the cause, and this had led to gene-targeted treatment to prevent the disease from occurring in the first place.

Gene therapy using the adeno-associated viral (AAV) vector has been developed for several inherited retinal diseases (IRDs), including advanced clinical trials for choroideremia, Leber's congenital amaurosis (LCA), retinitis pigmentosa (RP) and achromatopsia. The first approved gene therapy, voretigene neparvovec, is now available on the NHS for patients with biallelic mutations in the *RPE65* gene, a cause of autosomal recessive LCA and RP.[3] These IRDs may manifest early or later in life, resulting in progressive sight loss. A mutation in a gene may affect a specific retinal cell-type, e.g. photoreceptors, depending on its expression pattern, or subsequently (RPE), ultimately leading to cell damage and death as a consequence. The current delivery system of gene therapy involves a subretinal injection of the packaged gene so that it can reach the target cells easily, often the RPE or photoreceptor cells of the retina, whereby the AAV integrates into the hosts genome with subsequent activation of the packaged gene. There have been concerns about viral-host integration along with potential immune-related reaction to such integration. This has led to the development of non-viral gene therapy such as plasmids being used to express the faulty gene without host integration.[4]

Not all diseases are because of one faulty gene; there are multiple mechanisms and unknown precipitants of disease. Age-related macular degeneration (the commonest cause of blindness in the UK), although related to faulty complement pathway, involves multiple mechanisms such that replacement of the disease retinal pigment epithelium using a stem cell patch has been used with some success. It is by no means easy to replace such a small patch, and there is a limit to what the human hand can do; the use of robotics will help push the boundaries of this area of treatment.

## Surgical treatment

Surgical innovation in ophthalmology in the past 30 years has predominantly taken the form of advances in cataract and corneal surgery. With over 400,000 cataract operations carried out annually, the move towards phacoemulsification

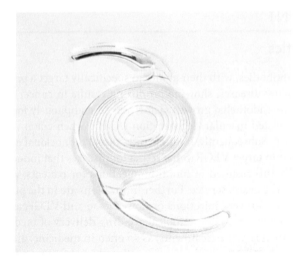

Figure 23.3 A multifocal intraocular lens. The lens permits the patient to view distant and near objects without need for glasses.

has led to smaller wound incisions, more efficient and safer day surgery and less post-operative convalescence and morbidity. Foldable intraocular lenses (Figure 23.3) allow for smaller wound incisions, and the lenses themselves have been developed to allow for multifocal vision.

Lasers have been used for many purposes in ophthalmology, including refractive surgery (reshaping the corneal surface), iridotomy (hole in the iris), capsulotomy (hole in the bag that holds the intraocular lens), retinopexy (scarring retina), retinal photocoagulation (RPE burn) and photodynamic therapy (drug activation within retinal vessels). Each aforementioned purpose uses different laser properties: photothermal, photochemical or photoionising. Eye-tracking devices are now incorporated into laser refractive surgery so that if the eye moves during the corneal reshaping, the laser corrects itself accordingly. More recently, laser has been utilised in cataract surgery to make the wound incision, opening up the lens bag and dividing the cataract in an automated robotic setting such that once the settings have been entered, the laser carries out the tasks on its own.

Robotics are still in their embryonic stage in ophthalmology compared to other specialties, such as general surgery. There are two broad themes in ophthalmic robotics, the first is referred to as "master–slave" or robot-assisted, whereby a surgeon directly controls the robot, through a joystick, to perform (part of) the operation – this removes the surgeon's fine tremor, improving surgical accuracy and dexterity.[5] The second theme is automation, in that a robot that may perform the surgery wholly or partly, without direct control, as mentioned above for femtosecond laser in cataract surgery. Robot-assisted systems (Preceyes BV) have been used in patients under local anaesthetic, to deliver subretinal medicine[5] and to perform membrane peels and were found to cause less retinal microtrauma.[6] However, the duration of surgery was nearly double that of standard surgery, which will in part reflect the initial learning curve.[6] This robot-assisted telemanipulation system offers a supra-human level of precision, which over time may be utilised in novel therapies such as gene therapy (see above), which requires delicate subretinal injection of medicine. For instance, manual injection of subretinal therapeutic products alone results in 50% reflux; hence some medicine is "lost" within the vitreous space. Robotic semi-automation of ophthalmology surgery using integrated OCT, notably intraocular robotic intervention surgical system (IRISS), has shown promise in cadaveric pig eyes.[7]

## CONCLUSION

Innovation has helped to reduce outpatient visits, improve diagnostic testing utilising AI and allow patients to undergo testing at home. Targeted therapies have resulted in breakthroughs in the management of previously untreatable disease, whilst the use of lasers and robotics will continue to improve the outcomes for eye treatment in the future.

## REFERENCES

1. Xiao S, Gaier ED, Mazow ML, et al. Improved adherence and treatment outcomes with an engaging, personalized digital therapeutic in amblyopia. *Sci Rep*. 2020;10(1):8328.
2. Kim HM, Woo SJ. Ocular drug Delivery to the retina: Current innovations and future perspectives. *Pharmaceutics*. 2021;13(1):108.
3. Chui W, Lin T-Y, Chang R-Chia, et al. An update on gene therapy for inherited retinal dystrophy: Experience in leber congenital amaurosis clinical trials. *Int J Mol Sci*. 2021;22(9):4534.
4. Toualbi L, Toms M, Moosajee M. The landscape of non-viral gene augmentation strategies for inherited retinal diseases. *Int J Mol Sci*. 2021.
5. Cehajic-Kapetanovic J, Xue K, Edwards TL, et al. First-in-human robot-assisted subretinal drug delivery under local anaesthesia. A randomised clinical trial. *Am J Ophthalmol*. 2021.
6. Edwards TL, Xue K, Meenink HCM, et al. First-in-human study of the safety and viability of intraocular robotic surgery. *Nat Biomed Eng*. 2018;2:649656.
7. Chen CW, Lee YH, Gerber MJ, et al. Intraocular robotic interventional surgical system (IRISS): Semi-automated OCT-guided cataract removal. *Int J Med Robot*. 2018;14(6):e1949.

# Index

Note: Locators in *italics* represent figures and **bold** indicate tables in the text.

T - #0130 - 111024 - C262 - 234/156/12 - PB - 9780367703004 - Gloss Lamination